WHAT MADE NOW IN
NORTHERN IRELAND

The very best
to you. Gerry,

Malachi O'Doherty

31. 7. 09.

WHAT MADE NOW IN NORTHERN IRELAND

December 2008

Northern Ireland Community Relations Council

Published by
Northern Ireland Community Relations Council
6 Murray Street
Belfast BT1 6DN

Email: info@nicrc.org.uk
Website: www.nicrc.org.uk

CONTENTS

Contributors   vii

Introduction
Maurna Crozier   xi

Chapter 1   From the earliest times to the Union
                Jonathan Bardon   1

Chapter 2   The Union on trial 1800-1921
                Jonathan Bardon   11

Chapter 3   Politics and the writing of Irish history: the Irish case
                Paul Bew   21

Chapter 4   The partition of Ireland
                Dennis Kennedy   47

Chapter 5   Explaining the Northern Ireland Troubles
                Richard English   61

Chapter 6   Falling out – Falling in
                Malachi O'Doherty   67

Chapter 7   20th Century incomers
                Marion Meek, Anna Lo, Nisha Tandon   79

Chapter 8   Recent migration experiences
                Anthony Soares   89

Chapter 9   Identities in Northern Ireland: nothing but the same
                old stories?
                Tony Gallagher   103

Chapter 10   Symbols in peace and conflict
                 Dominic Bryan   117

Chapter 11   Towards an oral history of the Troubles: *Conflict* at the
                 Ulster Museum
                 Jane Leonard   125

Chapter 12   Our tangled speech: languages in Northern Ireland
                 Aodán Mac Póilin   135

Chapter 13   The Northern Ireland peace process in comparative
                 perspective
                 Adrian Guelke   147

Chapter 14   Contemporary politics in Northern Ireland
                 Paul Arthur   157

Chapter 15   The meaning of history and experience for the future
                 Duncan Morrow   171

CONTRIBUTORS

Dr Maurna Crozier was Director of the Cultural Diversity programme of the NI Community Relations Council from 1990-2007.

Dr Jonathan Bardon is the author of several books on Irish history, including *A History of Ulster,* and he has written historical documentaries for the BBC, Channel 4 and RTE. *A History of Ireland in 250 episodes,* based on an acclaimed series for BBC Radio Ulster, was published by Gill and Macmillan in November 2008.

Paul Bew is Professor of Politics at Queen's University, Belfast.

Dr Dennis Kennedy is a writer, historian and political commentator, formerly a journalist, European Commission representative in Northern Ireland, and a lecturer at Queen's University, Belfast.

Richard English is Professor of Politics at Queen's University, Belfast. His books include *Armed Struggle: the History of the IRA* (2003) and *Irish Freedom: the History of Nationalism in Ireland* (2006).

Malachi O'Doherty is a writer and broadcaster based in Belfast. He is the author of four books on religion and politics in Northern Ireland, including *The Trouble with Guns*, an analysis of the political strategy of the Provisional IRA, and *The Telling Year*, a memoir of his work as a journalist covering the Troubles in 1972.

Marion Meek is the former Editor of the *Belfast Jewish Record*, and retired inspector of Historic Monuments in Northern Ireland.

Anna Lo is a Member of the Legislative Assembly of Northern Ireland representing the Alliance Party.

Nisha Tandon is Arts Development Manager of ArtsEkta, an organisation which is committed to promoting equality and understanding of different cultures through the arts, and which ensures that people of different cultures and backgrounds live and learn together in a supportive environment, with the aim of creating a world where there is no racial discrimination.

Dr Anthony Soares is Lecturer in Portuguese and Director of Queen's University Postcolonial Research Forum at Queen's University, Belfast.

Professor Tony Gallagher is Head of the School of Education, Queen's University, Belfast.

Dr Dominic Bryan is Director of the Institute of Irish Studies at Queen's University, Belfast, Chair of Diversity Challenges and has worked with the Northern Ireland Human Rights Commission and the NI Community Relations Council. He is an anthropologist researching political rituals, public space and identity in Northern Ireland; his book, *Orange Parades: The Politics of Ritual, Tradition and Control* (Pluto Press 2000), used theories of rituals to examine parades organised by the Orange Order in Ireland. He also works on issues around public order policing, human rights, ethnic politics and sectarianism and has done comparative work in South Africa and the USA.

Jane Leonard was History Outreach Officer at the Ulster Museum, Belfast, from 1997-2006, where she assisted community groups seeking to explore the legacies of conflict in Ireland. Her publications focus on how the experience of conflict shapes the postwar lives of survivors and bereaved. She is currently pursuing postgraduate research in the School of Politics at Queen's University, Belfast.

Aodán Mac Póilin is Director of the Ultach Trust, an organisation that promotes the Irish language on a cross-community basis in Northern Ireland. He has been active in the European Bureau for Lesser-Used languages, Foras na Gaelige, Comhairle na Gaelscolaiochta, the NI Community Relations Council and the Seamus Heaney Centre for Poetry at Queen's University, Belfast.

Adrian Guelke is Professor of Comparative Politics in the School of Politics, International Studies and Philosophy at Queen's University, Belfast and Director of the Centre for the Study of Ethnic Conflict. Publications include *Terrorism and Global Disorder* (IB Tauris, 2006), *Rethinking the Rise and Fall of Apartheid* (Palgrave Macmillan, 2005) and *A Farewell to Arms? Beyond the Good Friday Agreement* (Manchester University Press, 2006) (co-edited with Michael Cox and Fiona Stephen).

Paul Arthur is Professor of Politics and Course Director of the MA in Peace and Conflict Studies at the Magee Campus of the University of Ulster. He is the author of *Special Relationships: Britain, Ireland and the Northern Ireland Problem* (Blackstaff Press, 2000).

Dr Duncan Morrow is Chief Executive of the NI Community Relations Council.

Richard Froggatt was editor of International Marketing projects at Banque Privée Edmond de Rothschild Europe, Luxembourg and has worked as an editor at Law Reports International, Trinity College, Oxford; for the Northern Ireland Community Relations Council; and at Prolingua International Language Centre, Luxembourg. He also acts as English language advisor to an Austrian arts festival.

INTRODUCTION

This book reflects a seminar series of public lectures and discussions, organised by the Community Relations Council, to be of use and interest to those living and working in Northern Ireland.

Many issues being addressed both by organisations and by individuals locally, reflect the past histories of the many communities who have lived on the island of Ireland, from earliest times to the 21st century. The origins of such issues may be obscure to those who originate from elsewhere, as they may be unknown to younger local people.

The aim was both to cover earlier periods of history and to address the realities of life at the beginning of a new century. While the peace process will result in self-government and many proposals for new policies and directions towards a shared future, many debates and decisions, both public and private, are still likely to be based on long-held views and attitudes.

In order to reflect the actual diversity of the current population, and the different perspectives within it, the writers were drawn from journalism, academia, broadcasting, community relations, the arts, and heritage and culture. All were working as individuals or in organisations, which aim to present the society of Northern Ireland both to itself and to a wider world.

Maurna Crozier
December 2008

Chapter One

FROM THE EARLIEST TIMES TO THE UNION

Jonathan Bardon

Some thirty years ago I launched a flat-bottomed row boat on Lough Melvin at Kinlough, County Leitrim, and began casting with my fly rod in full expectation of a good hatch of mayfly. Then a strong wind sprang up in the west and, unable to scull against it, I was swept out into lake in my frail craft with every prospect of being engulfed by the rising storm. My only hope was a small island directly ahead of me.

As I took refuge in the lee of the island I realised that this was a place where peoples and cultures had clashed and blended. The island is an artificial one, a crannóg, laboriously created with rocks and wooden piles in the Iron Age. Here stand the ruins of Rossclogher Castle, a MacClancy fortress successfully defended by the Armada castaway Francisco de Cuellar in a snowstorm against the forces of Lord Deputy Sir William Fitzwilliam in 1588. I looked behind me and saw a line of buoys marking the artificial frontier between two jurisdictions, the Northern Ireland border. As I baled out my boat I reflected that Lough Melvin is home to four distinct races of trout: sonaghan, gillaroo, ferox and brown trout. Though they share the same streams at spawning time, these fish do not mate with each other. In short, there is more racial distinction between these four types of trout in one modest lough in the north-west of Ireland than amongst all the varieties of human beings on the face of the earth.

When looking at the history of Ireland we tend to be more aware of conflict than of integration. Yet blending on this island has been a consistent feature down the centuries. It is an arresting thought that humans had been living in Australia for at least 40,000 years before the first people set foot in Ireland. The earliest traces were found at Mount Sandel near Coleraine in 1973: here, from around 7500 BC, Mesolithic people had trapped eels, salmon and bass in the Lower Bann, hunted wild boar, gathered hazelnuts in the forest and fashioned stone implements from flint collected along the Antrim coastline.

Then the whole island, save for lakes, fens and mountain tops, was covered with dense deciduous forest. It was not until some time during the first half of the fourth millennium BC that the landscape began to be significantly altered. Any land bridges between Britain and Ireland had long been swept away. Intrepid family groups brought trussed cattle and other domestic stock by sea; trees were ring-barked to create clearings; and when the land was exhausted they moved on to make fresh pastures and cultivation ridges. These Neolithic farmers left permanent marks of their occupation: ceremonial sites such as the Giant's Ring near Shaw's Bridge and portal tombs and horned cairns where they buried their dead. From around 2000 BC there is evidence of gold, copper and bronze metal-working, the earliest remains of which were found by the awesome passage graves in the Boyne valley.

The first Celtic speakers may have come to Ireland as early as 1000 BC and in greater numbers from about 500 BC and the Gaelic ruling caste, equipped with iron weapons and advancing on horseback, brought the native peoples under subjection. Archaeological enquiry does not show evidence of formidable invasion; rather, there was a steady infiltration from Britain and the European mainland over the centuries. Indeed, Peter Woodman, who supervised the excavation of Mount Sandel, has concluded that the gene pool of the Irish was set by the end of the Stone Age.

The Celts were the first people north of the Alps to emerge into recorded history. At one time their civilisation stretched from Anatolia to Portugal, north to Scandinavia and west to the British Isles. That Iron Age culture survived longest in Ireland and north of the Highland line in Scotland. Ireland remained untouched by the legions of Rome and the Germanic peoples who brought about the destruction of the western Roman Empire. Indeed, the Irish attacking from the west did much to destroy Roman rule in Britain. And, as the Empire collapsed, aspects of Roman civilisation reached Ireland. Christianity and, with it, knowledge of writing arrived. The conversion of the Irish was a peaceable affair. Ireland lacked towns and cities so the Roman system of parochial and diocesan church organisation could not operate there successfully. Instead the Irish preferred the North African monastic tradition.

Irish monasteries, endowed with land by kings and nobles, became highly influential centres of piety and learning. Here many classical works were copied (some would have been lost to posterity otherwise) often in exquisite script and with intricate illumination. Wandering Irish monks and scholars were the first humans to reach the Faeroes and Iceland; St Colmcille spearheaded a Christian mission in Scotland; St Aidan and others did much to convert the Anglo-Saxons; St Columbanus of Bangor preached to the Burgundians; St Gall, also of Bangor, began the conversion of the Swiss; and Irish scholars were influential in the court of Charlemagne.

Ireland's long immunity from attack was abruptly ended by the Vikings. In 795 Rathlin was attacked and, negotiating coastal shallows and estuaries in their shallow-draught vessels, Norsemen penetrated deep into the island to plunder monastic centres. Later these men from the north overwintered and began to build Ireland's first towns. Dublin, and the area around it known as Fingall, became the first Viking kingdom, and together with Wexford, Waterford, Limerick and other urban settlements, brought Ireland into a flourishing trade network extending from Scandinavia to Constantinople.

Yet the Vikings never succeeded in conquering Ireland. The newcomers simply became embroiled in petty dynastic wars. Ireland had never been politically united but Viking intervention had the effect of increasing the importance of provincial kingdoms at the expense of lesser ones. In the early eleventh century Brian Boru of the Dál Cais was the first High King to rule the whole island but only briefly: in 1014 he defeated a coalition of northmen and Leinstermen at Clontarf but he was killed at the moment of victory. A century and a half of power struggles ensued as O'Briens, MacLoclainns, O'Connors and others attempted to make the high-kingship a reality. In the words of one annalist all were High Kings 'with opposition' and they made Ireland 'a trembling sod'.

This struggle for power led directly to the intervention of the English in Ireland. Dermot MacMurrough was driven out of his kingdom of Leinster in 1166 by the High King Rory O'Connor. Dermot travelled to the south-west of France to seek the aid of Henry II, the most powerful monarch in western Europe. Henry gave Dermot leave to enlist the support of Norman barons in south-west Wales led by 'Strongbow,' Richard FitzGilbert de Clare, Earl of Pembroke and Strigoil. The Norman conquest of England had been a ruthless affair, completed in just a few years. The Anglo-Norman intervention in Ireland was very different.

The Normans, first arriving in Wexford in 1169, did overwhelm Leinster and its Viking cities and defeated Rory in a couple of years. Then Henry II, fearing the establishment of a separate Norman state which could threaten his dominions from the west, came to Ireland in 1171. There he accepted the allegiance of Irish kings and the high-kingship of Rory and attempted to limit the conquests of Strongbow and his followers. In this Henry failed and over the next century the Normans (often assisted by Irish allies) extended their conquests over much of Munster, parts of Connacht and to the coastlands of Antrim and Down. From the early fourteenth century, however, the conquest began to falter.

Following his victory at Bannockburn in 1314, Robert Bruce and his brother Edward invaded Ireland: while the enterprise failed by 1318, the Scots nevertheless severely weakened the English colony. Thereafter, English kings concentrated on the Hundred Years' War in France and on a weakening struggle for the Crown between Yorkists and Lancastrians. Meanwhile, Gaelic rulers (most of them now lords rather than kings) built castles and adopted Anglo-Norman armour. They employed Scots mercenaries from the Isles known as gallowglasses (*gall óglaigh* – 'foreign warriors'). They included MacDonnells, MacSweeneys, MacCabes and MacDowells. In addition many descendants of the first Norman invaders went native ('more Irish than the Irish themselves' in the words of Gerald of Wales), adopting the Irish language and Irish customs and intermarrying with the Gaelic Irish (for example, Burkes, Lynches, Barrys, Dillons and FitzGeralds). The territory held by the English Crown contracted to the ports and an area, known as the Pale, stretching from Dundalk inland to Naas and south to Bray.

Victory for Henry Tudor at Bosworth Field in 1485 marked the beginning of a new era in Irish history. England became a strong, unified and wealthy state with a growing population seeking fresh opportunities abroad. Ireland was underdeveloped and underpopulated (perhaps with little more than half a million inhabitants), and it contained extensive woods – Britain was rapidly running short of timber for smelting, building, barrel staves and ships. In addition, English rulers became increasingly concerned that hostile foreign powers might use Ireland as a base for threatening England from the west – in the first half of the sixteenth century a French-Scottish coalition was feared; and in the latter part Spanish intervention was a constant anxiety. Henry VII was content to allow the Kildare Fitzgeralds to govern on his behalf. Henry

VIII was not: he made himself King of Ireland in 1541 (previously, English monarchs were Lords of Ireland) and extended royal power beyond the Pale.

In the end the Tudor monarchy decided on the complete conquest of Ireland but it was not until the end of the century that an all-out attempt was made to achieve this. Following inconclusive and expensive military campaigns, Henry VIII adopted the policy of 'surrender and regrant': Gaelic lords received English titles and royal protection in return for allegiance to the Crown. This was continued by Henry's successors but increasingly Elizabeth's viceroys counselled military conquest. The Armada in 1588 was a wake-up call – at one stage there were at least 3,000 Spanish castaways in Ireland at a time when the Lord Deputy had no more than a thousand men under his command.

The last straw for Gaelic lords was the attempt to divide their territories into numerous impotent freeholds (successfully accomplished in County Monaghan and in the Magennis lordship of Iveagh in Down). Hugh O'Neill, Earl of Tyrone, forged a coalition of Gaelic lords in Ulster and, following an overwhelming victory at the Yellow Ford near Armagh in 1598, won the adherence of powerful families in much of the rest of the island. Ultimate victory, he realised, depended on obtaining significant Spanish help. Yet that support (including munitions and silver landed at Teelin and Killybegs) ensured a concerted drive to defeat the northern lords. English naval power was used to effect: troops were brought in at Derry and Carrickfergus, and Ulster was close to subjugation when the Spanish landed at Kinsale in west Cork in 1601. O'Neill and his allies risked all by traversing the country in winter and the Irish were shattered in the open on Christmas Eve. Kinsale was Ireland's Culloden.

When O'Neill submitted to Lord Deputy Mountjoy at Mellifont in 1603 he did not know that Elizabeth was dead by a few days. James VI of Scotland was now James I of England, Scotland, Wales and Ireland. No major land confiscations followed but the Treaty of Mellifont was unstable: too many servants of the Crown felt frustrated because they had received puny rewards; and the Gaelic lords found it difficult to adapt to the new conditions. O'Neill held sway over three Ulster counties but he was constantly aware that attempts were being made to implicate him in conspiracies. He and the other lords resented the intrusion of royal officials, the loss of control of Church lands and the imposition of English law. To the astonishment of Lord Deputy Sir Arthur Chichester, the Earl of Tyrone, the Earl of Tyrconnell and around a hundred other members of the Ulster Gaelic élite sailed away from Lough Swilly in

September 1607, never to return. If their intention was to obtain Spanish help, they were doomed to fail: Philip III had made his peace with James I in 1604.

This was the backdrop to the most ambitious colonising project to be carried out in western Europe in modern times. The territories of the departed lords - encompassing six counties west of the River Bann – were confiscated and granted to undertakers (who undertook to remove the native Irish from their 'proportions' and 'plant' them with Protestant British), servitors (military men and servants of the Crown) and 'deserving Irish' (who had changed sides in time in the Nine Years' War). The counties of Antrim and Down were not included because piecemeal colonisation there after 1603 was progressing most successfully, partly because of depopulation resulting from the devastation of war. London livery companies were cajoled into colonising the county of Coleraine, increased in size and renamed Londonderry.

The 'Plantation of Ulster' was only a partial success. Certainly, great numbers of English, Welsh and Lowland and Border Scots came over to build towns (most Ulster towns are of Plantation origin), fell forests and open up great areas for more intensive cultivation. The Londoners created the last walled city to be built in western Europe. Everywhere, however, the Irish remained in a majority and undertakers failed to remove them from their estates. The problem was that the size of the proportions was estimated and not measured: plantation commissioners calculated that they had disposed of less than half a million acres whereas in reality the grants totalled 4.7 million statute acres. Planters could not find enough British (the word was first regularly used in Ulster) for their estates and so they allowed the natives to stay on. This did not mean that the Irish, having exchanged one set of landlords for another, were content. With no security of tenure, their burdensome rents set by informal arrangements from year to year, and their status severely reduced, the natives yearned for a return of the old order.

The Gaelic Irish were confronted by alien colonists adhering to a variety of Protestantism far distant from their own Catholicism. The tragedy for Irish history was that the Plantation took place at a time of intense religious conflict in Europe. The government was determined to impose a Protestant settlement but those most affected at this time were descendants of Norman settlers further south, the 'Old English'. In Ulster the Franciscans increased their numbers threefold between 1623 and 1639 to instil a new zeal. In Ulster, therefore, the uncompromising spirit of the Counter-Reformation faced the inflexible determination of both the Puritan settlers and the sporadic persecution of the Crown government. Hostility, suspicion and uncertainty created an unstable atmosphere of fear and division which was to persist to our own times.

Polical instability in England created the perfect conditions for fresh violence in Ireland. In 1641 the native Irish fell on the British settlements in Ulster and massacred thousands. As the English Civil War got under way the alienated Old English joined the Gaelic Irish for the first time. Under Eoghan Roe O'Neill the Irish won their greatest victory at Benburb in 1646 but they lost the war when Cromwell landed in Dublin with his Ironsides in 1649. Cromwell exacted fearful revenge in massacres at Drogheda and Wexford and confiscated great swathes of Irish land. Restored in 1660, Charles II found himself unable to undo the Cromwellian land settlement except to restore the Earl of Antrim to his estates. At peace, Ireland prospered and Dublin grew to be the second city of the Empire.

More political instability in England provoked further war in Ireland. James II, ousted by William of Orange in 1688, came to Ireland with a French army and rapidly gained control of the whole island, save for Enniskillen and the city of Londonderry. The epic defence of Derry for 105 days against the forces of King James would be celebrated by Protestants down the centuries. William landed in Carrickfergus in June 1690 with the largest army Ireland had yet seen. This multinational force routed the French and Irish at the Boyne on 1 July 1690 but the defeated retired in good order behind the River Shannon. Ultimate Williamite victory came on 12 July 1690 when Baron Ginkel overwhelmed the Jacobites on the plains of Galway at Aughrim – 7,000 Irishmen died in an afternoon in the bloodiest battle in Irish history.

William's victories were primarily a blow to Louis XIV's ambition to dominate western Europe. They also ensured constitutional parliamentary rule in Britain. In Ireland they spelled disaster for propertied Catholics. Further confiscations ensued and by the beginning of the eighteenth century only 14 per cent of Ireland's land remained in the hands of Catholics. By 1780 that proportion had fallen to five per cent. This was primarily the outcome of the Penal Laws. Except for small groups of Quakers, toleration was an alien concept. Protestants were expelled from France and persecuted in Bohemia. In Ireland laws enacted between 1695 and 1720 prevented Catholics from buying more land, forced Catholics to divide their estates equally among their sons, excluded Catholics from public service and the legal profession, and closed Catholic schools. Catholic worship was tolerated (it was in Cromwell's time that Mass was forbidden) but Catholics and Presbyterians had to pay tithes to an Established Church to which they did not belong. Catholics could not vote and they could not be Members of Parliament.

The Irish Parliament had been in existence almost as long as that of England. It was now a body which represented the Anglican élite, known later in the century as the 'Protestant Ascendancy'. Yet it was in this assembly that modern Irish nationalism was born. Ireland was, in effect, a colony but the colonists grew to resent laws enacted at Westminster to constrict Irish trade. An opposition group emerged in Parliament, calling themselves 'Patriots' and their moment came during the American War of Independence. The isolated and beleagured government at Westminster was forced to free up Irish trade in 1779 and, in 1782, to concede 'legislative independence'.

It would be quite wrong to think that Ireland was self-governing between 1782 and the Union. The Irish government, headed by the Lord Lieutenant and the Chief Secretary, was appointed (as under Direct Rule in Northern Ireland) by the Westminster government of the day. Westminster could no longer legislate for Ireland but, through patronage, could generally get its way in Dublin. In addition, the Irish Parliament was even more unrepresentative than that in London and one of the reasons it failed was that it steadfastly refused to widen its charmed circle.

The spirit of the Enlightenment was now filtering into Ireland. It had been given a fillip by the American War and Presbyterians in Ulster, finishing their education in Glasgow and Edinburgh, brought back with them ideas of toleration and liberty. It was the French Revolution, however, which had the most profound impact. A rising middle class (particularly Catholics and Presbyterians) sought wholesale reform. The Irish Parliament failed to respond. Most Penal Laws were repealed (though Catholics were still excluded from Parliament), in response to pressure from London, but demands to widen representation were constantly rebuffed. The Society of United Irishmen, founded in Belfast in 1791, had started out as a peaceful pressure group seeking equal treatment for all sects: by 1794 it was plotting revolution.

Bourgeois talkers could not by themselves carry out an effective revolution. A mass army was obtained, paradoxically, as a result of sectarian conflict. In Antrim and Down, Catholics were largely confined to inaccessible glens and mountains and to Newry – Protestants there felt secure and were strongly influenced by the new ideas of liberty. West of the Bann, however, Catholics and Protestants were roughly equal in numbers. Here ancient hatreds and memories of massacre and dispossession survived and festered as farmer-weavers competed to rent scraps of land near linen markets. Sectarian battles began in the 1780s at Markethill and steadily spread across County Armagh in the 1790s. Protestant gangs called themselves 'Peep-o'-Day Boys,' rising early to attack their Catholic neighbours and smash their looms.

Catholic gangs, though calling themselves 'Defenders,' were themselves aggressors in south Armagh. In September 1795 bands of Defenders made an ill-advised assault on north Armagh; they were routed with the loss of around thirty lives at the Diamond. The Protestant victors met at Loughgall to form the Orange Order, pledged to uphold the Protestant constitution and to celebrate the Battle of the Boyne every Twelfth of July. What followed was the expulsion of thousands of Catholics from County Armagh.

Fleeing Catholics spread Defenderism into neighbouring counties and into the province of Leinster. They applied to join the United Irish conspiracy and were accepted. Meanwhile the United Irish emissary, Theobald Wolfe Tone, got the aid of the French who sent a large expeditionary force in December 1796. Bad weather prevented a French landing but tens of thousands of aspiring revolutionaries were sure they would return. The strategic vulnerability of Ireland had been amply demonstrated to William Pitt's government in London. A new force, the Yeomanry, was created, quickly dominated by Orangemen.

Despite the arrest of nearly all the leaders and the failure of the French to return, the United Irish rebellion began on 23 May 1798. Soon most of Kildare, Carlow, Wicklow and Wexford fell under the control of the insurgents. Belatedly, Presbyterians in Antrim and Down joined in but were defeated at Antrim, Ballymena and Ballynahinch. The rebellion was strongest in Wexford but it was crushed there at Vinegar Hill on 21 June. A small French force landed at Killala Bay in Mayo in August but, after a striking victory at Castlebar, they and their Irish allies were defeated at Ballinamuck in Longford in September. A final French attempt in October was foiled in a stiff naval battle in Lough Swilly: Tone, on board one of the vessels, was captured and on being condemned to death he took his own life.

The moment he heard of the rebellion, Pitt decided to bring about the closure of the Irish Parliament and to rule Ireland directly from Westminster. It was he who created the United Kingdom of Great Britain and Ireland.

Chapter Two

THE UNION ON TRIAL
1800 – 1921

Jonathan Bardon

I f there was to be a Union of Britain and Ireland then it would require the parliaments in both London and Dublin to vote for it. Obtaining Westminster's approval was easy enough: arguments that the Protestant Ascendancy had failed to govern Ireland well and that Britain's strategic interests were paramount during a long war with France were convincing. Pitt thought a frightened gentry in Ireland would bow to the inevitable. He was wrong: the Irish Commons voted down the Union proposal in January 1799 and it took over another year to persuade, cajole and bribe the Irish Parliament into voting itself out of existence.

The Act of Union came into force on 1 January 1801. Henceforth, Ireland would be ruled from Westminster and send its peers to the House of Lords and a hundred MPs to the Commons. The United Kingdom of Great Britain and Ireland had a new flag incorporating the cross of St Patrick; the Church of England and the Church of Ireland were united into one Established Church; and there was to be free trade across the Irish Sea. Would it succeed?

'It is no Union,' Henry Grattan, the man who had done most to win legislative independence in 1782, declared at Westminster. He meant that Catholics were excluded, but in other respects there was not a full Union between Ireland and the rest of the United Kingdom. Though not mentioned in the Act, a separate Irish executive remained in Dublin Castle. Ireland was often treated differently from England, Scotland and Wales in the ensuing decades. The country was considered more violent than the rest of the kingdom and special powers (in the form of 'Insurrection' Acts and 'coercion') were in force during all but five years of the first half century of the Union. The government was more interventionist than it dared to be elsewhere. This was often beneficial: Ireland was well ahead of the rest of the UK in state support for education, hospitals, medical dispensaries, and road and bridge construction and in the provision of a police force, for example.

Pitt wanted 'Catholic Emancipation' (Catholics to be allowed to sit in Parliament and to be eligible for certain senior posts) to be incorporated in the Union. He was forced by colleagues and his Irish supporters to drop his proposal but he all but promised to bring in a Bill immediately afterwards. George III and, in consequence, his cabinet, refused to support him. Pitt resigned and numerous attempts by members of the Whig opposition to get emancipation at Westminster failed over the next twenty years. In this sense it could be said that the Union was holed beneath the waterline right at the start. Lord Cornwallis, the Viceroy in 1800, said that the mass of the people did not 'care one farthing' for the Union: he was right but educated Catholics generally supported the Union in the hope of emancipation. Outside of Ulster and in spite of penal laws a substantial Catholic propertied class had emerged in the eighteenth century. Pitt had hoped to incorporate them into the ruling élite where they would be in a safe minority, but not without influence, in Westminster. That hope had been dashed and now these Catholics formed an alternative alienated élite.

Daniel O'Connell, a brilliant lawyer, was one of the few notable Catholics to oppose the Union from the outset. In 1823 he formed the Catholic Association to obtain Emancipation, an organisation which was transformed when it enlisted ordinary people as associate members for a subscription each of a penny a month. The government faced a disciplined and peaceful popular movement and general election defeats as Catholic forty-shilling freeholders defied their landlords to vote for Emancipation candidates in 1826. Then in 1828, finding that there was nothing stopping a Catholic from being elected though he could not take his seat, O'Connell triumphantly won a by-election in Clare. Wellington's Tory government caved in and the last of the Penal Laws was removed in 1829.

Emancipation had not granted by the government, it had been wrung out of it. The Catholic élite was not reconciled. O'Connell announced in 1830 that his next objective was repeal of the Union. He was not consistent in this demand and, now that the Whigs were in power, he declared that he was putting the Union on trial – if the government would give 'justice to Ireland' he would drop his demand, if not, he would campaign for repeal. In the 1830s the Whigs did much for Ireland: National Schools were created in 1831; the Irish Constabulary was made an impartial force; Catholics were promoted; municipal corporations were reformed; the tithe was reduced; and Ireland was given a Poor Law. Many Whig measures for Ireland, however, were emasculated or killed by the peers of the realm – the power of a Tory-dominated Lords would continue to be a potent factor in Irish affairs. By 1840 O'Connell concluded that he had failed to get sufficient justice for Ireland. An all-out drive for repeal began.

The Loyal National Repeal Association held 'monster meetings' in Leinster, Munster and Connacht. The movement was as large and as disciplined as that for Emancipation. In contrast, however, O'Connell had little support in Westminster and no significant backing from Irish Protestants. When a monster meeting scheduled for Clontarf in October 1843 was banned, O'Connell called it off. Having witnessed the September massacres in Paris in 1792 he conclude that liberty was not worth the shedding of 'a single drop of blood' – he deserves to be remembered as one of the great pacifists of the nineteenth century. The Repeal movement slowly disintegrated.

If Catholics had changed their opinion of the Union since 1800, so too had Protestants. Members of the Ascendancy had mostly been opposed to the Union but they quickly discovered that the sky did not fall in after 1 January 1801. The separate Irish executive and the viceregal court remained and they had privileged access to jobs in public service, mostly in what were then known as the 'civil departments'. Successive governments thereafter steadily undermined the power of the Ascendancy by, for example: getting rid of the Yeomanry and introducing a centrally-controlled police force; setting up a Board of Works which took over many of the responsibilities of unelected Grand Juries; reforming municipal corporations in 1840 (O'Connell was immediately afterwards elected Lord Mayor of Dublin); introducing legislation to protect tenant farmers; and disestablishing the Church in 1869. This inexorable whittling-away of Ascendancy privileges produced the inevitable howls of outrage, but propertied and educated Protestants became fervent supporters of the Union as they witnessed the rise of Catholic nationalism – a restored Dublin parliament would have a Catholic majority more hostile to Ascendancy interests than even the most despised Whig government.

Only in the north-east did Protestants form a majority (Ulster as a whole did not have a recorded Protestant majority until the census of 1861). Here profound changes in opinion took place. Belfast in particular prospered under the Union: it was a thriving centre of cotton production and then, when competition from Manchester became too great, its manufacturers converted to the spinning of flax. Belfast was the fastest-growing urban centre in the United Kingdom. Tens of thousands poured into the town from the overcrowded and impoverished Ulster countryside to seek work in the mills. These people were mostly from mid-Ulster and they brought their fears and hostilities with them, settling with care in separate enclaves. They did not change their political opinions – they simply transferred them from west of the Bann to the Lagan valley.

What about those in Belfast, Antrim and Down and their descendants who had supported the United Irishmen? Many retained their liberal views but came to the conclusion that Westminster was governing them more fairly than the exclusive Irish Parliament. Besides, the Union was bringing them prosperity. Others were horrified by stories of sectarian massacre in the rebellion in Leinster. The Evangelical Revival swept across Ulster, reaching a climax in 1859, affecting all sects including the Established Church. This revival not only tended towards political conservatism but laid emphasis on Catholicism as a backward, superstitious religion. The Catholic Renewal (despite its similarity to the Evangelical revival) created alarm and the rising tide of Irish nationalism was to them Catholic nationalism. This O'Connell discovered for himself in 1841 when he was forced to leave Belfast protected by a force of armed and mounted constabulary.

In pressing the merits of his Union Bill, Pitt had argued that Irish prosperity would be assured. Irish economic growth had been impressive in the eighteenth century but, outside of the north-east, this faltered with the ending of the Napoleonic Wars in 1815. The performance of the Irish economy had little to do with either an Irish Parliament or the Union but rising levels of poverty certainly helped to strengthen nationalist feeling. After Waterloo agricultural prices fell and continued to fall: this may have benefited urban workers but it made it more difficult for tenant farmers to pay their rent. In normal times rents should have fallen in line with prices but they were reduced only slightly and in some cases not at all. The reason was that demand for land was increasing due to population growth. In the eighteenth century rapid population growth (from about two million to around five million) had been more than matched by an increase in wealth. From the Union onwards population growth (eight and a half million by 1845) outstripped productivity. To make matters worse mass-produced goods from industrial Britain and Belfast had a devastating effect on local crafts and the domestic textile industry (wool in the southern half of the island and linen in the northern half). Industrial progress was slow outside of the north-east and Dublin stagnated. Poor farmers and labourers were rapidly losing ways of supplementing their incomes from the soil.

The cultivation of the potato made it possible for a family to live at subsistence level for nine months of the year on just one Irish acre of land. The potato was no more vulnerable to failure than corn which was Ireland's principal export. It also fed huge numbers of animals, pigs in particular. Indeed, the consumption of the potato (if supplemented with cabbage and buttermilk) was a healthy diet and no major epidemic checked population growth. Then, in 1845, a new fungal disease struck the potato, by then almost the sole food of one third of the population. About half the crop was destroyed. Peel's Tory government took reasonably prompt action by setting up public works and by buying scarce maize from America and selling it at cost price or below from food depots run by the Army commissariat. Peel also got rid of the Corn Laws in the hope of reducing food prices but the gentry in his party cast him into the political outer darkness for this perfidy. The Whigs, with Lord John Russell as Prime Minister, came to power in 1846 with a passionate belief in the free market. Orders for American corn were cancelled, food depots were closed down and the starving were expected to earn money for food in the public works.

During the terrible winter of 1846-47 the public works simply failed to cope. Russell replaced this great inefficient bureaucratic structure with soup kitchens. For a time the soup kitchens were feeding three million every day. However, once the harvest was in during September, the soup kitchens were closed down. From now on the starving could get relief only within the workhouses. Appeals to provide 'outdoor relief' were ignored and the death toll in the overcrowded workhouses, where fever flourished, was appalling.

The Great Famine was declared to be over in 1847 but it raged on to 1850. One million people died and another million emigrated. The government spent about £10 million on relief (mostly in cancelling workhouse debts) but the Crimean War was, by comparison, to cost some £60 million. Many agreed with the republican John Mitchel that God had sent the blight but that the English had sent the famine. The Union had been put on trial and it had failed. There was something of a famine in Irish politics during and for some time after the Famine. Attempts to create an independent Irish Party in the Commons in the 1850s and 1860s yielded no lasting result.

Modern nationalism was born during the French revolution. It had been spread by Napoleon's victorious armies and travelled rapidly along newly-constructed railway tracks deep into eastern Europe by the 1840s. In the 1848 Revolutions dozens of peoples were demanding national self-determination. Irish nationalism took on the character of this movement and it continued to spread outwards and downwards. The revolutionary tradition barely flickered after the shambolic rebellion led by Robert Emmet in Dublin in 1803. It was revived by the Young Irelanders in the 1840s who made a pathetic attempt in 1848, derided as the 'Battle of Widow McCormack's Cabbage Patch'. Survivors of that rebellion formed the Irish Republican Brotherhood in 1858 (better known as the Fenians). This secret organisation, aiming to create a republic by force of arms, did much to reinvigorate nationalist passion. However, its attempt at revolution in 1867 was easily put down by the police.

The execution of three Fenians in Manchester in 1867 had a profound effect on the Liberal Party leader, W. E. Gladstone. When told as he chopped down a tree in 1868 that he was now Prime Minister he laid down his axe and said: 'My mission is to pacify Ireland.' He disestablished the Church in 1869 and made his first attempt to provide protection for tenant farmers in his Land Act of 1870. In 1870 Isaac Butt, son of a clergyman from Donegal and a former Conservative MP, formed the Irish Home Government Association. This became the Irish Parliamentary Party which won 59 seats in the 1874 general election – the first to be held under secret ballot. Charles Stewart Parnell, a Wicklow landlord, was returned for Meath in 1875: he soon outshone his leader and joined Joseph Biggar and others in a form of filibustering known as 'obstruction'.

Irish agriculture recovered remarkably well after the Famine. Then disaster struck in 1879: constant rain rotted the crops and, at the same time, imports of food from America depressed prices. Great numbers of farmers unable to pay the rent were evicted. Parnell, about to become leader of the Irish Party, realised that he had to champion the tenants. Farmers in the west of Ireland had formed the Land League under the leadership of the Fenian, Michael Davitt. A deal known as the 'New Departure' was struck: the Fenians would suspend their revolutionary plans to join the demand for Home Rule if Parnell would support the movement to end landlordism.

Parnell advised putting a tenant, who took over a farm from which a family had been evicted, into 'moral Coventry'. When applied successfully on Captain Boycott's estate in Mayo it became known as 'boycotting' and spread rapidly over the country. Landlords were powerless to resist this (largely) non-violent action. Gladstone produced an effective Land Act in 1881 which provided good protection for tenants and introduced the first rent controls anywhere in the UK. The 'Land War' was to continue but Parnell was able to return to the question of Home Rule.

The Third Reform Act greatly widened the franchise and increased the Irish electorate five-fold: not yet full democracy, it nevertheless enabled the voice of the people to be heard in elections for the first time. The 1885 general election is often regarded as the most significant in Irish history (though that of 1918 has a good claim): 86 Nationalists (members of the Irish Party) were returned. Equally significant was that all other Irish MPs were Conservatives (16 of them in Ulster) and that Liberal representation was wiped out in Ireland. Ireland was polarised: Catholics voted nationalist and Protestants voted unionist (the sprinkling of educated Protestants who were nationalists was not enough to make any electoral difference).

Parnell now held the balance of power in the Commons. After a somewhat inexplicable alliance with the Conservatives, in 1885 Parnell put Gladstone into power. Gladstone announced his conversion to Home Rule and put forward a Bill in the spring of 1886. But the great moment had not arrived: deserters from the Liberal Party ensured the Bill's defeat in June. Soon after these Liberals joined the Conservatives to create the Unionist Party (the name Conservative did not officially return until 1922). Passions ran high: fierce sectarian rioting ensued in Belfast.

Parnell's party was the first modern and disciplined political party in the UK. That unity was shattered in 1890 when Parnell was cited in a divorce case; he refused to step down and the party was split, a division not healed until 1900. Gladstone, returning to power in 1892, put forward a second Home Rule Bill in 1893; it passed the Commons but was easily defeated in the Lords. The lesson was clear – Ireland would not get a devolved parliament until the power of the peers of the realm had been broken.

The Conservatives, in office for most of these years, would not concede Home Rule but they did provide some useful measures for Ireland. Elected county councils replaced Grand Juries in 1898 and in 1903 Wyndham's Land Act effectively solved the land question: tenants were lent money by the government to buy out the landlords. In the ensuing years the Irish countryside was transformed: save for small demesnes the great estates disappeared and were replaced by family-owned farms. Ireland was one of the few countries in Europe where landlords were removed without widespread bloodshed. Meanwhile nationalism in Ireland continued to evolve, characterised in these years by a cultural renaissance including a revival of

Gaelic games by the Gaelic Athletic Association, the Gaelic League (which set out to restore the language where it had been lost), and the Anglo-Irish literary revival involving W. B. Yeats, J. M. Synge and others who set up the Abbey Theatre in Dublin.

In 1906 the Liberal Party won the greatest victory in its history. This was a disappointment for John Redmond, leader of the reunited Irish Parliamentary Party, because the new government did not need Irish support. That situation was transformed in 1909-1911 when the government was locked in a titanic struggle with the Lords. In 1911 the Parliament Act ensured that the House of Lords could reject legislation only for three successive sessions (about two years). Following two general elections in 1910, the Liberals lost their overall majority and were dependent on the Irish Party to stay in power. Home Rule was the obvious price of support.

Why did the Third Home Rule Bill, introduced by Asquith's government in 1912, not become law? Unionist resistance is the main explanation. Led by Sir Edward Carson, Ulster Unionists pledged themselves in a covenant ('Ulster's Solemn League and Covenant') signed by 471,414 people to 'use all means which may be found' to prevent a Home Rule parliament being set up in Ireland (not just in Ulster). Belfast was the biggest city in Ireland, the port of third importance in the UK after London and Liverpool, with the biggest shipyard, rope works, linen mill, flax machinery factory, tobacco works, handkerchief factory, tea machinery factory and aerated waters factory in the world. All were owned by Protestants and their industrial and commercial strength was crucial in this struggle.

Led by Andrew Bonar Law, the Conservatives gave their full support. 'All means' included the threat of violence and in 1913 the Ulster Volunteer Force was formed. Asquith put forward complex partition proposals but neither Unionists nor Nationalists would consider them. Civil war seemed closer when the Irish Volunteers were formed in Dublin in 1913. The UVF ran in 216 tons of German rifles and ammunition at Larne, Bangor and Donaghadee in April 1914. When a small consignment of antiquated Mauser rifles were landed openly at Howth for the Irish Volunteers in July 1914 violent conflict seemed inevitable.

War in Europe postponed civil war in Ireland. Asquith put the Home Rule Bill on the statute book but only to be implemented after the war and with a general pledge to make special provision for Ulster. Irish and Ulster Volunteers alike flocked to join up and Ireland never seemed so peaceful and prosperous. But the Irish Republican Brotherhood determined on revolution

and persuaded some Irish Volunteers and members of the left-wing Irish
Citizen Army to fight to set up an Irish Republic with German help. The
insurrection in Dublin, beginning on Easter Monday 1916, lacked German
help and was put down in less than a week. It lacked popular support but,
following the execution of its leaders, a seismic shift began to take place in
Irish nationalist opinion.

A new umbrella separatist party, Sinn Féin (meaning 'ourselves'), formed
in 1917. Led by survivors of the rebellion, it won a series of by-elections in
1917-1918. Attempts by the government to introduce conscription in 1918
and the imprisonment of separatists suspected of being in a (non-existent)
German plot cut the ground from under the more moderate (and ageing)
Nationalists. When the war ended in November 1918 it was followed rapidly
by a general election. The franchise was widened still further by giving all
men and some women the vote. Sinn Féin won 73 seats, reducing the
Nationalists to six. Just as significant, Unionist representation was raised from
18 to 26, and the Conservatives in David Lloyd George's coalition formed an
overall majority in the House of Commons.

Pledged not to take their seats at Westminster, the Sinn Féin MPs formed
their own assembly, Dáil Éireann, in January 1919 and declared that Ireland
was a republic. Some Irish Volunteers (becoming the Irish Republican Army
the following year) began a guerrilla campaign against Crown forces and civil
servants. What was Lloyd George to do? He proscribed the Dáil and prepared
a new Home Rule Bill. Back in 1916 the Ulster Unionists had made the
decision to accept partition. Crucially, they decided to call for the exclusion
of just six counties because they feared that the addition of Monaghan, Cavan
and Donegal would endanger their majority. With no Sinn Féin MPs and only
a handful of Nationalists led by Joe Devlin of West Belfast in the chamber, the
Ulster Unionists got their way in a Conservative House of Commons. The
Government of Ireland Act of 1920 had an unexpected feature, however:
'Northern Ireland' was to have its own devolved parliament in Belfast, just as
'Southern Ireland' was to have its own Home Rule parliament in Dublin.
Ulster Unionists were quietly delighted by this arrangement – a local
parliament could be a vital defence if a future Liberal or Labour government
tried to reunite the island.

This 'Partition Act' was naturally rejected by Sinn Féin. The IRA fought
on in a spreading guerrilla war until in July 1921 a truce was agreed. Clearly
a fresh political arrangement was needed. Talks between Eámon de Valera, the
Dáil president, and Lloyd George were inconclusive. Eventually, the Dáil sent
a delegation to negotiate with the British government in October. Sir James

Craig, now Prime Minister of Northern Ireland, refused to join in the discussions. At 2 am on 6 December 1921 the Anglo-Irish Treaty was signed. Twenty-six counties were to form a Dominion called the Irish Free State. The Royal Navy was to retain three ports and the frontier with Northern Ireland was to be settled by a boundary commission.

Lloyd George and his cabinet – and indeed most of the Opposition – were satisfied that the Irish Question had at last been solved. But as the year 1921 was coming to a close the Dáil was bitterly debating the Treaty with de Valera leading opposition to it. Members of the IRA were preparing to fight again, this time against each other. North of the border Catholics felt that they were in a worse position than before, though many hoped that a boundary commission would assign their area to the Free State. And Craig was presiding over a devolved part of the United Kingdom rent by intercommunal and political violence resulting in more bloodshed than all the riots and sectarian clashes in Ulster in the previous century put together.

Bibliography
A History of Ulster, Jonathan Bardon, Blackstaff 2001
Ireland: The Politics of Enmity 1789-2006, Paul Bew, Oxford, 2007
Contested Island: Ireland 1460-1630, Seán Connolly, Oxford, 2007

Chapter Three

POLITICS AND THE WRITING OF IRISH HISTORY: THE IRISH CASE

Paul Bew

In his Wiles lectures, given in Belfast in 1985, Eric Hobsbawm declared: 'To be Irish and proudly attached to Ireland – even to be proudly Catholic Irish or Ulster Protestant Irish – is not in itself incompatible with the study of Irish history.' He adds: 'To be Fenian or an Orangeman, I would judge, is not so compatible...unless the historian leaves his or her conviction behind when entering the study.' These are interesting remarks. The issue of objectivity in the writing of Irish history is a fraught one. The fact remains that very many people in Ireland, Fenians and Orangemen in particular, regard their history as almost a personal possession and resent what is often seen as a subversive and impious challenge by scholars in ivory towers. Given the scale of emotional investment that has traditionally been made, it is difficult to contemplate the possibility that for all its sound and fury, the tale might not entirely have the comfortable significance attached to it.

These issues first received serious historiographical treatment in the nineteenth century from two great scholars, James Anthony Froude (1818-1894) and William Edward Hartpole Lecky (1838-1903). Both published extensively on the great issues of the day – issues of secularism, freedom and political morality. Both men were outstanding researchers and were recognised as such by the academy: Froude was appointed Regius Professor in Modern History at Oxford in 1892, while Lecky was awarded a LittD at

Cambridge in 1891. Nonetheless, they had very different styles. Lecky was obsessed with precision and calibration of judgment; Froude, on the other hand, enjoyed dramatic presentation above all. Froude was always inclined to present history as a matter of harsh choices, which, when fudged by those in power, only made matters worse: paradoxically, he was capable of escapism himself. In the spring of 1879 he privately advocated a policy of extermination of black Africans (according to Lord George Hamilton's memoir) but when he came to make a public statement he spoke of treating them with 'perfect justice'. Hamilton, an Ulster aristocrat, remarked that after this he never took Froude seriously again.

The greatest Victorian historian of Ireland, Lecky was driven by a conviction that Irish history was 'so steeped in party and sectarian animosity, that a writer who has done his utmost to clear his mind from prejudice, and bring together with impartiality the conflicting statements of partisans, will still, if he is a wise man, always doubt whether he has succeeded in painting with perfect fidelity the delicate gradations of provocation, palliation and guilt.'[1] Lecky was the heir to a small landed property in Queen's County and Carlow. As a student at Trinity College, Dublin, Lecky had been deeply concerned about a perceived malaise in Irish political life. Whilst acknowledging that sectarianism, the greatest evil in Irish life, was the cause of the absence of local legislature, the absence of a native parliament, nonetheless, in nineteenth-century Ireland carried a profoundly negative implication. The public opinion of Ireland was naturally hostile to the existing government. Shortly after graduating from Trinity, Lecky published *The Leaders of Public Opinion in Ireland* (1861), a powerful analysis of Irish political culture from Grattan to O'Connell. It contained a measured and not unsympathetic portrait of its major figure, Daniel O'Connell. The 1871 edition of this work was, in fact, even more 'nationally-minded' in tone; over time, Lecky's respect for O'Connell appears to increase significantly. It is tempting to suggest that the Irish born and raised Lecky's immersion in Irish life and society was greater than Froude's, and this explains their differences as scholars. For Lecky, Grattan's liberal patriotism is highly attractive and O'Connell's political mobilisation for Catholic Emancipation, at the least, defensible; for Froude, both Grattan and O'Connell were windy demagogues. Lecky's life and being were indeed dominated by Ireland. Nevertheless, Froude's connection and intimacy with Irish affairs, though less profound than that of Lecky, was also significant.

A Tory radical and Imperialist, Froude always wrote with 'nerves on the stretch' and 'obsession' near the 'surface'.[2] Froude, in fact, came to hold a stance unprecedented in English historiography: friendly to puritanism and a strong monarchy, hostile to the monasteries, and by no means tender to early capitalism.[3] What interested Froude was not liberty in the constitutional or liberal sense – frequently he uses the word 'constitutional' pejoratively – but acts of 'good authority'. He studied Ireland with these assumptions always dominant in his mind: inevitably the Irish, who felt they had suffered much from both imperialism and puritanism, often bitterly mocked his work. Yet, Froude, in a curious way, respected Ireland and the Irish experience: in other Victorian histories, the Irishman is a mere foil to English virtues, but for Froude he is altogether more seductive and intriguing. 'The Irish who had been conquered in the field revenged their defeat on the hearts and minds of their conquerors: and in yielding, yielded only to fling over their new masters, the subtle spell of the Celtic disposition.'[4] Each new English politician sent to Ireland to deal with its problems was possessed with 'the belief that he, at last, was the favoured knight who would break the spell of enchantment'. For Froude, Ireland and the Irish embodied a 'fatal fascination' which he saw as 'certain perennial tendencies of humanity, latent in all mankind and which opportunity may at any moment develop…an impatience of control, a deliberate preference for disorder…a reckless hatred of industry'.[5] 'Putting aside the question of the justice of the observation, it can be said of Froude,' as Professor JA Burrow has observed, that, in contrast to other leading Victorian historians, Froude 'could imagine what it might be to be someone else, lead another kind of life.'[6]

Born into a wealthy clerical family, James Anthony Froude was educated at Westminster College and Oriel College, Oxford. Soon after graduation he took up a position as the tutor for the son of an Evangelical clergyman in Ireland. In 1845, Froude returned to make a long tour with his friend, George Butler, during which he suffered a serious illness. Froude's personal reaction to the Famine is very striking. There was no cold indifference, no sense that an inferior race was meeting its just deserts. He wrote to an Oxford friend, Arthur Hugh Clough from Ireland: 'I hear horrible stories…I think it is very lucky for us that we are let to get off for the most part with generalities and the knowledge of details left to those who suffer this. I think that if it was not so, we should all go mad or shoot ourselves'.[7] Three decades later, talking of pre-Famine Ireland which he knew 'intimately,' he recalled the 'potato in its glory' and the subsistence peasantry, which relied upon it, 'the singular intelligence in the midst of helplessness'.[8] He noted a local gentry, wonderfully hospitable, but more than a little feckless.[9] He was perfectly clear as to the impact of the Famine: 'Hundreds of thousands perished…England voted ten millions and exerted herself to send food, but the food was insufficient and most of the money was wasted'. Froude also grasped the full political implications.

An Irish Catholic bishop said bitterly to me that every death lay at England's door. England, it seemed, was expected to work a miracle, like the multiplication of the bread at the sea of Galilee. Yet, what the Bishop said was true, after all. The condition of things which made such a calamity possible was due essentially to those who had undertaken the government of Ireland, and had left Ireland to her own devices.[10]

Froude realised that the Irish diaspora in America would retain an enmity towards the British Government.

It was a law of nature that the people should increase like rabbits while the potato flourishes, and perish like rabbits when the potato failed. The economist sees no objection; but there are natural laws there and also spiritual laws, and by the action of these spiritual laws, there are now five million Catholic Irish citizens in the United States whose one hope is to revenge the loud agony of their fatherland on guilty England.[11]

Yet, this sympathetic and insightful commentator on the Famine and its effects was determined to make himself a figure of controversy in Ireland. In the late 1860s, Froude took a house – 'Dereen' – in Kenmare, Co Kerry. In 1868, Froude and his family began a tradition of entertaining the local Laragh schoolchildren at Dereen House. The local press hailed the Froude family as 'the kindest, most pleasing persons that England could send to the sister island'. In 1870, the local parish priest and old Repealer, Father Callaghan McCarthy, getting wind of some of Froude's opinions, denounced Froude's work as anti-Catholic, but having made his point in public, attended the occasion at Dereen, allowing, in Froude's phrase, a 'feast of reconciliation'[12] to go ahead. Froude's own wry comment is worthy of note: 'We held our feast of reconciliation, at which he was generously present, with the schoolchildren on the lawn. They leaped, raced, wrestled, jumped in sacks, climbed greasy poles and the rest of it – 100 stout little fellows with as many of their sisters – four out of five…to grow up citizens of the United States, the fifth to be a Fenian at home.'[13] At Laragh, he worked on his manuscript for *The English in Ireland in the Eighteenth Century*, which he published first in 1872. Its tone, unlike that of Lecky's early works, was deeply offensive to Nationalists. Inevitably, Froude became an ogre: this time, his critics were not to be so easily appeased as Reverend Callaghan McCarthy.

It is important to convey the sense of shock created by Froude's book, not just in Ireland but in England. As the nineteenth century progressed, the

British Establishment, irritated by the failings of the Irish landlord class, was prepared also to sponsor exposure of the Cromwellian legacy. The de-legitimisation of the Irish landlord class became an entirely permissible activity. Particularly important here was the work of Lecky's friend, JT Prendergast, on the history of the Cromwellian era. Prendergast's *The Cromwellian Settlement in Ireland* was first published in London in May 1865. On 26 October 1865, JT Delane, editor of the *Times,* away from his London base on an Irish trip, wrote to GW Dasent in the *Times* office in London: 'I am glad you put in the review of *The Cromwellian Settlement.* It is making a great sensation here, many of the reigning families being traced either to private troopers or to sharpers who bought up their claims.'[14] The Prime Minister, Gladstone, read Prendergast's book while he was preparing his first Irish Land Act in December 1869.[15]

Against such a *bien pensant* consensus, Froude chose to claim that Cromwell, alone of British statesmen, had understood the requirements of Irish society. Froude followed the position established by his intellectual hero, Thomas Carlyle, who, in 1848, made it clear that he regarded English government in Ireland as a sham since Cromwell's time.[16] Carlyle's essay 'Ireland and the British Chief Governor' sharply criticised the administration of Lord John Russell, Prime Minister in 1848, for not facing up to the harsh choices involved in ruling Ireland and instead investing time and effort in legislation which dealt with minor issues. Thomas Carlyle himself was prepared to argue for state intervention to mould the hard-working Irish into organised labour forces which would revive the country.[17] Face to face with Russell over dinner in 1864, Carlyle made it clear that he had not changed his mind.

> He said the Irish had never been well governed except under Cromwell: they had too much freedom to talk to every man, whatever folly came into their heads. What they wanted was someone to enforce silence and keep them working. They were a fine race when under control, but unfit to be their own masters.[18]

Froude defended Cromwell from some of the worst charges of cruelty in arms and mocked Prendergast's depiction of 'Irish hearts ... full of the noblest fire ... under the poorest rags.' It was, however, Cromwell's 'mode of government' which attracted Froude's praise.

> But had Cromwell's mode of government been persisted in – had there been no relapse into the old combination of iniquity

and feebleness – events would have justified his resolution. He meant to rule Ireland for Ireland's good, and all testimony agrees that Ireland never prospered as she prospered in the years of the Protectorate'.[19]

All testimony, of course, did not agree, but Froude insisted that, under Cromwell, Ireland's interests were not sacrificed to England's commercial advantage. For Froude, Cromwell answered the deepest needs of the Irish character: 'He allowed no wrongdoing – no tyrannous oppression of the poor ... He abolished licence, which the Irish miscalled liberty.'[20] Froude insisted that if Cromwellian policy had been consistently applied, 'the two nations would, at least, have become one'.[21] He added: 'The best hope of really uniting the two countries was to make Ireland Protestant in the best sense of the word.' In his lecture 'Ireland under Cromwell,' delivered in the Academy of Music, New York, on 19 November 1872, Father Thomas N Burke gave the inevitable angry Irish Catholic reply: 'Cromwell retired from Ireland, having glutted himself with the blood of the people,' his final action being to send 80,000 Irish slaves to work in the sugar plantations of Barbados – 'fair, beautiful, stripling youths.' 'Oh! Great God! Is this the man who has an apologist in the learned, the frank, the generous and gentlemanly historian, who comes in oily words to tell the American people that Cromwell was one of the bravest men that ever lived, and one of the best friends that Ireland ever had'.[22]

Nor was it simply Froude's treatment of the Cromwellian era which caused offence. Consider his treatment of the case of the execution of Father Nicholas Sheehy, who was hanged for the alleged murder of a Whiteboy informer in 1766. Thomas Moore, in his *Memoirs of Captain Rock*, described Father Sheehy's execution as 'one of those *coups d'etats* of the Irish authorities which they used to perform at stated intervals, and which then saved them the trouble of further atrocities for the time being.' After his execution, Nicholas Sheehy rapidly achieved the status of revered martyr. His tomb became a place of pilgrimage – the stone which lay above his body was chipped to pieces by enthusiastic relic hunters. More than a century later, when the Meaghers of Kilkenny, a substantial Catholic farming family, found themselves the focus of the conflict with landlordism in Tipperary, it was proudly recalled that Mrs Meagher had the blood of the martyred Father Nicholas Sheehy in her veins.[23]

All this reverentialism was a deep provocation to a mind like Froude's. Froude noted contemptuously: 'The execution is among the stereotyped enormities which justify an undying hatred against the English rule and connection.' But he added with a decided brutality of tone: 'Yet, the Government was essentially right; and if treason and murder are crimes at all in Ireland, Father Sheehy was as deep a criminal as ever swung from a crossbeam.'[24] It was, of course, rather a big 'if': for John Mitchel, this was truly poisonous stuff; many believed, after all, that Father Sheehy's alleged victim had not been murdered at all, but lived on safely in Newfoundland. The execution of Father Sheehy, in Mitchel's view, was 'judicial murder, pure and simple'.[25] He completed his lengthy demolition with the words:

> He [Froude] had done evil as he could; he has sought grievously to injure people, which have done him no wrong. I would now commend him, after the example of his Cromwellian heroes, to fall down upon their knees and seek the Lord...so that peradventure, Grace might be given him to repent and receive absolution of his sin.[26]

Mitchel's rebuttal was widely admired. WJ O'Neill Daunt, for example, largely agreed with Mitchel, describing Froude as an apologist for torture.[27] But Froude could hit back effectively. He also had a gift for getting under Mitchel's skin. His remark to an American audience was a double blow against John Mitchel's view (as a northern Protestant himself) that northern Protestants ought to be Irish nationalists, and Mitchel's other great cause – the defence of slavery in the US South: 'If I know anything of the high-spirited, determined men of the north of Ireland, they would no more submit to be governed by a Catholic majority in Dublin than New England would have submitted to a convention of slave-owners sitting at Richmond.'[28]

Lecky refuted Froude's negative portrayal of the Irish character and insisted on the genuine nature of Irish grievances. Referring to Froude's hostility to Catholic Emancipation, Lecky observed icily: 'However much it may please literary gentlemen in search of sensational paradox to coquet with such views, any responsible statesmen who acted on them would be very properly regarded as more fit for a place in Bedlam than for a place in Downing Street.'[29] Professor Roy Foster has shrewdly argued that Lecky feared that Froude's tone would actually intensify Nationalist sentiment and thus weaken the Union.[30] This was a widespread view amongst Irish liberal unionists. John E Cairnes wrote to Lecky to share his indignation provoked by Froude's book: 'Gross perversions of history and malignant attempts to stir up the worst and most dangerous passions of the sensitive and excitable people.'[31] This liberal Irish Quaker economist and close friend of John Stuart Mill, had told an Irish nationalist friend, Dr Robert McDonnell: 'What I feel on the subject of nationality is that the elements of a nation do not exist in Ireland, and were English power withdrawn, we should fall into chronic civil war.'[32] He was particularly keen, therefore, to draw McDonnell's attention to his own refutation of Froude in the August 1874 *Fortnightly Review*: 'I am particularly pleased that you approve my review of Froude, and to think it may do something towards countering the influence of a pestilent book.'[33] Cairnes had brutally mocked Froude's pretensions. Froude's work bore much the same relationship to good history as bad novels with a simplistic 'moral' lesson did to the best of imaginative literature. Froude's 'scholarship' was irresponsible: both because it intensified irrational Nationalism, kindling 'new ardour in the ranks' of Home Rule, while at the same time 'fortifying the worst prejudices of Irish Protestants.'[34]

Against Froude's Cromwellianism, Lecky had another model in mind for the best development of Ireland. This was an Ireland ruled benignly by its own patrician class – hence Lecky's admiration for Grattan, whom Froude saw as a bombastic figure. Lecky admired this project of a restrained, moderate eighteenth-century patriotism. He felt it was destroyed by William Pitt[35], the Prime Minister at the time of the Act of Union of 1801, linking Britain and Ireland.

In his *History of Ireland in the Eighteenth Century* (1878), Lecky had censured Pitt. Not everyone accepted Lecky's argument on this point. In the 1903 edition of *Leaders of Public Opinion,* Lecky returned to the issue of Pitt's role in the 1790s; he acknowledged that recent scholarship had attempted to place Pitt's efforts in a more sympathetic light. Lecky had, in fact, written generously to the author of one of these works.[36] But Lecky acknowledged that he remained personally unconvinced; Pitt's culpability remained all too clear.[37] He had sent Fitzwilliam to Dublin in 1795, with the hint that the Government would support Catholic Emancipation, but then left his Viceroy in the lurch. The Viceroy's tactical errors in tact in handling the powerful local Protestant interests were acknowledged; but for Lecky, the real blame for the débâcle lay in London. Pitt had then used Castlereagh and Cornwallis to gain Catholic support for the Union project by offering a rapid process of full emancipation. When the King refused the Catholic claims on pain of abdication, Pitt, in Lecky's view, should have faced the monarch down. After all, the King had been similarly outmanoeuvred on other issues. Nor was Lecky mollified by Pitt's resignation on the Catholic question in 1801: 'There has seldom been a resignation which deserves less credit.'[38] Froude, on the other hand, delighted in puncturing what he saw as reformist self-deception and using the testimony of a revolutionary like Tone to do it, as when, in 1795, Tone dismissed moderate liberal opinion on the Irish question and 'proves' the greater honesty and purchase on reality of the conservative hardliners.[39] In particular, while Lecky venerated the memory of Edmund Burke, a strong believer in a reformist accommodation between Irish Catholics and the British state,

Froude's account of the Burke family's influence on Irish politics was less flattering, drawing both on radical and government sources to achieve its effect.

In the short term, Lecky's worst fears were justified. It became fashionable to employ Froude's work in defence of nationalism. Froude was gradually turned into a witness in unwitting support of Irish separation. In Dennis Dowling Mulcahy's lecture, given in Cambridge Hall, London, to a large audience of advanced Irish Nationalists and English radicals, Mulcahy, a Tipperary Fenian insurrectionist of 1867, who practised medicine in the United States after his release from jail, conceded that Froude was an anti-Catholic bigot, all too ready to excuse the cruel Cromwellian massacres of Drogheda and Wexford as 'necessary'. But he insisted that Froude was not really an enemy to Irish freedom and national independence. Rather, Froude, by outlining the brutality which lay at the heart of the Anglo-Irish relationship, gave the best possible case for Irish revolutionary violence. Froude's condemnation of the Irish as 'a nation which at once will not defend its liberties on the field, nor yet allow itself to be governed,' was a clear invitation, incitement even, to defend these liberties. Froude admitted the 'sacred rights of revolution,' adding only the caveat: 'It is sacred only when the insurgents have the power to achieve it.' 'Should they achieve such an enterprise,' says the well-known Englishman, 'I shall willingly release them as another among the nations of the earth.'[40] In short, Dennis Dowling Mulcahy regarded Froude's apparent adherence to a 'might is right' doctrine[41], as a justification for Irish revolutionary violence. Froude was being treated as an invitation to Irish Nationalists to do their worst. This was precisely the type of intellectual contagion generated by Froude's work which Lecky deeply feared. Froude stands condemned as an irresponsible blowhard. But, in fact, matters were rather more complex. Froude saw and grasped earlier than Lecky the crisis of British rule in Ireland. A discussion which focuses simply on Froude's greater offensiveness will lose sight of the fact that he, in some ways, possessed the greater insight.

In the early and mid 1870s, Lecky still believed in a *via media* between the claims of Irish nationality and the Union. He respected the social conservatism of Isaac Butt's Home Rule movement, even if he did not accept the doctrine of Home Rule. Lecky believed instead, as did the Whig statesman Lord John Russell, that local government reform could satisfy national sentiment in Ireland. He hoped that Gladstonian liberalism, reform from above, could assuage Irish discontents. Lecky was particularly optimistic about the impact of Gladstone's 1870 Land Act. Froude took a rather different view. He invested less in the 1870 Land Act than Lecky. He accepted the potentially destabilising seriousness of the Home Rule movement, which he saw, above all, as a movement which allowed the Fenian activists who had been defeated in the insurrection of 1867 to regroup and prepare for their next advance. In short, Froude was inclined to believe that the Gladstonian liberal unionist project for Ireland was dead. He was certain, at any rate, that Irish agrarian grievances remained. James Macauley observed:

> In Ireland, says Froude, the law is not yet what it ought to be. The tenant must be compensated when he is evicted, but he may still be evicted. The landlord must now pay the tenant five years' rent if he wishes to be rid of him, but I have known of Irish peasants who so loved their houses, that they would not leave them for a 100 years' rent. I would have no evictions.[42]

In the same year, he asked an Irish American audience[43], why, if he despised Ireland, 'did he keep a house there?'[44] In fact, said Froude, he loved Ireland. In September 1873, in 'A Policy for Ireland'[45], the leading article in *Fraser's Magazine*, which he edited, Froude rejected the common English dismissive attitude to the formation of the Home Rule League in Ireland.

The problem was the existence since 1801 of a mongrel Union, which encouraged

> Irish nationality in name but denies it in fact, which accords just enough independence to foster a morbid longing for more, but not enough for any good purpose whatsoever, which establishes sufficient connection with England to draw the Irish nobles and gentry to the metropolis of the Empire, but not sufficient to make English wealth flow back – sufficient to destroy the generous rivalry which independent Ireland could feel towards the powerful and prosperous neighbours, but not sufficient to prevent everything Irish from being daily more petty and provincial, which boasts a Vice-regal court that serves to make the middle classes ape their better and live beyond their means, while it fails to keep the aristocracy at home or to make the Irish capital anything more than the principal town of a struggling province.[46]

Froude continued in a way which raises doubts about his subsequent reputation as a writer who, at all times, believed that the Irish were unfit for self-government: 'It is not to be taken for granted that Home Rule is a madman's dream and itself as proof is proof of Irish folly ... No race is more instinct with love of the country than the Irish, and it may be that, if the nation were sobered by the responsibilities of independence, good and wise men among them would be found to administer the government.'[47] The logic of all this was clear enough: some great conflict with London was looming.

In an attempt to stave off such a conflict, Froude advocated a policy of 'amalgamation'. Ireland was to be governed by an English Home Secretary, with responsibility also for Scotland and Wales. The legal professions of the two countries should be amalgamated – Irish rural criminals could then be tried before juries in Liverpool courts. The Prince of Wales should be given £20,000 a year to take up permanent residence in Phoenix Park. But, as Froude was well aware, there was insufficient political will to make such proposals work: the whole object of establishing a more sustained Royal presence in Ireland had always floundered.[48] The notion of a permanent Royal residence in Ireland had been championed by Sir Colman O'Loghlan, a former ally of Daniel O'Connell. O'Loghlan pointed out how little time was spent by Royalty in Ireland. After 1821, 28 years elapsed before the British crowned head paid a visit to Ireland. This was followed by two visits of five days each in 1853 and 1861. Could the Irish be expected to be loyal when they were so neglected by Royalty? Then there was the matter of the mentality of the Irish people themselves. The *Cork Examiner* derisively commented on Froude's essay: 'If the writer could add a scheme for the wholesale transportation of the Irish people and the resettlement of the country by English and Scottish immigrants, he might have some chance of success, but only a chance.'[49]

In fact, Froude's skill was in pointing up the inconsistencies and weaknesses of British policy rather than suggesting any viable 'new departure'. The difficulty lay with Froude's alternatives to existing policy; alternatives which were both brutal and unconvincing. 'The Irishman is instinctively loyal to an authority which is not afraid to assert itself. He respects courage; he despises cowardice. Rule him resolutely, and he will not rebel; rule him justly, and he will follow you to the world's end.'[50] In the posthumous 1895 edition of *The English in Ireland*, Froude asserted that, were England 'even now at this eleventh hour' to say that she would 'pass no hurried measure at the dictation of incendiaries' and that 'the constitution would be suspended, and that the three southern provinces would, for half a century, be governed by the Crown, the Committee of the Land League are well aware that, without a shot being fired in the field, their functions would be at an end.'[51] Froude was well aware of the likely objection. In the 1895 edition, he also wrote: 'But I am told it is impossible … Not impossible in the nature of things, but impossible from the nature and condition of English parliamentary government – impossible because inconsistent with the interests and ambitions of the parties into which the English parliament is divided.'[52] If in 'a moment of panic,' an English cabinet followed a strong policy, it would be 'undone by the next.' Froude added, with an air of resignation: 'The very quiet which would ensue would be an excuse for a demand for the restoration of constitutional rights. Despotism is out of date. We can govern India. We cannot govern Ireland.'[53] But Froude was not afraid of the consequences of his line of reasoning. He stated his startling conclusion with firm resolution: 'Be it so. Then let Ireland be free.'[54] Michael Davitt, in his *Fall of Feudalism in Ireland*,[55] one of the great early twentieth-century texts of Nationalist advocacy, seized on the passage with delight in support of what he called a 'future racial programme of Irish self-government.' But was Froude right to lay stress on parliamentary competition as the clue to English weakness in Ireland? In 1879, the Irish Land War erupted: thousands of tenant farmers were mobilised in the Land League movement by a radical Nationalist leadership. Froude was not surprised: he had always seen the 1870s as a period of rebuilding for those who had been involved in Fenianism. He was called upon to comment and produced some interesting work.

One important member of the British ruling élite, Lord Derby, accepted much of Froude's analysis, but rejected it in part for a strikingly different, perhaps more profound, reason. In his diary, he noted his response to Froude's typically wide-ranging historical and political analysis contained in his article 'Ireland,' which appeared in the *Nineteenth Century* in September 1880. 'Read to Lady D an article by Froude on the state of Ireland: clever, well written, containing much truth on the analysis of the causes which have led to the present situation. But utterly without help as to the future.' Indeed, Froude hardly conceals his belief that the best thing which could have happened in the past would have been that the penal laws should have been effectively put in force so as to convert or drive out of the country 'the Catholic population'. Derby then made an observation which expresses well the difference between a man with practical experience of politics and an academic, albeit a brilliant one.

> He ignores, I think, the fact that, though laws of extreme severity may be passed by governments or parliaments, sitting at a distance and impressed by motives of state policy, such laws require to be executed by officials or private persons resident among the persons against whom they are directed – and the personal contact of man with man produces a state of feeling which necessarily mitigates the law in its practical administration. In fact, the Irish penal laws never were enforced, nor could be.

Yet, Derby conceded that Froude reflected something in the public mood in both countries. 'Froude represents a very general feeling in the kind of hopelessness as to the future of Ireland which pervades his article. What is to be done with people who seem to hate us more and more, the more we do for them?'[56]

The effect of the agrarian upheaval in Ireland was in some ways more shocking in its impact on the mind of Lecky rather than Froude, though even Froude expected in the autumn of 1880 that there was enough 'virtue' in the Liberal party to resist the tide of agrarian militancy in Ireland.[57] Lecky was appalled by what he saw as the rise of communistic doctrine in the Irish countryside. In early 1880, Lecky significantly told a nationalist friend, WJ O'Neill Daunt, that the speeches of Land Leaguers were far more damaging to Ireland than Froude's work.[58] Lecky was profoundly disturbed to discover that the title of the Irish landlord to land, even though it had lasted for 300 years, had no popular legitimacy: Edmund Burke's theory of prescriptive rights was cruelly cast aside, though Lecky knew well that Burke had argued that for these rights to be respected required a disavowal of triumphalism. Even more depressing for Lecky was the unwillingness of British Liberalism – in which he had invested so much – to defend the legal rights of Irish landlords, or, indeed, any kind of credible economic and social order in the countryside.[59] In consequence, Lecky moved much closer to Froude's world view.

By November 1881, Lecky's break with Gladstonian Liberalism was complete. 'It seems to me that the net result of Gladstone's legislation has been that there are now two predatory bodies instead of one in Ireland, and I do not know whether, in the long run, the Land Court might not prove the worst of the two.'[60] By 1 January 1883, he was writing to his friend Booth: 'It is curious how Irish affairs turn us all into Tories. My old friend, Mr Prendergast, whose *Cromwellian Settlement* is one of the most fiery works of Irish history I know, has become quite so; and, as far as I can find out, the Catholic gentry are, at least, as much so as the Protestant.'[61] By the end of 1885, Lecky and Froude were both guests together of Derby at Knowsley; they were now in 'total agreement about Ireland' and the clashes feared by their host never materialised.[62] Then Froude moved on to another country house, where he met and impressed Wilfrid Scawen Blunt, a strong English supporter of Irish Nationalism: 'He recognised in the Irish a people belonging to a different age of ideas from our own, and thinks that Parnell might well, if he is a man really of courage and prepared to fight, rule them with a strong hand. He believes home rule must come, on account of our democratic weakness here, which is incompatible with Empire. He has little belief in its dangers to England.'[63] In fact, it is striking how the two historians – once bitterly opposed in controversy – now found themselves drawn together and sharing a common fate. No longer were Froude's provocations an excuse for Irish nationalist violence as Lecky and Cairns had feared. Rather, the admissions of both Froude and Lecky as to the defects of British rule in Ireland were exploited by Nationalists and Liberals as part of the case for Home Rule.

In 1880, Parnell exploited Froude's criticisms of the Irish land system in his appeal to influential American audiences.[64] JA Fox's *A Key to the Irish Question* utilised Froude's negative commentaries on Irish absenteeism and the landlord system.[65] Gladstone in particular read Froude for his arguments in favour of the land purchase proposals, which he had made an integral part of his Home Rule legislation. He admitted that Froude did not support his land policy. Nonetheless, Froude was declared by Gladstone to be a man of truth and honour, whose description of Irish peasant life as a 'grinding tyranny, a tyranny the more unbearable because inflicted by aliens in blood and creed' was all the more significant, because it came from a 'man who, if he sees what he believes to be an injustice, will not allow his heart and his conscience to tamper from the principles involved in his exposure.'[66]

Lecky was subject to the same type of subversive reading. R Barry O'Brien, a serious Parnellite historian, always remained a strong admirer of Lecky's historical work. He found it useful for his own self-appointed task of constructing a liberal genealogy of Gladstone's Home Rule policy. But he was not afraid to point up the apparent contradiction between that body of work and Lecky's political opinions in the 1880s and 1890s. O'Brien seized on a passage in Lecky's critique of Froude in *Macmillan's Magazine* for January 1873: 'The two fundamental principles of all constitutional government – that the will of the majority should rule, and that the scruples of the minority should be respected and equally anticipated.' O'Brien's critique of the critique was highly effective. 'But the effect of allowing the majority to rule in Ireland is to throw power into the hands of the Catholics.' This trend was irreversible, because 'both in England and in Ireland at the present day, democracy is growing in influence.'[67]

But if Lecky was to be exasperated by O'Brien's article, five years later, Froude was to be subject to an even more annoying experience. Spotting Froude in the hall during an election meeting in Salcombe in 1892, J S Swift MacNeill, a Home Rule MP, yielded to the moment 'to seek some humour at his expense.'[68] MacNeill then deliberately sprinkled his speech with quotations from Froude, which condemned British rule in Ireland. At first Froude responded impassively, but eventually – indignation rising – he left the room. MacNeill sent him on his way: 'Alas! I see that some people do not desire to hear the truth, even in the words of Mr James Anthony Froude.'[69]

But infuriating as such moments were, the deepest anguish for Froude and Lecky lay elsewhere. They both knew that the Irish popular mind had been captured by another historical writer, a writer whose message was distinctly more welcome – the Young Irelander John Mitchel (1815-75), whose writing Lecky rightly saw as the inspiration for the revolutionary politics of the Land League era. Lord Derby recorded: 'With Lecky … some conversations about Ireland … he admits that the "English garrison" had disqualified themselves from that position by reckless extravagance, being, in fact, three quarters ruined before bad times … He holds that Mitchel's Irish history has had more effect on the popular mind than any other book – it is circulated everywhere at a low price and is to be found in most farm houses and cottages. It is, of course, written in the most bitter anti-English spirit'.[70] Lecky's remark reminds us of a vital truth. John Mitchel had come to dominate the popular Irish, especially Irish American, understanding of the relationship between Ireland and Britain. It was not just the Irish masses who were transfixed by Mitchel: Gladstone read his *Ireland, The History of* on 24 and 29 September 1886, and discussed it sympathetically with James Bryce on 28 December. Father Burke was both too dogmatically Catholic and too politically moderate – 'I do not believe in insurrectionary movements in a country so divided as Ireland'[71] – to become a fashionable literary reference point.

Mitchel might well have been surprised by such a posthumous success. In his lifetime, he had made little money from his historical writing. He had observed gloomily: 'To be the historiographer of defeat and humiliation is not a task to be coveted, especially by one of the defeated. Neither can the world bring itself to take much interest in that side of human affairs. It sympathises with success; it lends an ear to the successful and inclines to believe what they affirm.'[72]

Lecky may have been exasperated by Mitchel's popularity: but he must have been uncomfortably aware that his friend Ernest Renan's celebrated lecture, given at the Sorbonne in 1882, 'What is a Nation?', had declared that the defining feature of nationality was the shared acceptance of a subjectively agreed, but probably erroneous, view of the past. 'Forgetting, I would even go as far as to say historical error, is a crucial factor in the creation of a nation, which is why progress in historical studies often constitutes a danger for [the principle of] nationality.'[73] In the Irish case, one of Renan's observations is particularly suggestive. 'Where national memories are concerned, griefs are of more value than triumphs, for they impose duties and require a common effort.'[74]

One other embattled nineteenth-century historian of Ireland is worthy of note. Like Lecky, William O'Connor Morris (1824-1904) had been shocked by Froude's tone, which had 'turned into ridicule too many distinguished Irishmen.' Although a friend of Froude's – they had both been scholars at the same Oxford college, Oriel – on the publication of *The English in Ireland*, he had sent Froude 'an angry letter'. But like Lecky, O'Connor Morris was later reconciled to Froude: 'I am willing to admit that subsequent events have, in some measure, proved his theories true.'[75] In this sense, O'Connor Morris is a significant figure. Living a year longer than Lecky, he is, in a more important sense, post-Lecky, historiographically speaking. His principal historical work, produced in the 1890s, after the close of a long career on the Bench, has that sense of liberal political disappointment, which permeates Lecky's later historical essays but not his major books. O'Connor Morris was thus forced, much more directly than Lecky, to face up to issues of possible bias. It was no longer possible to assume – as Lecky certainly did in the 1870s – that good historical research principally supported, and was vindicated by, a decent moderate reformed impulse in politics. As a result, the standpoint of the historian was problematised: the emotional stance of a moderate liberal historian of Ireland in the 1890s, as opposed to one in the 1870s, was now more fraught. Lecky seemed to hand the baton of embattled Irish liberalism on to O'Connor Morris. In 1896, he wrote to praise the historical work of O'Connor Morris: 'I am full of admiration for the admirable sanity and judicial spirit you display on subjects about which very few people are either sane or impartial.'[76]

But how to be 'sane' and 'impartial' and be accepted as such, that was the big question. In a striking passage, devoted to this problem in 1895, William O'Connor Morris wrote: 'To this hour, Ireland has produced no genius who has been able to bridge the chasm existing between her divided people, to do justice to the sons of English and Scottish colonists, and to portray the habits and life of the Celtic Irishry.'[77] Three years later, he offered his own valuable *Ireland 1798-1898* as a serious attempt 'to rise above the blinding dust of party conflict, and to be strictly just with the conclusions I have formed as to men and things'.[78] But he added realistically: 'The greatest historical writers, when describing contemporaneous events, or those near their own times, have not been free from the prejudices…caused by tradition, education, personal experience and the circumstances of life.'[79]

In the century or so since William O'Connor Morris penned these remarks, the Irish historiographical tradition has become vastly more rich and complex. One of its most important features is the way in which Irish historians have had to write frequently against a backdrop of violence and turmoil. In the period between 1918 and 1923, three major general studies appeared from the pens of Irish authors: in this epoch, a strong nationalist campaign faced stern resistance in Protestant and unionist Ulster. A founding editor of the magazine *The New Republic*, Francis Hackett, produced his *Ireland: A Study in Nationalism*, published by BW Huebsch in New York in 1918. Emily Lawless and Michael MacDonagh's *Ireland*, published by Fisher Unwin of London in the same year, and Stephen Gwynn's *The History of Ireland*, published by the Talbot Press, also appeared. All these works are characterised by a sympathetic recounting of Irish national grievance. Francis Hackett was the son of an ardently Parnellite doctor in Kilkenny, to whom his book was dedicated; Emily Lawless, also a 'great friend' of Lecky,[80] a liberal Unionist, was the granddaughter of prominent O'Connellite Lord Cloncurry, while her co-author, Michael MacDonagh, who added his material to the work she had completed by the time of her death in 1913, was a mainstream Redmondite Nationalist. Grandson of William Smith O'Brien, the Young Ireland leader, and a child of a distinguished Church of Ireland clerical and academic family, Stephen Gwynn became the Nationalist MP for Galway 1908-1918. He was active in the Gaelic League but also was, like MacDonagh, above all, a particularly loyal and close follower of John Redmond. Gwynn, too, had been positively influenced by Lecky.[81] Yet, all three broadly nationalist writers treat the Ulster Unionist case with great seriousness.

Hackett, though born and raised in Ireland, first achieved professional success in America. He was seen as a sophisticated Irish-American analyst.[82] The first section of his volume, 'Causes,' was devoted to a summary of Irish history, that 'angry memory of conquest and confiscation'[83] which 'Irishmen are conveniently accused of cherishing when the purposes of Imperialist policy would be better served by forgetfulness.'[84] Hackett acknowledged that many people in America were quite unable to reconcile Ireland's indictment of England with their own knowledge and experience of Englishmen. But it is 'precisely for this reason'[85] that any proper discussion of the Anglo-Irish problem must be preceded by an examination of the historical facts. A strong believer in the long-term psychological impact of the British domination of Ireland[86], Hackett deftly painted a portrait of the well-meaning Britisher, who, having made the 'most adequate acknowledgement of the sins of his grandfathers,' is straightaway convinced that 'verbal atonement suffices'. Hackett insisted instead upon the absurdity of the comfortable English notion that the crimes and blunders afflicting Ireland belong to the 'dim past, and cannot be compared with, say, the evils under which the Czecho-Slovaks and Poles have suffered.' There was, according to Hackett, no possibility of a 'social settlement until this meaning of Irish history is accepted and statesmanship granted accordingly.'

In 1922, in a frenetic burst of writing, Francis Hackett wrote – in just a few days – his *The Story of the Irish Nation*. He analysed the conflict of 1919-1921 in striking terms: 'The wickedness of conquest was re-enacted with English soldiers shouting "Halt!" to Irishmen as in the days of Elizabeth, and English mercenaries burning houses and murdering prisoners as in the days of "98"'. Hackett then offered a qualification to his judgement: '[n]ot the whole wickedness of conquest, not the war on the Catholic religion or the venom of the yeoman, not the quartering of the soldiers and the demonism of rape.' But he added decisively: 'And the Irish Republican Army fought back, harassed the enemy, planned ambushes and carried out the killing of hundreds of individual men.'[87]

But despite the impassioned language in this later, more polemic, work, in *Ireland* Hackett was remarkably circumspect on the Ulster question. Hackett laid great stress on the economic basis of Ulster Unionism. Ulster, he stated, had, for a 'long time,' associated its 'superior fortunes' in the matter of 'material wellbeing' with the Union.[88] He was suspicious, therefore, of racial explanations for Ulster Unionism. 'It is no less probable that the homogeneity of Irish and Scotch "unionism" is not so much of racial sentiment, etc., as of capitalist industry. In its economic utterances one finds the Belfast Chamber of Commerce entirely dispensing with racial sentiment'.[89] Hackett concluded: 'Under the circumstances, there is case for Ulster's particularism. It ought never to be dismissed.' He added: 'It ought never to be dismissed, because it is the business of statesmanship to face problems, not to stifle them.' 'Orange Ulster,' therefore, had to be dealt with 'by understanding, not blows.'[90]

Michael MacDonagh's decision to publish his own work within the same covers as that of Emily Lawless is a very striking one. Michael MacDonagh, a distinguished *Freeman's Journal* commentator, was the sympathetic historian *par excellence* of constitutional nationalism. He was the author of important books on William O'Brien and the Home Rule movement; as late as 1947, he published a significant article on Parnell and his family. Lawless, on the other hand, was a convinced Unionist, the eldest daughter of Baron Cloncurry. In the eighteenth century, the Lawless family, like many other able and wealthy Catholic families, sought to make their way on the Continent. Nicholas Lawless (1733-1799) purchased a very considerable estate near Rouen – but, according to his son's memoirs, 'he was not long, however, in finding out that they did not order things much better in France than in Ireland.' Lawless sold his French estate, returned to Ireland, where he conformed to Protestantism and became 'thereby qualified to hold a territorial stake in the country.'[91] His son, Valentine Lawless (1773-1853), despite high social and political connections, became embroiled in the radical currents of the 1790s and was imprisoned. Released from prison, Lawless (later Lord Cloncurry) became, over time, a skilled operator; always a sceptic about the merits of the Union, he effectively operated as a reformist Whig, who exercised considerable influence behind the scenes in the struggle for Catholic Emancipation and its immediate aftermath.

By the 1880s, the Cloncurry family was perceived to be considerably less 'popular' in its political sympathies. During the Land League crisis, the then Lord Cloncurry was identified as a hard-nosed English market-orientated agrarian capitalist, who was less than concerned with general well-being in the Irish countryside.[92] Cloncurry even stymied the efforts of other landlords to defend the rights of agricultural labourers against farmers and thus split the popular movement.[93] Perhaps inevitably, his tenantry at Murroe became actively involved in the Land War.[94] Perhaps inevitably also, *The Nation* (20 February 1886) responded to Lawless' novel *Hurrish* by claiming that Lawless looked down on the peasantry 'from the pinnacle of her three-generation nobility' and had written a work 'slanderous and lying from cover to cover.' The *Freeman* comment rather misses out on Lawless' irony: *Hurrish* satirised the depth of Irish Anglophobia but admitted a similar phenomenon could be found in English middle-class attitudes towards France in earlier epochs. She presented a picture of a violent, brutalised peasantry, egged on by malignant old crones – hence the *Freeman's* anger – but also a society where the state's law and order had no respect. Gladstone, however, was impressed: the Prime Minister felt she had presented to her readers 'not an abstraction, but as a living reality, the estrangement of the people of Ireland from law and order'.[95]

Lawless published her historical novel *Essex in Ireland* in 1890; the 'diary' of an Englishman during the Essex campaign in Ireland, it gained her Gladstone's great admiration, though on a slightly false basis. Gladstone loved it but oddly took the book to be an authentic record rather than a work of the imagination. As Edith Sichel observed: '*Tour de force* though *Essex in Ireland* is, it required perhaps a man of Gladstone's Homeric *naivete* and immense power of belief to take it for a contemporary document; its very correctness and regularity would have aroused suspicion in minds more critical and conversant with the luxuriant waywardness of Elizabethan English.'[96]

MacDonagh's own chapters contain a series of brilliant insights into the era of high Redmondism and the emergence of the Irish Free State from 1914 to 1922. Decisively, however, the book concludes, when it turns to the issue of partition, that it was 'left to the future to decide whether the north would come voluntarily under the Free State, satisfied that she could do so without any fettering of her commercial enterprises. Then, and only then, can there be assured a peaceful and prosperous future for all Ireland – nurtured, her kindred peoples mingled as one.'[97] The emphasis here on 'voluntary' choice is decisive: it echoes precisely Hackett's argument. There is absolutely no suggestion that the partition of Ireland is simply an imperialist project worked by the British state. In *Ireland*, a volume published in 1924 in HAL Fisher's series 'The Modern World: A Survey of Historical Forces', Stephen Gwynn addressed the same issue with a particularly impressive and profound eloquence: 'A fully developed Irish nation can only issue from a voluntary alliance of the two national states which lie at present almost with a naked sword between them. A romantic match is out of the question: the future Ireland must be the offspring of a *mariage de convenance*.' He added wryly: 'This prospect is the less objectionable, because in the Gaelic Ireland that we know, no other type of marriage is customary or approved. But a great deal of hard bargaining precedes such alliances.'[98] Stephen Gwynn concluded with a sharp refutation of the notion that partition represented the triumph of British strategy. 'Nothing that is not Irish stands in the way of its accomplishment: and if it can not be accomplished by Irishmen, no outside power can convert our national aspirations into a reality.'[99] Taken together, these three texts deserve to be regarded as important precursors of the professional historiographical tradition in Ireland.

Inevitably, however, the coming of Irish independence would incite institutionalised pressures in favour of a more heavily one-sided version of the Irish experience. These intensified with the election of the more nationalistic Fianna Fáil government of 1932. In the spring of 1935, Professor Timothy Corcoran SJ, Professor of Education at University College, Dublin, published an important article on the training of young graduate historians in Ireland. The article was a passionate plea for a more explicitly Catholic direction of the process. Professor Corcoran argued that the Institute of Historical Research in London was dominated by a Protestant Anglocentric world view; in future, it was important that young Irish historians learning their trade should not be sent to London. Rather, they should be sent to the 'excellent schools of historical research and of palaeography connected with the Vatican, with the Catholic colleges of France and with the Catholic University of Louvain.'[100] Corcoran's article, which appeared originally in the *Irish Monthly*, received strong endorsement in the editorial of the *Catholic Bulletin* in June 1935. The *Catholic Bulletin* stood for a particular and highly distinctive vision of Ireland's place in the world: an Ireland, especially conscious of the responsibility of being the world's largest English-speaking Catholic country. The world's only Anglophone Catholic country, it held the line within Fianna Fáil against a tendency towards a dilution of the case of Irish Catholic

Nationalism against Britain. When the young Erskine Childers (son of the Republican martyr and a later President of Ireland) gave a public lecture in 1937, stating that Ireland and England had one 'quality in common – they were devoted to the idea of democracy against the wave of Fascist autocracy.' The *Bulletin* was not pleased: 'We rubbed our eyes. Was this the doctrine to expect from Erskine Childers?' England was not a real democracy: had not Erskine Childers' father had to take up arms against British hypocrisy and repression in Ireland? The *Bulletin* preferred the Salazar Fascist regime in Portugal: 'Such a land as Portugal is a better model of a fine friend than England, which Mr Childers recommends to us.'[101]

But Corcoran's intervention was already too late. In 1931 Robin Dudley Edwards of University College, Dublin, joined up with Theo Moody of the Queen's University of Belfast – who had been there already for a year – at London University's Institute of Historical Research. The two men became friends. Edwards later recalled: 'For nearly a year we had a most pleasant exchange of historical views when we met in the evenings.'[102] Moody, Edwards explained, was much obsessed with the 'complexities of historical research,' as revealed by the seminars at the Institute of Historical Research. In 1933, Edwards completed his doctorate, entitled 'The History of the Penal Laws against Catholics in Ireland from 1534 to the Treaty of Limerick (1691)' and in 1935, published his *Church and State in Tudor Ireland: A History of Penal Laws against Irish Catholics 1484-1603*, with the Talbot Press in Dublin and Cork.[103] Moody finished his doctorate on the Londonderry Plantation of Ulster in the early seventeenth century. Out of this 'detailed and elaborate investigation' came a series of articles and a book, *'The Londonderry Plantation, 1609-41: The City of London and the Plantation of Ulster.*[104] In February 1936, Moody established the Ulster Society for Irish Historical Studies in Belfast. In November of that year, Edwards established the Irish Historical Society in Dublin. Within two years, the Ulster and the Irish Societies had agreed to collaborate, and reflecting his decision, the Irish Committee of Historical Science was created in 1938. In March 1938, the first number of *Irish Historical Studies* appeared. This not only gave Ireland the first professional journal of history it had ever possessed, but from the outset established standards of scholarship that gained international recognition.[105] As Dr Ciaran Brady has expressed it, Moody and Edwards were 'determined to bring about a revolution in the aims, method and style of Irish historical writing.'[106] I hope it can now be seen why such a revolution was necessary and why, unlike most revolutions, it was entirely benign in its effect.

Notes

1   Brian Maye, 'An Irishman's Diary,' *Irish Times*, 27 October 2003.
2   JW Burrow, *A Liberal Descent: Victorian Historians and the English Past*, Cambridge (1981), p 236.
3   *ibid,* p 243.
4   *ibid,* p 262.
5   *ibid,* p 262.
6   *ibid,* p 262.
7   Eileen Reilly, 'JA Froude's Use of History and his Irish Prescription,' in Lawrence W MacBride, *Reading Irish Histories: Text, Context and Memory in Modern Ireland,* Dublin (2003), p145; L M Cullen, 'Home Economics,' *Bullan: An Irish Studies Journal,* vol 2, no 2 (winter/spring 1996), p 101.
8   *The English in Ireland,* p 369.
9   JA Froude, 'On the Use of a Landed Gentry,' *Short Studies in Great Subjects,* vol 3, London (1877), pp 408-9: 'I was staying the year before the Irish famine at a large house in Connaught. We had a great gathering there of the landed gentlemen of the country; more than a hundred of us sat down to a luncheon on the lawn. My neighbour at the table was a Scotchman, who was over there examining the capabilities of the soil. "There," he said to me, "you see the landed gentry of the country. In all, the number there may be one, at the most two, who believe that the Almighty has put them into this world for any purpose but to shoot grouse, race, gamble, drink or break their necks on the hunting field"'.
10   *The English in Ireland,* p 571.
11   *The English in Ireland,* p 573.
12   Gerard J Lyne, *The Lansdowne Estate in Kerry under WS Trench 1849-72,* Dublin (2001), p 399.
13   JA Froude, 'A Fortnight in Kerry,' *Frasers Magazine,* 83 (January 1871), p 45.
14   G W Dasent, *John Delane 1817-1879,* vol 2, London (1908), p 149.
15   HGC Matthew, *Gladstone Diaries,* 7 December 1869, p 191.
16   *The Spectator,* 13 May 1848, 'Ireland and the British Chief Governor'.
17   Simon Heffer, *Moral Desperado: A Life of Thomas Carlyle,* London (1985), p 266.
18   JR Vincent (ed), *Disraeli, Derby and the Conservative Party: The Political Journals of Lord Stanley,* Hassocks (1978), 25 February 1864, p 209.
19   JA Froude, 'Romanism and the Irish Race in the United States,' *North American Review,* vol CXXX (January 1880), p 34.
20   Froude, *The English in Ireland,* vol I, p 153.
21   'Romanism and the Irish Race in the United States,' *North American Review,* vol CXXX, January 1880, p 34.
22   *Ireland's Vindication: Refutation of Froude and Other Lectures; Historical and Religious,* London (1873), pp 210-1.
23   *Tipperary People,* 28 January 1881.
24   James Anthony Froude, *The English in Ireland in the Eighteenth Century,* vol II, London (1895), p34.
25   *Freeman's Journal,* 6 April 1872.
26   *Freeman's Journal,* 22 January 1873. An excellent selection of press cuttings covering this controversy may be found in NLI Ms 7516, Larcon Papers.
27   *Lecture on the Rt Hon Henry Grattan: His Character and Career,* Dublin (1875), p 25.
28   Norman Vance, 'The Problems of Unionist Literature: Macaulay, Froude and Lawless,' in DG Boyce and Alan O'Day, *Defenders of the Union,* London (2001), p 183.
29   *ibid,* p 61.
30   'History and the Irish Question,' *Paddy and Mr Punch: Connections in Irish and English History,* London (1994), p 9.

31   Elizabeth Lecky, *A Memoir of the Right Hon William Edward Hartpole Lecky,* Cairnes to
     Lecky, 5 June 1874, London (1909), pp 96-7.
32   NLI Ms 18,490, J E Cairnes to Dr Robert McDonnell, 25 June 1870.
33   NLI Ms 18,490, same to same, 7 August 1874.
34   Tom Boylan and T Foley (eds), *John Elliott Cairnes: The Collected Works*, vol 6, p324.
35   This paragraph owes much to the material presented in Anne Wyatt, 'Froude, Lecky and
     the Humblest Irishman,' *Irish Historical Studies*, vol XIX (1974-5).
36   PRONI Ashbourne Papers, F6/1.
37   *Leaders of Public Opinion,* London (1903), p xvii.
38   *Leaders of Public Opinion,* 1903 ed, vol 1, p 259.
39   *The English in Ireland,* vol III, p 335.
40   Dennis Dowling Mulcahy's lecture in London, 31 March 1876, *The Irishman,* 11 June
     1876. I owe this reference to Dr Patrick Maume. Mr John Ryan of Notting Hill was in the
     audience, and many English radicals and Liberals were present. Thomas Mooney, writer of
     The Transatlantic Column in the Irish World, was on the platform, as was Stephen Joseph
     Meany, a Clare man and Fenian, who had been sentenced to 15 years' penal servitude in
     1866, released after two years on condition he did not live in Ireland or Britain. In March
     1880, he became a member of the founding committee of the American Land League.
     WO'Brien and D Ryan (eds), *Devoy's Post Bag,* vol 1, Dublin (1948), p 393.
41   In fact, Froude was a true follower of Carlyle on this point, believing himself a supporter
     of the 'right is might' doctrine.
42   James Macauley, *Ireland in 1872: A Tour of Observation,* London (1873), p 178.
43   For the derisive Fenian attitude towards this speaking tour, see John O'Leary to J J
     O'Kelly, 8 November 1872, in W O'Brien and D Ryan (eds), *Devoy's Post Bag,* vol 1,
     Dublin (1948), p 63.
44   NLI, Larcom Papers 7516, cutting of address delivered 30 November 1872.
45   *Fraser's Magazine,* vol VIII, no xlv.
46   Froude in *Cork Examiner,* 4 September 1873.
47   'A Policy for Ireland,' p 278.
48   *Freeman's Journal,* 18 May 1868. Gladstone was sympathetic to O'Loghlen's campaign,
     but nothing was done. Gladstone to Sir CM O'Loghlen MP, 20 April 1872, BL ADDMS
     44541, fl 12.
49   *Cork Examiner,* 4 September 1873.
50   *The English in Ireland,* vol 3, p 558.
51   *ibid.*
52   *ibid.*
53   *ibid.*
54   *ibid.*
55   Michael Davitt, *The Fall of Feudalism in Ireland or the Story of the Land League
     Revolutionary,* London and New York (1904), p 717.
56   JR Vincent (ed), *The Diaries of Edward Henry Stanley, 18th Earl of Derby (1826-1893),
     Between 1878 and 1893,* 2 September 1880, Oxford (2003), p 268.
57   'Ireland,' *Nineteenth Century,* vol VIII (September 1880), p 369.
58   WJ O'Neill Daunt, *A Life Spent for Ireland: Being Selections from the Journals of the Late
     WJ O'Neill Daunt,* ed by his daughter, London (1896), p 180.
59   Michael Bentley, *Modernising England's Past: English Historiography in the Age of
     Modernism,* Cambridge (2005), p 75.
60   Elisabeth Lecky, *Lecky: A Memoir,* p 157.
61   Lecky to Arthur Booth, 1 January 1883, p 169.
62   JR Vincent (ed), *Derby Diaries,* p 824.
63   Wilfrid Scawen Blunt, *The Land War in Ireland,* diary entry 1 January 1886, London, p 13.
64   Jane ML Cote, *Fanny and Anna Parnell: Ireland's Patriot Sisters,* pp 112-4.

65   *ibid,* pp 117, 246.

66   *Evening Standard,* 17 April 1886.

67   R Barry O'Brien, 'Mr Lecky on Home Rule,' *Irish Wrongs and English Remedies,* London (1887), p 177.

68   JG Swift MacNeill, *What I have Seen and Heard,* Boston (1925), p 73.

69   *ibid.*

70   JR Vincent (ed), *The Diaries of Edward Henry Stanley, 15th Earl of Derby, 1826-1893, Between 1878 and 1893,* Oxford (2003), 22 December 1889, p864. For Mitchel, see James Quinn, 'John Mitchel and the Rejection of the Nineteenth Century,' *Eire-Ireland* (fall-winter 2003), pp 90-108.

71   *Ireland's Vindication,* p 283.

72   Patrick Maume (ed), *The Last Conquest of Ireland (Perhaps),* Dublin (2005), appendix

73   Ernest Renan, 'What is a Nation?' in Geoff Eley and Ronald Gregor Suny (eds), *Becoming Nationals: A Reader,* Oxford (1996), p 45.

74   *ibid,* pp 52-4.

75   *Memories and Thoughts of a Life,* p 140.

76   WEH Lecky to W O'Connor Morris, 4 June 1896, in E Lecky, *A Memoir of WEH Lecky,* p 283.

77   *Memories and Thoughts of a Life,* London (1895), p60.

78   *Ireland from 1798-1898,* London (1898), v.

79   *ibid,* vi.

80   Elisabeth Lecky, *A Memoir of WEH Lecky,* p 322.

81   S Gwynn, *Experiences of a Literary Man,* London (1926), p217; Gwynn to Winston Churchill, 29 July 1910, Churchill Archives Centre, Churchill College Cambridge, CHAR 2/246. Gwynn is here responding to a request from Winston Churchill, then a member of a pro-Home Rule Liberal cabinet, for advice on appropriate historical reading on Ireland, 'Lecky doesn't need mention,' Gwynn noted.

82   *Freeman's Journal,* 18 January 1919, 'Ireland under the Microscope: An Irish-American's View of the Situation'.

83   Hackett, *Ireland,* p 11.

84   *Freeman's Journal,* 18 January 1919.

85   *Freeman's Journal,* 18 January 1919.

86   Hackett's wife, Signe Toksvig, recorded on 10 May 1931: 'F was saying this morning about the Irish character, as exemplified in the so-called lower orders, that it contained a curious mixture of gentleness and spitefulness, which used to be considered feminine. He traces it all to the eighteenth-century oppression and deprivation of self-respect.' Lis Pahl, *Signe Toksvig's Irish Diaries,* Dublin (1994), p 107. Hackett was not original in offering this type of interpretation. Father Burke explained the Irish propensity for drink thus: 'What made us so impudent, so reckless? Ah, was it not the cruel blooded-stained Government of England, that robbed us of every penny of our possessions? ... What hope had the Irishman at home? He tilled his field and drained it: he made a piece of bog choice arable land; but the moment it was worth twice its former value, the landlord turned him out,' *Ireland's Vindication,* p 109.

87   Francis Hackett, *The Story of the Irish Nation,* Dublin (1924), pp 387-8.

88   Francis Hackett, *Ireland: A Study in Nationalism,* p 92.

89   *ibid,* p 88.

90   *ibid,* p 92-93.

91   *Personal Recollections of the Life and Times with Extracts from the Correspondence of Valentine, Lord Cloncurry,* Dublin (1859), pp 18-9.

92   *Freeman's Journal,* 4 September 1880.

93   Padraig G Lane, 'Landlordism and the Farm Labourers in the 1880s,' *Journal of Waterford Archaeological and Historical Studies,* no 60 (2005), pp 179-83.

94   Anna Parnell (ed with an introduction by Dana Hearne), *The Tale of a Great Sham,* Dublin (1986), pp150-1. This is actually a rather complex case, revealing relatively comfortable farmers against an Irish landlord who happened to be 'a little better off than most of his kind.'

95   Betty Webb Brewer, 'She was Part of it,' in *Eire-Ireland,* vol 18 (1983), p 121.

96   Edith Sichel, Emily Lawless, *Nineteenth Century,* July 1914. Patrick Maume's *Containing Granuille: Nineteenth-Century Novelistic Portrayals of Grace O'Malley,* paper given at the Irish Studies conference, University of Sunderland (November 1994).

97   *Ireland,* 3rd ed (1923), p 480.

98   Gwynn, *Ireland,* London (1924), p 218.

99   Gwynn, *Ireland,* p219. For Gwynn's formal debt to Lecky see his *Experiences of a Literary Man,* p 217.

100 'Protestant Historical Training,' *Catholic Bulletin,* vol XXV, 6 June 1935, p 442.

101 Patrick Walsh (ed), *The Catholic Bulletin: On Peace, War and Neutrality, 1937-39,* Belfast (2004), p 14.

102 RW Dudley Edwards, 'TW Moody and the Origins of Irish Historical Studies: A Biographical Memoir,' *Irish Historical Studies,* vol XXX, no 101 (May 1988), p 101.

103 For an interesting discussion, see James Murray, 'Historical Revision: R Dudley Edwards, Church and State in Tudor Ireland, 1935,' *Irish Historical Studies,* vol XXX, no 118 (November 1996), pp 233-41; see also Aidan Clarke, 'Robert Dudley Edwards 1909-1988,' *Irish Historical Studies,* vol XXVI, no 102 (November 1988), pp 121-7.

104 FSL Lyons, 'TWM,' in FSL Lyons and RAJ Hawkins (eds), *Ireland Under the Union: Essays in Honour of TW Moody,* p 3.

105 Lyons, 'TWM,' p 6.

106 'Constructive and Instrumental: The Dilemma of Ireland's First New Historians,' Ciaran Brady (ed), *Interpreting Irish History: The Debate in Historical Revisionism,* Dublin (1994), p 3.

Chapter Four

THE PARTITION
OF IRELAND

Dennis Kennedy

The partition of Ireland in 1921-22 – and of the then United Kingdom of Great Britain and Ireland – created two entities on the island that no one had set out to achieve, and no one ideally wanted.

For a century Irish nationalists had opposed the Act of Union and sought Home Rule for the island within the United Kingdom, not total separation from it. After 1916 the more extreme form of nationalism represented by Sinn Féin demanded total separation, but with great reluctance, and at the cost of civil war, had to accept the compromise of virtual rather than *de jure* independence, and a 26-county state instead of the whole island.

About a third of the island's population had strongly opposed Home Rule, creating unionism as a political movement. It began as opposition to Home Rule, and evolved into opposition to the inclusion of Ulster in a Home Rule Ireland. A six-county Northern Ireland as a devolved entity within a reduced United Kingdom was a final Hobson's Choice. Each entity was left with a disappointed minority.

These unsatisfactory states of affairs found expression in the violence that surrounded the births of both entities. In the South the former comrades in arms of Sinn Féin turned on each other over the degree of compromise involved in the settlement. In the north bitter sectarian violence preceded partition, nationalists vehemently opposed the settlement, and the IRA launched a terrorist campaign against it.

There the similarities end. The Irish Free State was a virtually independent state intent upon asserting, and over time able to assert, its full independence. Northern Ireland was a small province within the unitary state of the United Kingdom, with a limited degree of devolved authority over internal matters exercised through a regional parliament and government.

The most fundamental difference between the two entities lay in the size and disposition of their minorities. In the South the Unionist minority, largely though by no means entirely Protestant, of approximately 300,000 at the time of Partition was about ten per cent of the new state's population.[1] That was not an insignificant number, but it was too small to oppose the will of the great majority or pose any threat to it, had it wished to do so.

The situation in the North was different. At partition the Nationalist minority constituted one third of the total population, and was almost entirely Catholic.[2] Not only was this a very significant number, the distribution of population meant that in some local authority areas nationalists were in a majority.

The differences in the attitudes of the minorities in the two jurisdictions were even more marked. When the Irish Free State was established there was, in fact, no political minority – that is there was no organised political opposition to the new state. The identifiable minority that remained was religious – it was Protestant – and by the 1926 census was down to just over 200,000. But it was also a minority which openly declared its loyalty to the state.

In December 1921, before the Free State was formally constituted, the Archbishop of Dublin, Dr Gregg, the most senior Church of Ireland prelate in the new jurisdiction, publicly pledged the loyalty and good will of the Church to the new state, and declared that the new Constitution would claim the allegiance of Church of Ireland members.[3] A few days earlier, *The Irish Times,* speaking not specifically for Protestants but for 'Southern Loyalists,' backed the Treaty and said if it was accepted the new state would have their support.

In the North the reverse was emphatically the case. The nationalist minority refused to recognise the new state and its institutions. Prior to the May 1921 election which launched the Northern Ireland Parliament the Catholic Bishop of Down and Connor, Dr MacRory urged every Catholic to vote against partition.[4] Cardinal Logue boycotted King George V's formal opening of the Parliament, Nationalist MPs refused to take their seats, and nationalist-controlled local councils ignored the new authorities in Belfast. Catholic school-teachers initially refused to accept their salaries from Belfast. Instead of pledging its loyalty to the new state, most of the minority in the North gave enthusiastic support to the IRA campaign of terror against it, and to the IRA-enforced boycott of Belfast goods.[5]

The Green South

In the South, the minority's protestations of loyalty did it little good. In May 1922 a group of leading Protestants, alarmed at instances of murder and intimidation of Protestants particularly in county Cork, went to Collins and Cosgrave to seek assurances that Protestants were indeed wanted in the new state, and would be protected.

While assurances were given, and the attacks on Protestants dwindled, the state took little or no account of the existence of a minority which was not Catholic and which did not see Gaelic culture as central to its identity. The minority had to take its compulsory Gaelic medicine along with everyone else, and the Catholic ethos ruled in areas such as health, education, and public morality as enforced, for example, through censorship. The majority, admittedly a very large majority, defined the 'Irishness' which was to be enshrined in the laws and practices of the new state, and took no account of a minority which had a different view of Irishness.

How this worked in practice is seen in the example of divorce legislation. When this question arose in the early years of the Free State, the government's first reaction was to consult the Catholic Church. When the Attorney General advised that refusing to make any provision for divorce would be seen by non-Catholics as an invasion of their rights and as a failure to honour the promises of protection for the minority in the new state, Cosgrave asked the Catholic hierarchy to consider the matter. In October 1923 Cardinal Logue on behalf of the hierarchy declared that it would be 'altogether unworthy of an Irish legislative body to sanction concession of such divorce, no matter who the petitioners may be.'[6] The 1937 Constitution formally prohibited any legalisation of divorce, a prohibition that was to remain until 1995, three quarters of a century after the foundation of the state.

The comparatively minor question of divorce is illustrative of how narrowly Irishness was defined in the independent Irish state – similar lessons could be drawn from examining contraception, abortion, compulsory Irish, censorship. The minority was certainly loyal to the new state, but not entirely comfortable within it. More than a decade after Partition, Protestants in east Donegal felt sufficiently threatened, economically and in other ways, that they formally requested the British Government, as a party to the 1921 Treaty, to intervene to 'restore them their former rights and liberties.' More than seven thousand signed a petition to this effect.[7]

The state that arose from Partition was intensely Catholic and conservative, inward if not backward looking, illiberal – even obscurantist – and obsessed with nationalism. It remained so at least until late in the 20th century.[8] Despite inheriting a reasonably healthy economy, and good social, educational and political infrastructures, under self-government the southern state did not prosper and by the 1950s was experiencing unprecedented, and by European standards almost unparalleled levels of emigration.[9]

The transformation began in the 1960s. Irish society became progressively less Catholic, less Gaelic and more liberal, as the state looked outward rather than inward, seeking and attracting foreign investment, and abandoning the isolationism of non-participation in World War II for participation in UN peace-keeping forces and enthusiastic membership of the European Community. The tide of emigration receded, and was eventually reversed; the economic growth was under way which produced the Celtic Tiger before the end of the century.

In many ways the Irish Republic today is the envy of Europe: it is the promised land for immigrants, it attracts large-scale foreign investment and has the fastest growing European economy, its infrastructure is being spectacularly transformed, its lifestyle is eulogised, and it is regarded as a bastion of culture and human values in a crassly materialistic world.

But this is not the whole picture; the modern Republic still carries a deal of historical baggage, and the rampant Celtic Tiger is not entirely healthy. The modernisation process, while dramatic, has been uneven; public attitudes and behaviour – 'popular Ireland' – in many areas changed much more rapidly than did the state, 'official Ireland'. Long before 1995 many Irish couples had terminated their marriages either by getting church annulments, or divorcing outside the state. Contraceptives were widely used for years before it was legal to import them, and thousands of Irish women travelled to Britain for abortions, and still do. In the 21st century Irish state radio and television continues to observe the daily Angelus while most Irish families abandoned it generations ago, and mass-going among Catholics has plummeted.

The state continues to insist that Irish is the first official language and spends millions of Euros each year to finance its teaching and its official use. Yet in 2004 the legislators who insist on this status conducted less than one per cent of their own debates in Irish. After 13 years studying the language at school, pupils struggle to speak it.[10]

The political divide is not between left and right but between parties peculiarly Irish, born out of the Civil War of 1922-23. All parties still put the nationalist goal of reunification of the island as their theoretical top priority, even though all acknowledge that this cannot happen without the consent of the majority in Northern Ireland, and despite the strong evidence that the southern public regard it as among the least of its political concerns. A recent survey showed that just over half the respondents in the Republic favoured a united Ireland.[11]

While reunification is not the burning desire of the general public, a populist, sentimental nationalism has replaced the political variety, characterised by supreme self-confidence, rather embarrassingly displayed in the reverent adulation of *Riverdance*, or the collective mania over the Republic's soccer team. (Surveys show that percentage of Irish citizens 'very proud' to be Irish rose from 55 per cent in 1994 to 71 per cent in 2003.[12]) This new nationalism may also help explain the surprising degree of tolerance shown towards Sinn Féin and the IRA in the course of the so-called Peace Process, not just by Government, but by the public at large.

President Bush's special envoy Mitchell Reiss's remark in March 2005 that it was hard to understand how 'a European country in the year 2005 can have a private army associated with a political party' [13] is a pointed reminder of how the hangover of history has delayed the modernisation process in some key areas of both official and popular thought. Not only has the Irish Government insisted that such a party with a private army must be given government office in Northern Ireland,[14] it has effectively cooperated, via the International Decommissioning Body, with the private army in its own jurisdiction to allow it to retain control of its illegal armoury.

Despite widespread belief that the IRA was involved in the December 2004 £26 million Northern Bank robbery and in the McCartney murder in Belfast, a rather surprising 28 per cent in an opinion poll in March 2005 deemed Sinn Féin suitable to be a partner in Government in Dublin.[15] In the same month, with criticism of Sinn Féin over its IRA links at its height, the party won 12 per cent of the vote in the Meath by-election – a share inflated by a low turn-out, but also by the party's exceptional ability to maintain its numerical support.

The IRA is believed to be deeply involved in major organised crime in the Republic, working at times with British-based criminal gangs. This has involved cigarette smuggling, the laundering and smuggling of diesel fuel, and of alcohol, and has cost the Dublin exchequer millions of Euros in lost revenue, as well as seriously embarrassing the government. The Northern Ireland Security Minister, Ian Pearson, has described the IRA as 'perhaps the most sophisticated organised crime gang to be found in Europe, possibly anywhere in the world.'[16] The Republic has also been beset by a series of allegations of corrupt practices in both public authorities and in the business world, one recent case resulting in the jailing of a former senior government minister.[17]

The Black North

But even with these imperfections, the Republic is generally viewed as a model, modern European state in stark contrast to a Northern Ireland seen as still wrestling with religious hatreds more appropriate to the 16th century than the 21st, once described by the British Minister responsible for it as a 'bloody awful place' and only now emerging from 30 years of communal violence.[18]

It did not entirely begin like that. The Unionist leadership in 1921 initially showed keen awareness of its responsibilities towards the minority in its jurisdiction – a minority which had suffered in the inter-communal violence that preceded Partition, and which was fearful of its fate. Sir James Craig told a Reform Club lunch in February 1921 that the rights of the minority had to be sacred to the majority, and called for broad views, tolerant ideas and liberty of conscience. In May he said that Unionists would do what they could to manage the six counties, not in a one-sided way, but with the full responsibility that rested on any executive to govern all the people. In July, against the background of increasing attacks in the South on Protestants by anti-Treaty elements, the *Belfast News-Letter* declared that Ulster had the opportunity of showing the rest of Ireland how minorities can exist and flourish without oppression.[19]

What went wrong? At the outset, the hand that Craig seemed to be extending towards the minority was pretty savagely bitten by the IRA campaign that greeted the beginnings of Northern Ireland, by the Belfast

Boycott, and by the refusal of nationalists to have anything to do with the new institutions. The strong public support from the Catholic Church leadership for nationalist rejection of the new state cemented the perception that it was the minority as a whole, not just extreme elements within it, who were 'enemies of Ulster.'

Much of the violence was sectarian, and Catholics as well as Protestants were victims, but in the circumstances of the time, and with the new authorities in Dublin backing the IRA campaign and financing the Boycott, Unionists saw it essentially as an assault on the very existence of Northern Ireland.

When the Northern Ireland Parliament met in 1921, and for four years thereafter, it was indeed a Protestant Parliament simply because Nationalists refused to take their seats in it. The politics and governance of the new entity were framed within an entirely Protestant and Unionist context. Far-sighted Unionists may have, should have, seen that the stability and permanence that they wanted for Northern Ireland was unlikely to be achieved without the consent of at least some sections of the minority, but it is not difficult to see why this did not happen.

Nationalist belief that the Boundary Commission would see off Northern Ireland dominated the minority's approach to the new state for its first three years, but even after the settlement of 1925 the minority continued, in the words of one historian, to flaunt its disloyalty, or at best maintain an attitude of surly resentment.[20]

Minority representatives first took their seats in the Belfast Parliament in 1925, though abstentionism remained a factor in nationalist politics. They took their seats as Nationalists, with reunification their prime political goal. Unionists have been pilloried for running a 'one-party state' in Northern Ireland, but they had little option, for by making its main political goal the elimination of the state, the minority was effectively excluding itself from any share in government, and was ensuring that the minority-majority divide would dominate all political debate.

This suited Unionism, particularly those elements in it which had never shared Craig's professed view that the rights of the minority had to be sacred to the majority, and who felt that they were now relieved of any responsibility to 'govern all the people'. The public identification of the Catholic Church leadership with political Nationalism helped feed the rabid anti-Catholicism which had been one of the strands in the formation of political Unionism.

By ensuring that Partition remained the overriding issue in politics generally, the nationalist minority also helped ensure that Unionism remained on the defensive. The pressure on Craig and the leadership came not from those who wanted a more liberal approach – and there were some, notably Lord Londonderry in the early 1920s, and men like Lord Charlemont and Hugh Montgomery, founders of the Irish Association in the 1930s – but from the hardliners. Only briefly, in the 1960s and with the founding of the SDLP in 1970, did minority political leaders show signs of moving beyond anti-partitionism. But by 1979 the SDLP had parted company with Paddy Devlin and Gerry Fitt and was primarily a nationalist party.

When the 'New Ireland Forum' met in 1983-84 it was hailed as a redefining moment, as nationalism coming to terms with reality. But in fact the Forum report presented a largely traditional Nationalist account of the origins – and iniquity – of Partition, and of Unionist misrule. It did not address the fundamental issue confronting any political minority – does it condemn itself to permanent minority status by making its prime goal something which is unobtainable, or does it embrace 'consent' and work within it? Instead, the Forum was happy to blame successive British Governments for allowing 'a system of untrammelled one-party rule in Northern Ireland to be exercised by and on behalf of the majority Unionist population.'[21]

Even after the minority's overt acceptance of the principle of consent, and by implication of the legitimacy of Partition and the Northern Irish state, it has continued to define itself as a nationalist, *ie* anti-partitionist, minority. Sinn Féin has overtaken the SDLP as the main representative of the minority, riding on the back of IRA violence and its own vigorous presentation of traditional nationalism. The SDLP has sought to respond by re-emphasising its own nationalist credentials, and has restated its fundamental aim by declaring it is '100 per cent for a united Ireland,' and wants a referendum on unification in the lifetime of the next Assembly.[22]

Thus for Northern Ireland's entire period of existence, the nationalist minority has helped ensure that the political debate has never advanced far beyond the fundamental issue of partition, and in so doing the minority has also condemned itself to permanent opposition, and therefore to a form of second-class citizenship in the political context. In these circumstances parties which have tried to take the Border out of their politics and draw membership from both the Protestant and Catholic communities – such as the Northern Ireland Labour Party in the 1950s and 60s, and recently the Alliance Party – have had little success.

Nationalist Nightmare?

Have nationalists also been second-class citizens in a more general sense? Were they, as the New Ireland Forum Report asserted, the victims of systematic discrimination, deprived of the means of social and economic development? Nationalist leaders firmly assert that this was so, and argue that equality cannot be fully achieved within the present constitutional arrangement, hence their continued pursuit of Irish unity. Republicans claim that the IRA campaign was, at least in part, a struggle for justice. The language used by both British and Irish Governments in the course of the 'peace process' suggest some sympathy with this viewpoint.

Few now would deny that there was discrimination against Catholics in the areas of public housing, employment and local government boundaries. The figures show that there was significant Catholic disadvantage in employment generally; since the foundation of Northern Ireland, Catholics have been twice as likely to be unemployed as Protestants. Some local authority areas where nationalists were clearly in a majority, such as the city of Londonderry, somehow managed to elect Unionist councils.

Experience of personal, or family, disadvantage and of overt acts of discrimination help fuel nationalist belief that there was, indeed, a nationalist nightmare. Observers, including the present writer, documented serious incidences of anti-Catholic discrimination in public housing allocation in the years preceding the civil rights campaign.[23] But there are now serious doubts as to the extent of such discrimination, over whether discrimination was even a major factor in causing the Catholic disadvantage in employment, and in particular over whether there was systematic and widespread anti-Catholic discrimination to the extent that the minority was denied the means of social and economic development.[24]

The groundbreaking survey work done by Professor Richard Rose, in the 1960s, suggested otherwise.[25] Undertaken in 1966-67, forty-five years after the creation of Northern Ireland, and at a time when nationalist sentiment had been reinvigorated by the 50th anniversary of the 1916 Rising, and when events in the United States had stimulated interest in civil rights and discrimination, the survey concluded that there was no evidence of systematic discrimination against Catholics.[26]

His survey did show that there was a wide perception among Catholics that they were discriminated against. But the details on housing showed that while more Protestants than Catholics owned their own homes, more Catholics than Protestants lived in local authority housing.[27] Similarly on public employment, his survey showed that the proportions of each community employed in the civil service or other public agencies were almost identical (8 per cent of Protestants, and 7 per cent of Catholics) and his conclusion again was that there was no great aggregate discrimination in public employment. On employment in the private sector those surveyed were asked what difficulties they thought there were for themselves in finding a job in Northern Ireland. Only five per cent – mostly Catholics – cited religious discrimination.

Rose's work does not prove, nor even suggest, that there was no discrimination, but it refutes the contention that discrimination was widespread and systematic at the time of the civil rights movement.

Most of specific grievances that formed the civil rights platform in the late 1960s were addressed in the reform programme of late 1969, yet it is since then, ironically, that belief in the 'nationalist nightmare' as the root cause of the Northern Ireland problem has grown, and this despite the fact that for almost all of that period the province has been governed, not by Ulster Unionists, but by London.

Central to the argument has been the higher rate of unemployment among Catholics. The introduction of progressively stringent fair employment legislation has tended to imply that the elimination of discrimination would mean the end of Catholic disadvantage, but this has not been the case, and the disparity has remained stubbornly high. Very few complaints of discrimination have been upheld at tribunal. It is now seen that the main causes of disparity in employment are long-standing 'structural' features of society such as geographical distribution of population, age structure, different reproduction rates of Catholic and Protestant communities.[28]

Perhaps the strongest argument against the 'nationalist nightmare' is to be found in the population statistics. Adverse economic conditions in both parts of Ireland up to the 1960s meant high unemployment and large-scale emigration, but the pattern was vastly different in the two parts of the island.

The Catholic population of the south actually declined by 2.8 per cent between 1926 and 1961, while the Catholic population in the North increased by 11 per cent.[29] The difference arose from a much higher rate of emigration in the south. The records show just that; net emigration from the South between 1926 and 1961 was almost 900,000, from the North during the same period it was less than 50,000. (The figures for Northern Ireland include estimates for war years when returns were not made.) In the decade from 1951 to 1961 more than 400,000 emigrants left the South, and just over 30,000 left Northern Ireland.

Economic conditions on either side of the border were not exactly the same, and the war years produced a boost for the North, but both parts of the island suffered from high unemployment and related problems. Emigration from the South, mainly to Britain, meant moving to another jurisdiction, to what many emigrants thought of as a foreign country; emigration from Northern Ireland meant moving from one part of the United Kingdom to another. If conditions for the minority in the North had approached anything like the nightmare of oppression and discrimination frequently painted, then why were its members so much more reluctant to emigrate than their Southern cousins enjoying independence after centuries of subjection?

None of this suggests a nightmare for the Catholic citizens of Northern Ireland.

Conclusion

In the course of the past eighty years the two parts of the island have passed each other on the stairway of history, the South coming up, the North going down. At the outset the unionist North was brimming with confidence, boasting the largest shipyard in the world, the biggest ropeworks, the greatest linen industry and its share in the imperial heritage of the United Kingdom. It knew what it was and where it was going. The South, by contrast, was extremely poor, isolated and seriously underdeveloped by European standards. It was obsessed by nationalism, but seriously divided by it, and unsure how to proceed along the trail of nationhood.

By the 1970s an increasingly confident South was climbing the stairway of economic growth up out of poverty, isolationism, and church-dominated conservatism, just as a beleagured North, having lost its industrial base, seemed to be sliding down in a cloud of communal bitterness, terrorism, and general opprobrium. In the new context of the European Community, Northern Ireland was a historic throw-back, an embarrassment to the United Kingdom, while the Republic of Ireland was already gearing up to be the brightest young star on the European flag.

Today the South's problems are those of over-development – uneven distribution of wealth, corruption, environmental damage and a high level of immigration. The 'national question' remains, though it is now a problem for 'official' Ireland, for the state and for the political parties, rather than for the unofficial man in the street. That 'national' question now is not how to unite Ireland, but how to shed the burden of history and learn to live with and make the best of the two entities on the island.

Mitchell Reiss's surprise at a European country in the year 2005 having a private army associated with a political party must be even greater when that country is the United Kingdom, President Bush's strongest ally in the war against terrorism. Not just has it one such party, it has several. Surely even more startling to Mr Reiss must be the fact that a party with a private army has also had Ministers in government in part of the UK. Such is the very strange world that has been brought about in Northern Ireland, and in these islands, by the 'peace process'.

Northern Ireland is peculiar in other ways. For most of thirty years now it has suffered not from one-party government, but from no-party government. Under Direct Rule no party could be involved in government since both major UK parties declined to organise in Northern Ireland, and Labour, until 2004, refused to admit any resident of Northern Ireland to its membership – a stance maintained partly in response to strong SDLP lobbying. Direct Rule has meant, in effect, very indirect rule via Northern Ireland Office Ministers with no personal, party or constituency link to Northern Ireland. With short intermissions in 1974 and under the Belfast Agreement, the North has been in a democratic limbo.

London has sought to modify that defect by creating innumerable and often overlapping agencies and 'quangos,' quasi-autonomous non-governmental organisations, to advise and oversee various areas of public or governmental activity, to the extent that the province has been dubbed 'quangoland'. Public money has readily been found for new quangos at a time when public libraries have no money to buy books, and both the physical infrastructure – roads, water supply, sewage – and the social infrastructure – schools, hospitals and related services – are seriously under-funded.[30] Finance for both the Irish language and the reinvented Ulster Scots is made available, to the bewilderment of an already confused population.

In a short period of time, Northern Ireland has begun to look like the poor relation on the island, its citizens glancing enviously south to new motorways and other signs of rampant development. But in fact its economy has performed surprisingly well for the past two decades, despite the sustained IRA terrorist campaign. Unemployment is low, and there is even a recovering tourist industry. Belfast, and other towns show signs of vigorous if not always tasteful reconstruction and development.

Against the black picture of inter-communal political polarisation, and segregated settlement patterns that amount almost to apartheid, have to be set more positive elements. There is general acceptance that Northern Ireland has to be shared by the two communities, and that devolved government can only be restored on some basis of power-sharing. There is similar acceptance of cross-border cooperation, as both beneficial in practice and essential politically to help satisfy the minority's sense of Irishness.

Nor is the majority-minority divide as rigid as generally assumed. The latest *Conflict and Consensus* study showed a significant 21 per cent of Catholics preferring Northern Ireland in the UK to a united Ireland, and another 11.2 per cent opting for an independent Northern Ireland rather than Irish unity.[31]

The crisis of early 2005, starting with the collapse of the latest government initiative to restore devolution, and deepened by the Northern Bank robbery and the McCartney murder in Belfast, has focused attention on what some analysts have long argued is the fundamental problem – the toleration, and appeasement, of a political party with a private army as the key element in a process aimed at finally disposing of the unfinished business of 1921-22.[32]

Notes

1   See FSL Lyons in Francis MacManus (ed) *The Years of the Great Test* Mercier Press, 1967. Also Census figures for 1926 in WE Vaughan and AJ Fitzpatrick (eds) *Irish Historical Statistics, Population 1821-1971*, Royal Irish Academy, 1978.

2   Eamon Phoenix, *Northern Nationalism*, Ulster Historical Foundation, Belfast, 1994. p 129. also 1926 Census in Vaughan and Fitzpatrick *op. cit.*

3   Dennis Kennedy *The Widening Gulf*, Blackstaff Press, Belfast, 1988, p 115.

4   Phoenix, *op. cit*, p 128.

5   See Kennedy, *op. cit*, Chapter 5.

6   Ronan Fanning, *Independent Ireland,* Helicon History of Ireland, Dublin 1983. pp 54-57.

7   Kennedy, *op. cit,* p 169.

8   For a comprehensive discussion of this area see Tom Garvin *Preventing the Future; Why was Ireland so poor for so long?* Gill & Macmillan, Dublin 2004.

9   See J.J Lee, *Ireland 1912-1985*, Cambridge, 1989, pp 77, 335.

10 First annual report of the Irish Language Commissioner, Dublin 2005.

11 See *Irish Times*, 23/03/2005.

12 *ibid.*

13 Quoted in *Daily Telegraph* 13/03/2005.

14 See Foreign Minister Dermot Ahern's speech to Irish-American Partnership, Boston, 15/3/2005.
15 *Irish Times* 5/03/2005.
16 Interview on BBC Radio Four's 'File on Four,' 15/03/2005.
17 Former Foreign Minister Ray Burke was jailed for six months in January 2005 for making false tax returns.
18 Reginald Maudling. Widely reported as making the remark as he boarded a plane out of Belfast in June 1970.
19 See Kennedy, *op. cit,* Chapter 4
20 Michael Laffan, *The Partition of Ireland 1911-1924*, Dublin Historical Association, 1983, p 109.
21 New Ireland Forum Report, Stationery Office, Dublin 1984.
22 Policy document on SDLP website, www.sdlp.ie. This policy was later amended in its 2007 election manifesto to calling for such a referendum "when the Agreement's institutions are operating stably".
23 See 'Religious Houses', a series of articles by Dennis Kennedy, *Belfast Telegraph,* November 25, 26, 27, 1964.
24 See Graham Gudgin, 'Discrimination in Housing and Employment under the Stormont Regime' in Barton and Roche, *The Northern Ireland Question, Nationalism, Unionism and Partition,* Ashgate, 1999, for a discussion of this debate.
25 Richard Rose, *Governing without Consensus; An Irish Perspecitve,* Faber, London 1971.
26 Rose, *op. cit,* p 293. See articles 'Religious Houses' by author in *Belfast Telegraph*, February 1963.
27 The 1971 Census figures show that Catholic households actually had a disproportionately large share of local authority housing.
28 Gudgin, *op. cit.*
29 *Irish Historical Statistics, op. cit.*
30 By 2005 Northern Ireland had about 100 quangos, with a total annual budget of £6 billion. Report, *Belfast Telegraph,* 22/03/2005.
31 *Conflict and Consensus.* Institute of Public Administration, Dublin 2005.
32 See *Picking up the Pieces*, Cadogan Group, Belfast, 2003. p 5.

Chapter Five

EXPLAINING THE NORTHERN IRELAND TROUBLES

Richard English

The Northern Ireland Troubles, to which one might perhaps naively attach the dates 1968-98, have generated a vast explanatory literature. Some of this has been essentially narrative-historical, some based around interpretive schemes such as colonialism or ethno-nationalism; some has focused on specific organizations or individuals, while some again has analysed the literature itself in thematic ways.[1]

But seven years on from the 1998 Good Friday Agreement – which many people saw as an agreed end to the conflict – is it possible now to make sense of why the Troubles occurred, and to understand more clearly the central themes within their turbulent history?

As in Oscar Wilde's description of truth, the history of Northern Ireland has been 'rarely pure and never simple'. And if the complexity and nastiness of that history have been off-putting for many observers, then so too has been the length of the problem's historical roots.

From the twelfth century onwards there has been English political involvement in Ireland (perhaps unsurprisingly, given the proximity of the two islands). By the time of Henry VIII, declared King of Ireland in 1541, a lasting religious ingredient had been added to Anglo-Irish relations. For the sixteenth-century Reformation left England overwhelmingly Protestant, but Ireland mainly Catholic in allegiance. The distinctly religious flavour to Anglo-Irish politics was intensified by sixteenth- and seventeenth-century plantations, with Protestant planters being settled in parts of Ireland with the mission of civilising the predominantly Catholic island. Indeed, by the seventeenth century it was religious rather than ethnic divisions which dominated Irish politics: state and colonists were Protestant, while their opponents (whether ethnically Gaelic or Old English) were united by their emphatic Catholicism.

At the end of the eighteenth century – and under French Revolutionary inspiration – the first clearly Irish nationalist attempt to transcend these religious divisions was made by the United Irishmen. Initially a propagandist, reformist society, by 1798 the United Irishmen had developed into a revolutionary group intent on breaking the connection between Ireland and England, and on achieving this goal by force. As such, they have long been celebrated by latter-day Irish republican militants. But their double-failure (inability to erode religious divisions; defeat in the 1798 rebellion), perhaps serves as a caution against over-optimistic assessments of the possibility of uniting Irish people around an aggressively anti-English, revolutionary project.

Following the failed United Irish rebellion, London responded with the 1800 Act of Union. This established the United Kingdom of Great Britain and Ireland, with the following hundred and twenty years witnessing an uncomfortable relationship between the UK state and its Catholic Irish inhabitants. Religion, economics and culture separated much of Catholic Ireland from the state of which it formed a part, and various Irish nationalist leaders and movements (Daniel O'Connell, Charles Stewart Parnell, Young Ireland, the Fenians), in divergent ways pursued redress of Irish nationalist grievance and greater Irish autonomy from Britain.

By the early years of the twentieth century, an answer to the Anglo-Irish question seemed to have been found in the notion of Home Rule. This involved significant autonomy for Ireland within a UK framework. But pro-Union – or Unionist – opposition to being incorporated in what was seen as an economically backward and Catholic-dominated Ireland, helped to thwart such an arrangement. So, too, did the baneful effects on Ireland of the First World War. During that conflict, divisions between pro-British Unionists (especially in Ulster) and increasingly disaffected Irish Nationalists grew more acrimonious. The 1916 republican Easter rebellion helped to intensify Irish Nationalist sentiment, and by the post-war period it was a militant and aggressive Irish republicanism (embodied in the political Sinn Féin and the paramilitary Irish Republican Army [IRA]) that represented Irish Nationalist interests.

Conflict during 1919-21 between these Irish republican forces and the British state resulted in the settlement of 1921 from which Northern Ireland was born. Under that deal most of Ireland was granted substantial independence from Britain (developing, in time, into complete independence in the form of the current southern Irish state); the six counties of Antrim, Londonderry, Tyrone, Fermanagh, Armagh and Down were kept (as Northern Ireland) within the UK, reflecting the preference of the majority of the population within that area for retaining the union with Britain.

This partitioning of Ireland came to be seen by Northern Unionists as merely a reflection of divided Irish opinion; by nationalists – north and south – it was regarded as a British mutilation of what should have been a united Ireland. More importantly, Northern Nationalist hostility to the new Northern Irish state made the nationalist minority an object of suspicion as far as the Belfast unionist government was concerned. In the confessionalized context of twentieth-century Irish politics, there emerged two states built to suit the religious-political majorities within their boundaries: in the south, a Catholic nationalist culture prevailed; in Northern Ireland, the Protestant Unionist majority enjoyed a state which reflected their interests and their politics.

Argument still rages about the extent of anti-Catholic discrimination during the 1921-72 period of Northern Irish government. The evidence is clear, however, that very many Northern Nationalists held the state to be neither legitimate nor fair, and it is this central fact which explains the genesis of the Northern Ireland troubles. Indeed, in Northern Nationalist eyes, the state's illegitimacy and its unfairness were interwoven: since this British state had been wrongly carved out of Ireland to serve Unionist interests, what else could be expected there but pro-Unionist political and economic bias?

When, therefore, the late 1960s witnessed a civil rights movement, campaigning for an end to the unfair treatment of northern Catholics, it was unsurprising that familiar lines of political and religious allegiance became sharpened. Protestant loyalists saw the civil rights project as merely another anti-Unionist ploy and so responded in hostile – at times, violent – fashion. The Belfast government did produce reforms, but these managed to be simultaneously too little and too tardy for nationalist appetites, and yet too much for many unionists to stomach. Turbulence on the streets ensued, and order broke down in Belfast and Derry. The police force – the largely Protestant Royal Ulster Constabulary (RUC) – was seen by many Nationalists as failing to police this crisis fairly, and the state-versus-Nationalists battle lines began to be ever more firmly drawn.

When the British Army was deployed to address the civil disorder, friction rapidly developed with the Catholic working class. Ill-judged or tragic military episodes – a one-sided curfew in Belfast in 1970, mass internment of suspected republicans in 1971, the killing of civilians in Derry in 1972 on Bloody Sunday – ruptured relations between the authorities and working-class Catholics, and seemed to validate the logic of aggressive republicans (after 1969, embodied in the Provisional IRA), who argued that Northern Ireland was systematically unfair, illegitimate and irreformable. To such eyes, only the violent destruction of the north would suffice.

The IRA thus embarked on a lengthy campaign of violence which would see them emerge from the modern Troubles as the group responsible for more killings than any other (during the conflict, for example, the RUC was responsible for 50 deaths, the IRA for 1,778). But while the IRA used force in an attempt to force London to withdraw from Northern Ireland, Protestant loyalist paramilitary groups such as the Ulster Defence Association (UDA) or the Ulster Volunteer Force (UVF) used force with a directly opposite purpose. The IRA argued that only with British withdrawal would their violence come to an end; loyalist violence suggested that British withdrawal would, in fact, not end paramilitary killings, but rather generate far worse inter-communal conflict as rival groups fought over territory and sovereignty without the containing restraint of the British state.

Thus the three agents of political violence in Northern Ireland – republican paramilitaries, loyalist paramilitaries, and the forces of the UK state – became locked in a triangular war of attrition. In the early years of the conflict, each showed some conviction that force would bring them victory. But by the end of the 1980s it was clear instead that stalemate, rather than anything more decisive, was the likeliest outcome of further conflict between three combatants – none of whom could be militarily defeated.

In particular, militant republicans came to the pivotal conclusion that there existed greater opportunities for forward momentum towards their goals without, rather than with, their military campaign dominating their politics. There had, over the years, been many attempts at solving the Northern Ireland conflict, some of them (such as the 1973 Sunningdale Agreement) prefiguring the eventual 1990s deal in terms of power-sharing, north-south dimensions across the Irish border, and the recognition of the northern majority's right to remain within the UK. But the crucial difference between such earlier attempts at a solution and the more successful 1998 Agreement lies less in differences between the various proposals themselves, than in the 1990s emergence of a paramilitary recognition that violence would not produce victory and that some form of compromise therefore made sense. The lengthy Northern Ireland peace process has represented the working out of that decisive logic.

The evolution of Irish republican thinking has been central to this process. Where once violence was seen as the necessary mechanism for producing victory (as Brighton bomber Patrick Magee expressed it, 'that was the only avenue open to us, to engage in armed struggle'), now Sinn Féinish political argument together with gradual demographic change would supposedly do a more effective job. To those who had long stressed the sectarian and counterproductive qualities of IRA violence, this latter-day shift by republicans might appear tragically slow in its arrival. The constitutional nationalist Social Democratic and Labour Party (SDLP) had stated as early as 1974: 'The Provisional IRA can achieve nothing by carrying on their campaign of violence but they can achieve almost anything they desire by knocking it off.'

Whether the 1998 deal will indeed yield sufficient redress of nationalist Irish grievances remains yet to be seen. Moreover, Ulster unionist opinion – evenly divided at the time of the May 1998 referendum on the Good Friday Agreement – has shifted away from the deal as a result of a perceivedly nationalist bias in its implementation. Political change in Northern Ireland during the Troubles has frequently been seen by unionists as unwelcome, in so far as change was thought likely to involve an irreversible weakening of unionists' existing position. As Democratic Unionist Party (DUP) leader Ian Paisley flintily put it, 'The Unionists are not aspiring for anything: they've already got their aspirations, they're in the Union, and they mean to maintain the Union.'

The DUP's emergence as the largest party in Ulster politics in elections in 2003 makes this an unavoidably significant point. But neither side in Northern Ireland looks likely to be in a position to ignore the other's beliefs and fears sufficiently for them to be able to achieve a straightforwardly dominant position. Some form of compromise – a nuanced approach to self-determination, a commitment to effective power-sharing between the two communities, a recognition both of majority UK preference and of minority dissatisfaction with the UK's record – seems compelling for the foreseeable future.

The UK has long found it difficult to accommodate Catholic Ireland, and there are those who doubt that it can perform this trick any more effectively in twenty-first century Northern Ireland than it did for Ireland under the nineteenth- and twentieth-century Union. But, if the violent Troubles of the past generation are indeed to prove completed, then it is hard to see any arrangement which attempts to force Unionists out of the UK; in the absence of such expulsion, the imperative is surely to make Northern Ireland a truly inclusive and mutually satisfactory polity for both communities, Nationalist as well as Unionist.

Northern Irish politics has embodied the key forces shaping the modern world, involving as it has the intersection of nation, state, religion, socialism and political violence. The regrettable failure of the UK to accommodate Irish Nationalism, and of Irish nationalist ideology to accommodate Ulster Unionism – a double failure which explains the essence of the Northern Ireland problem – can now be studied through a depth of available and often painful sources open to historians. Serious study of the problem suggests that it would be misleading simply to apportion blame to one or other participant in the conflict: historical explanation will involve a recognition of the complex roots to the Troubles, just as political remedies will need to involve subtle and complicated compromise.

Notes

1   T. Hennessey, *A History of Northern Ireland 1920-1996* (Dublin: Gill and Macmillan, 1997), D. Miller (ed.), *Rethinking Northern Ireland: Culture, Ideology and Colonialism* (London: Longman, 1998), B. O'Leary/J. McGarry, *Explaining Northern Ireland: Broken Images* (Oxford: Blackwell, 1995); R. English, *Armed Struggle: The History of the IRA* (London: Pan Macmillan, 2003), H. McDonald, *Trimble* (London: Bloomsbury, 2000), J. Whyte, *Interpreting Northern Ireland* (Oxford: Oxford University Press, 1990).

Chapter Six

FALLING OUT –
FALLING IN

Malachi O'Doherty

On April 10, 1998, I drove from Donegal to Derry to record a response to the report that political parties in Northern Ireland had agreed a peace deal. That morning, when I heard the news, I punched the air with delight. It seemed hardly likely, right up to the end. My radio talk was an emotional reflection on some of my worst moments of the troubles. It was my way of discharging the last of my anger and pain, I think; my small contribution to the new mood.

Driving back over the border, I stopped to give a man a lift. I regretted it as soon as he was in the car and it was clear that he was a bit drunk. I asked him if he heard the news, the Northern parties had agreed a peace that included disarmament and the release of prisoners. He would believe it when he saw it, he said. This man was some kind of affiliate of the INLA. Did he think that Republicans would adapt to the new state structures and support the police. 'Now, I can't ever see that happening,' he said. Well, we would see.

What we overlooked at first in our enthusiasm for the deal was that it was flawed. Far from being a closed compact between former enemies, it was just the more dramatic device in a long series of such devices, contrived to keep the peace process alive. It hardly mattered that it was flawed then. What mattered was that it was agreed. A better deal, that is a more logical deal, a more practical deal, might never have been agreed. The flaws were in a democratic structure pegged as they were to community allegiance and thereby in danger of entrenching sectarianism forever. There was also a failure to achieve a clear trade-off between prisoner releases and arms decommissioning. Yes, paramilitary-related parties might have refused such a pairing but they could not rationally have refuted the justice of it.

This latter problem was the hurdle that made the Agreement difficult to implement. On the very day of the agreement, Jeffrey Donaldson, a member of the Ulster Unionist party negotiating team, left Stormont and disassociated himself from it. David Trimble, the party leader, stayed in, assured by a promissory note from the Prime Minister, saying that if the mechanisms for excluding those not committed to peaceful means did not work, he would seek new ones and that he expected decommissioning to start immediately.

The whole peace process had been dogged by the refusal of armed groups to disarm and the refusal of first the Government and then Unionist parties to enter talks with Sinn Féin until the IRA got rid of its weaponry. There had been several compromise devices which tried to gloss over the deadlock and these had succeeded in getting the talks completed, though with one major Unionist party, the DUP, and some smaller others, refusing to participate. Now Trimble refused to play his necessary part in establishing an Executive for the new legislative assembly until decommissioning started. Deadlock again.

Many are probably familiar with the devices employed to gloss over or defer that problem. One device was that used several times by the Prime Minister. He would say that he had witnessed huge progress, a seismic shift, a radical change of attitude by the IRA. He said these things in order to create a moral climate in which the Unionists would have to reciprocate the IRA's generosity of spirit. Another device, deployed by the US President Bill Clinton, was to urge the Unionists to lift their bar on forming an Executive – to make it easier for the IRA to disarm with dignity – and then to walk back out of the Executive and collapse it if the IRA did nothing of the kind.

At one point, the British and Irish governments tried to establish a day of disarmament in which all paramilitaries would participate. No one bought the idea. Then David Trimble went for a sequencing plan, shored up by a post-dated resignation letter. He would allow the Executive to be formed, take his place as First Minister, and invite the IRA to disarm – 'jump' – afterwards. If they didn't, the resignation would take effect and the Executive would collapse. That was what happened.

Even as he agreed to enter the Executive, Republican spokesmen Pat Doherty and Martin Ferris briefed supporters that no deal on disarmament had actually been agreed with Trimble. George Mitchell, who had chaired the negotiations towards the sequence, was asked afterwards if the IRA had in fact agreed to disarm and reneged on that agreement. He said he would not like to get into that degree of 'specificity'.

When decommissioning eventually started, it came after the September 11 attacks on Washington and New York. Whether arising from political developments at home or not, the new world mood probably made it inevitable. Later it would emerge that the IRA had been spying inside the Northern Ireland Office and that Sinn Féin had been able to calculate its moves according to baselines of the governments, always conceding the least it needed to, the latest it could. Brian Lennon SJ, an insightful commentator on Northern Ireland, rightly argued that this delay helped. It created time in which the unthinkable might become thinkable, for nearly all parties. But delay has also exhausted the popular enthusiasm for the Agreement and eroded faith that it can ever settle.

I can trace my own loss of engagement with the process. The early deadlines produced high tension and suspense. I was part of the press pack that would gather at Stormont or Hillsborough Castle to feast on the excitement. There was once a carnival atmosphere to these occasions. They were huge professional reunions for journalists and politicians and activists. The carnival attracted its eccentrics and protesters. We waited outside for briefings, watched from a distance the politicians coming out for a stroll. We believed that great historic things might be happening. Sometimes the Northern Ireland Office erected a marquee for us, provided coffee and pizza. And sometimes, as our deadlines slipped past without anything from inside, we interviewed each other as commentators.

I was one of those who tried to interpret events for some political figures. When the IRA agreed to the inspection of weapons dumps in May 2000, on the deadline for the completion of decommissioning, I assured Unionists that this meant that weapons had at last become expendable for the sake of the process. I said that in terms of Republican theology this was a fundamental change.

But a time came, probably half way through 2002, when I decided I simply could not afford to invest so much emotional apprehension in our politics. Once I joked with another journalist I would rather do programmes on hillwalking and then by chance I got an invitation to do just that. It was great.

I had reached the point where the politics was not even interesting. The pessimistic view had been born out. The IRA was an old lecher who – even once married – could not help running after skirts. The Loyalists had succumbed to a brute leadership and lost political interest. The Unionists were split and simply were not able to ride out further compromises of the kind that Blair specialised in. And the content of the dispute became more and more ridiculous.

When the Government came up with the joint declaration of measures that were balanced to assuage all fears, it included practical measures like allowing offenders and suspects on the run to come home – but its other nonsense, like extending the signal from an Irish language channel and funding for an Ulster Scots Academy, conveyed the impression that we had run out of serious things to argue about. We were down to the fantasy that an English-speaking region was split down the middle over languages that very few of us spoke. Indeed one of the languages had been invented for the purpose of providing a balance.

The Government had now apparently conceded that only acts of completion would satisfy. That would mean total disarmament by the IRA and a stable Assembly. Very soon, it meant only more decommissioning, a promise that the IRA would expire at the completion of the Agreement and an assembly election. The sequencing for that broke down when the IRA pledged the Decommissioning Commission to secrecy on what had been decommissioned, but not before an election had been announced. That election would – as we saw – eclipse the Ulster Unionists and the SDLP. The deal now would have to be between the DUP – which wanted changes to the Agreement – and Sinn Féin, a party the DUP refused to speak to because of its association with the IRA. The question then was whether there was a momentum in the process that would call these two parties together.

Sinn Féin was all for it and was briefing eagerly that it had received overtures from the DUP already. The DUP said it wanted a new agreement but could offer in return the stability that Sinn Féin craved. There was no 'anti' party behind them to set limits to what they could concede or to pull them down if they conceded too much. But the process has been, if nothing else, an intense political education for everyone who was involved in it or watched it closely. For me, I think it was more valuable than any university course could have been.

I bring that training to bear on reading political developments elsewhere. For instance, I read the Anglican Communion's Windsor Report on how to manage the crisis over gay bishops with a closer understanding of the tactical mind that wrote it – because I have seen so many tactical manoeuvres inside our own politics.

It was an education for our absolutist politicians too, to watch an operator like Blair at work. He showed them that you can stamp your feet and be as emphatic in your deadlock as you like, and still find ways to keep the game in play. In the end it does not matter that you stick to your undertakings – what matters is how many people you bring with you. I think it must have been a revelation to our overly-principled politicians to see that this is how real politics works. It is always about adaptation and compromise, never about getting everything you told your electorate you would get for them. A negative outcome of the politics of the process was polarisation. Parties thrived on deadlock.

The Unionist refusal to form an Executive and the constant blaming of Sinn Féin – however rational – inflated the importance of Sinn Féin to the nationalist electorate. It was Republicans who were making David Trimble go red in the face, so it was Republicans who would get the votes. I spoke to one of Trimble's team about this and suggested, only half facetiously, that he should pick a fight with Mark Durkan and lose if what he really wanted was that the SDLP would keep its lead over Sinn Féin. In a sectarian society, it is the party which most annoys the other side which thrives. Had the Agreement worked from the start, the SDLP and the Ulster Unionists might still be the premier parties in their own camps. One of the big disappointments about these two parties is that they did not pull together and secure the middle ground, but then it might not have worked if the other two parties had loudly kept sectarian issues in play.

Anyway, the decommissioning deadlock delivered its result and it is a reward for the parties that were most intransigent on it. Now comes a time to ask if the parties really want the Agreement to work or if they have their own dark sides, if they ultimately gain more in the old sectarian game of annoying the other side.

The party that has been most emphatic in its assertion of its good intentions on the Agreement has been the SDLP. But it failed to form a firm partnership at the heart of the Executive with the Ulster Unionists.

The two men that led the first Executive, David Trimble and Seamus Mallon, made each other bristle, even as press photographers tried to contrive friendship poses between them. One of the most embarrassing moments was on a popular television programme, "The Kelly Show", involving David Trimble and Seámus Mallon. The producers must have imagined that just because these people led parties into partnership with each other they would at least, for the sake of appearances, behave like friends in front of an audience.

Mallon's protest resignation after Trimble refused to enter the Executive in 1999 – a resignation which he later withdrew – made him dependent on the dexterous machinations of Peter Mandelson to save the executive. The contrivance by which he was enabled to withdraw his resignation was probably the first nationalist gerrymander inside Stormont. Mallon had almost scuppered his own Executive. These two charges must be levelled against the SDLP, that they did not do enough to secure partnership and that in times of crisis they succumbed to an almost suicidal umbrage.

As for the Ulster Unionists, it seems clear that David Trimble would have much preferred to join with the SDLP against Sinn Féin. Unionism had split on the agreement and it might have seemed more fair and balanced to him if nationalism could be split too. Yet when Mallon, in the autumn of 1998, offered to exclude Sinn Féin if decommissioning was not complete by 2000, the Ulster Unionists made nothing of that offer. Yes, the decommissioning demand was reasonable, but a two-year wait for it, in which the Executive would gather experience and credibility might not have been too much to ask for.

Sinn Féin has always played a tactic of minimal and deferred movement. Have they been playing for breakdown? More, are they playing just to prolong the process because of the rewards it yields in terms of international attention and patronage?

The most hopeful thing that can be said is that the Peace Process now is coming to a conclusion and that the two parties best equipped to secure an enduring deal are now face to face – metaphorically at least.

If you are one of the pessimists then perhaps the least that you will have to concede is that the parameters of the game have changed. I liken the old game to a vicious circle and the new one to a virtuous circle. The manner in which David Trimble's Ulster Unionist party and Sinn Féin engaged with each other, up to 2003, was one which promoted tension and division. Even in conceding ground both parties sought to irritate each other. They may have had sound pragmatic political reasons for doing that. There were forces behind them who were much more hesitant about change and had to be assuaged of any fears that they were about to be sold out.

So, for example, after the Mitchell review, when David Trimble chose to write a post-dated resignation and enter the Executive with Sinn Féin without arms having been decommissioned, allowing time in which the process might start, he couldn't help firing a barb at the very people he was trying to coax into constructive partnership with himself:

> We have done our bit now Mr Adams, it is over to you. We have
> jumped. You follow.

No-one could imagine that this relationship was any form of courtship. Some people get a little giddy when they talk about peace and reconciliation and imagine that it is about enemies becoming friends. The conduct of the peace process so far has always been about enemies repositioning themselves to find new ways of prolonging their enmity. In the Trimble era it was not just Sinn Féin that behaved like an enemy and was treated like one. The larger nationalist party at that time, the SDLP, failed to establish the most elementary amicability with the Ulster Unionists. David Trimble and Séamus Mallon were so uncomfortable together that no one could have failed to notice it in their body language. The peace process has not been a process of deepening love. It has been a transformation of conflict into a forum in which enemies might continue to irritate each other and grasp advantages over each other.

The Ulster Unionist Party insisted on decommissioning of weapons and some there at least saw pragmatic advantage in not seeking to poke Sinn Féin's eye. But the party leadership was vulnerable to a large section of the party council which would routinely oppose compromise and seek to undermine Trimble's position. Republicans toyed with language and made repeated promises which were not kept. They always worked to the very end of every deadline and always conceded less than was called for while trying to present this as heroic and historic.

The two governments confused things further by repeatedly claiming larger moves on behalf of the IRA than the IRA itself was willing to make. When Gerry Adams came out with a form of words under pressure to concede that the IRA campaign was ended he said: 'The violence we have seen must be a thing of the past, over done with and gone.'

This is a line that has no meaning. It is purely aspirational and entirely unfocused. What is 'the violence we have seen'? For all anyone knew he was talking about British or Loyalist violence. Yet Downing Street briefed the London media that it could celebrate the end of the IRA and the headline writers obliged. Again, Tony Blair came to Stormont and declared that there had been a seismic shift. It only took Pat Doherty to explain to Channel 4 News that he was talking through his hat. Again in September 2004, after the Leeds Castle talks, Blair came out and announced that the decommissioning issue was now resolved. That is what he always has done. Maybe this time he was telling the truth. Certainly many things are different about how peace processing is now done.

The optimistic rationale says that Sinn Féin has better reason to disarm the IRA for the DUP than it had for the Ulster Unionists. This rationale says a deal with the DUP was always going to be more secure than a deal with Trimble because there would be no one behind the DUP to pull it down, to usurp a leader who had compromised. The DUP happily reminds Republicans of this when it gets a chance. 'A deal with us will cost you more than a deal with Trimble would have cost you, but it will be a sounder, safer deal.'

Ostensibly this is reasonable. SDLP leader Mark Durkan appears to believe that Sinn Féin has been saving the goodies for a DUP leader who contributed nothing to the Agreement. Having done that, Sinn Féin has jeopardised the architecture of the Agreement itself for it can only now deliver to a Unionist party which will demand changes in that Agreement. He is saying it was not such a smart thing to do after all. And for how long would any deal remain unchallenged if much of the DUP base did not accept it?

I would not be confident that, especially after the departure of Paisley, new dissident forces within Unionism would not be rallying to bring it down. A Sinn Féin calculation, made last year or the year before, to save the guns for Paisley may not have been so smart, may have squandered the last two years for little more than the next two.

Still others made serious miscalculations too. For instance, had David Trimble stood down as Ulster Unionist leader and made way for the Empey/Donaldson team as many in his party urged him to in 2003, that would have tied Donaldson into the Ulster Unionist party and made it impossible for him to defect to the DUP even after electoral eclipse.

If we look at how the character of the exchanges between the rival parties has changed. we should forget any fanciful notion that the desired or remotely possible outcome of this is respect and affection between Adams and Paisley, Robinson and McGuinness. These are what I would describe as Corrymeela dreams.

Neither Paisley nor Adams has behind him in this a hardliner to make him drop the prize. Neither can play the game of referring to that hardliner and pleading for patience or further concessions. Trimble was able to say, in effect, 'look, I'm a decent guy and I see your point but I would never get this one past Donaldson.' The DUP has no Donaldson yet. It does not play hard cop/soft cop though it is not inconceivable that it will learn to. Paisley is hard-cop. Robinson may be the soft cop but in these negotiations hard-cop comes to the table and put his own prints on the documents. In the Ulster Unionist Party, it was the other way round. For such a relationship to deliver, the hard cop must be just a little weaker than the soft cop.

Adams, in the past, might have suggested that were he to concede too much he might be assassinated by the IRA or that the armed struggle would resume. These worries have also faded away. At an earlier phase of the process the arms were discussed by mediators, by Hume and later by Adams, as if belonging to someone else, a someone else who might be constructively influenced if political circumstances changed. This is how protection rackets operate too. That conceit was useful to a government which did not want to be seen to be negotiating with those it branded as terrorists or conveying the impression that it was ready to barter constitutional change for reductions in terrorist weapons stocks.

Nobody cares about these niceties any more. It is quite clear that the arms were on the table at Leeds Castle and that they have been accepted as a legitimate bargaining counter. Indeed they have little other reality now than as a bargaining counter.

In the old Trimble days the vicious circle of mounting suspicion and minimising of concessions evolved into what thc media easily called the blame game. The objective of the big high-profile summits at Hillsborough or Castle Buildings or Weston Park was not to finalise agreement at all but to emerge at the end of all the wrangling looking like the party that had done its best in the face of the other's obstinacy.

The surprising change in the past year has been the speed with which obstinate positions have apparently relaxed. Sinn Féin and the DUP are the lead negotiators now and neither wants to be thought intransigent or difficult. There was the quaint image used by Paul Bew to describe the hints at amenability dropped by Gerry Adams in the run-up to talks last year. Bew said he believed that Adams was 'showing a lot of leg.' You may extend that metaphor however you like to describe the altogether more tantalising hints that have come from Gerry Adams in recent weeks.

He said that the IRA arms were just an excuse by Unionists for a refusal to share power and that Republicans should be willing to remove that excuse. The shadow side of his assertion included the implied prediction that even once the arms were gone the DUP would still refuse to share power with Sinn Féin. In recent days Sinn Féin has been perhaps overeager to imagine that prediction fulfilled.

The DUP, which was determined to show that it was not the pushover that Trimble had been, has turned out to be keen to work for an agreement, and not wanting to be wrongfooted into appearing to be the main obstacle to agreement, finds it tactically necessary now to be sweet and considerate, however much out of character.

The blame game has speeded up. The parties involved are monolithic. They have nothing to focus on but each other, no internal wrangles to resolve or anticipate. Each is now able to give an unambiguous statement of position to the other. Each is now able to consider the other's position quickly, without worrying about internal dissent, and reach early conclusions.

If this is a game, then these conditions are not conducive to long play. They produce a danger that the game will either be resolved too quickly or exposed as a sham. Resolving it quickly might not strike you as a great danger. Perhaps it is not, though you might think that those wary old dogs, the Provos and the Paisleyites, might benefit from more time to sniff around each other. It is a danger, if the peace process is our real politics now and viurtually the only politics we have. Parties which have enlarged their electoral base through their conduct of the peace process must surely by nervous about it passing.

We have a paradox here; yes, a majority voted for the Good Friday Agreement but since then, majorities have always favoured those parties which obstructed its implementation and played for sectarian advantage.

Both the new sleeker architecture of the game and pressure from the governments may tend towards a completion or to collapse. I suspect neither party wants either. There are early indications that Sinn Féin wants to play the game much as it has before, by hinting at greater generosity on arms by secret briefings that can be qualified or withdrawn rather than by declaration of commitment. Even when Danny Morrison, writing in the *Examiner* after the Leeds Castle talks, anticipated the retirement of the IRA, he based his prediction on the confidence of the two prime ministers, not on any personal insight into Republican strategy. This allows him to disown that observation more easily.

As before, Blair validated Republican promises. Republicans were quick to turn the pressure on the DUP and the DUP to respond with smiles and assurances that it is not remotely interested in majority rule. But Blair would like this settled. It would have been nice if it could have been done before the party conference in September 2004. He pushed for that, operating on metropolitan time.

The DUP may feel that it has not had the time yet to enjoy its victory at the polls. It had presented the peace process to the electorate as a sequence of concessions to Republicans facilitated by Unionist gullibility. It may like to demonstrate its power to reverse that flow of concessions before sealing a deal, but then it could achieve one of the most powerful demonstrations of Unionist advantage simply by walking into the assembly tomorrow and taking the leadership of a Unionist majority there.

Sinn Féin may be teasing us all with promises of decommissioning yet to come but it too has a substantial prize to gain by getting on with it – a possible coalition with Fianna Fáil at the next election in the South. The arms are an obstacle to that. After Leeds Castle, Bertie Ahern, standing beside Tony Blair, told us that the arms were not a problem any more; only the DUP's concern with accountability is a problem. He has hardened that position again to clarify his insistence that Sinn Féin will not share power with Fianna Fáil until the IRA is defunct.

But the political objections to the Agreement raised by the DUP raise the prospect that an unresolved peace process in the North, in which the arms aren't a problem, because they only exist as a bartering counter on hold anyway, might reasonably be no hindrance to Sinn Féin's ascendancy in the South.

It is hardly likely that Fianna Fail would allow perceived DUP intransigence to prevent it forming a new partnership with Sinn Féin. In that event there would be a new psychological border in Ireland, more real than the territorial one, between Nationalism and Unionism on the whole island. The peace process would be an all-island project and its only perceived obstacle would be those mad intransigent Unionists.

What a prize for Adams if he could achieve that without standing down the IRA.

Postscript

Two major events, elided into one, followed the delivery of this paper on 19 October 2004 and changed the course of the peace process. These were the IRA's raid on the Northern Bank on 20 December and the murder of Robert McCartney on 31 January 2005. These exhausted all toleration of Provo messing and forced them towards final decommissioning and a deal. They even created space for the DUP to insist that Sinn Féin endorse policing and join the police board, which they had not had to do to settle with Trimble. The bank robbery and murder also appear to have helped scupper Sinn Féin's parliamentary growth in the south.

Chapter Seven

20TH CENTURY INCOMERS

I. JEWS IN NORTHERN IRELAND

Marion Meek

When Jews are scattered around the world, they adapt to their host countries. This has been going on for thousands of years and we should not really think of them as a race, only a religion. With the combination of integration and extermination, their numbers are shrinking all the time.

There are two main blocks of tradition: to the north, in areas of Russian and German influence, (Russia, Lithuania, Germany, Poland) is the Ashkenazi tradition, and to the east and south, (Arabia, Syria, Iraq, Iran, Morocco, Ethiopia, Egypt, Spain) there were Arab/Moslem-influenced traditions known as Sephardim. The Ethiopians include black Jews who claim their origin from Solomon and Sheba. In western Europe there are mainly Ashkenazim, although the Netherlands has a Sephardi connection through its historic trade with the east.

Jews were scapegoats at any time where religion became extreme. In the Middle Ages, when heresy was punished by Christianity, Judaism was treated as another heresy with Jews forced to a choice of conversion or death. Many Jews in Spain went through the motions of conversion, but kept underground prayer groups. One of the best known excuses for killing Jews was the blood libel. It was a generally-held belief that Jews made their Passover bread, matzo, with the blood of a Christian child. As recently as 10 years ago when BBC Radio was looking for what was called its 'ethnic spot' in news broadcasting, I pointed out that Passover was one of our most important festivals. 'Oh we couldn't have that' said the programmer, 'it would offend our Christian listeners.' I did not dare ask what he meant.

In the last 150 years there have been two waves of persecution. In the mid-19th century, Russia and Lithuania attacked their Jews – you know the story from the musical 'Fiddler on the Roof'. All who could moved to Germany, Czechoslovakia, Poland and further west, to France, Britain and America. Small numbers were scattered everywhere. My father's ancestors came then. The Macaborskis settled in Manchester, and eventually started a raincoat factory, and lived near Strangeways Prison – in streets like 'Coronation Street'.

Jews came to the UK and Ireland by several paths. Some came with enough money to establish businesses. They were prepared to work at languages, and traded goods, often linen. In Manchester, cotton and fashion was the draw, and in Leeds, woollen goods. The successful survivor had a portable trade. Tailors needed only needles and scissors. Furriers, coming from Russia, the same, though their raw materials were expensive. Musicians and writers could go anywhere, though they could have difficulty making a living. Many people on the run have nothing at all. If they are lucky, they find employment. The rest try to buy and sell. The east end of London with its markets was a starting point for many generations of immigrants. In Ireland too, the markets were starting places. Some of those who could not afford a pitch would end up as packmen, carrying suitcases around the farms, bringing useful items to the housebound women – sewing materials, gadgets, linen stockings and underwear. All sorts of immigrants worked this way. In the country they were all called 'Indians', no matter where they were from. This kind of trade lasted until the 1960s, when women started to have cars and could shop in towns.

The beginning of an organised Jewish community in the north of Ireland began with Daniel Jaffe, born in Germany in 1809. He came to Belfast with his brother Isaac in 1845 to set up a linen export business, shipping to Dundee, Paris, Hamburg and even to Russia and South America. This was a tremendously successful business and the family became well-known. The known Jewish population in what is now Northern Ireland was 55 souls. In 1864, services were held in Martin Jaffe's house in Holywood, and on 7 July 1871, the foundation stone was laid for the first synagogue in Great Victoria Street. The building included a flat for the minister, a study and a school.

Daniel Jaffe paid for the whole building. He died in 1874, and a piece of the
City cemetery was set aside as a Jewish cemetery. Today the Jewish cemetery
is at Carnmoney.

Daniel Jaffe had four sons and five daughters. John was president of the
Chamber of Commerce; Alfred was made a Justice of the Peace in 1886 and
served on the Belfast Harbour Trust. The most distinguished was Otto, born
in Hamburg in 1846. He was elected as a city councillor in Belfast in 1894
and as Mayor in 1899: he was knighted, and in 1904 was Mayor for a second
time. He was a patron of all levels of education, making gifts to Queen's
University and Belfast College of Technology, and his wife promoted a school
in the Cliftonville Road, close to an area of Jewish homes. Many people know
the little Jaffe Fountain, in Victoria Square. By 1904 the Jewish community
had risen from 55 to over 1000, and a new synagogue was built in Annesley
Street near Carlisle Circus, in the area where many Jewish families lived.
That remained their synagogue for 60 years, even though they moved further
north on the Antrim Road and owned two properties in the Somerton Road
area for social purposes. Another resident from that time was Chaim Herzog,
son of a Rabbi, and later President of Israel.

The next great catastrophe for Jews came in the 1930s with Hitler. My
mother was brought up as a German in Berlin. Her father and other men of
that generation had been in the First World War. But when, as a ten-year old,
she wrote about 'our Fatherland' her teacher wrote 'not *your* Fatherland;.
Many Jews in Germany, Austria, and Czechslovakia hardly thought about
religion. But in these circumstances, if the authorities decided you were
Jewish, you were. My grandfather and grandmother stayed and were killed in
the death camps. My mother, like many other refugees, was rescued in 1938
when she was seventeen, by two Quaker ladies in Manchester. The best book,
with a local Belfast connection, about the terror of the time is *A Time to Speak*
by Helen Lewis. Helen survived the death camps by teaching dance to provide
entertainment for the prison guards. Here in Belfast she taught dance, and
directed a dance company in the 1950s and 1960s.

The Belfast Jewish community worked hard to rescue as many as they
could from persecution. They bought a house to act as a hostel in Cliftonpark
Avenue, and found jobs for adults and foster parents for children. One of the
most important rescue schemes was the *Kindertransport,* trainloads of young
children – some 10,000 of them, sent west and arriving in London for onward
transfer to whoever would take them – many of whom never saw their parents
again. In a country at war and with rationing of food and clothes, this was a

wonderful commitment. Ireland would not help, and a richer Britain today is not so open-hearted. Three-year old Alfie Dubbs went to Cookstown, County Tyrone, where his Christian mother found him. Lord Dubbs told locals of this connection when he worked here as Minister of State.

In 1938, the Belfast Jewish community thought up a marvellous idea which saved over 300 people all in one place. They set up a little home in Millisle, Co. Down, on a 70-acre farm, which was kept going until 1948. The aim was that it would be self-sufficient, and milk cows, keep chickens and grow vegetables as well as fields of barley, wheat and oats, and learn new skills which would be appropriate for Palestine, if the plan for a national Jewish homeland came about. Marilyn Taylor's book *Faraway Home*, is a fictional account of this enterprise. The Belfast Jewish community had to pay the rent, keep the residents clothed, the children in school, and much else besides. It was a remarkable achievement, and its survivors, now scattered around the world, still remember it with affection. Sadly, the buildings have now been demolished.

Small pockets of Jews gathered in other towns – Derry, Lurgan, Newry, each of which had meeting places in a house at some time. Now that transport is so easy, all religious activity is concentrated in Belfast, but there are still little Jewish enclaves in places like Kilkeel and Portadown.

By 1964 Annesley Street was too far from the community and it was difficult to run a wedding or even organise a cup of tea at the 1904 synagogue. Barney Hurwitz, then President of the community, thought that a new synagogue should be built at the property in Somerton Road, where there was more space to provide social as well as religious needs. At that time there was a rabbi, a cantor, a teacher, two Jewish butchers and someone who could circumcise baby boys. In 2004 there was a celebration of two anniversaries, 100 years since the opening of Annesley Street and 40 years in the current synagogue.

At the end of the 1960s, the Troubles started, and affected Jews in the same way as others. Murder, bombs and threats were mostly related to money. Lawyers were targeted too. People left, students went elsewhere and did not return. Sometimes the Jewish community provided 'neutral venues' for talks between political factions.

To-day the Jewish community has shrunk to fewer than 300 souls. Mostly we manage to keep a rabbi, but nobody else. Half of the buildings and land have been sold Meat comes once a week from Manchester, as there is no local kosher provision. We have a wonderful volunteer burial society, and a club for old folk. I was editor of a quarterly magazine which keeps us in touch both internally and with those who have left. As a child in Belfast I went to Hebrew school five or six times a week. Today the children meet on Sundays but have not learnt enough of either language or tradition to cope with a service. Weddings are very rare. An interesting new initiative is the Council for Christians and Jews. This meets at Somerton Road and produces audiences large enough to welcome visiting speakers and concerts.

How do we fit into modern society? Mostly fine. If we are identified with Israel, we get the benefit of current views. Political Protestants compare Israel to Ulster. Sinn Féin identifies with Palestinians. Israeli flags actually go up in some districts. There are attacks on the City cemetery, as there are on graveyards elsewhere. And we get occasional insults, but nothing violent. There are no restrictions in our lifestyle, and my generation speaks without an immigrant's accent, so we are not easily distinguished, except by name – Cohen, Levey and such. Our problems are largely of our own making, losing interest in religion, or moving to centres where more people allows for more facilities, such as kosher food and Jewish schools.

I have been asked what we should like for ourselves in the future. With our dwindling numbers, I find this a hard question. What I would really like is for a chance to help in the present by way of thanks to the kind people who helped us when we arrived here in the 1930s and 1940s. In England, I got a lot of pleasure teaching English to Vietnamese refugees. And in that emergency, some special ideas were thought up for instant homes and schools. But do we have a good system for welcoming new arrivals, providing an introduction to the language and customs of the district now? In Israel, where virtually everyone has to learn a new language, they have a special college, the Ulpan, geared to helping the incomer. Is it time for us to establish a new Millisle farm?

References:

The Jews of Ireland, Louis Hyman, (The Jewish Historical Society of England and Israel, Universities Press) 1972

Shalom Ireland, Ray Rivlin, (Gill & MacMillan, Dublin) 2003

Faraway Home, Marilyn Taylor, (O'Brien Press, Dublin) 1999

A Time to Speak, Helen Lewis, (Blackstaff Press, Belfast) 1992

Belfast Jewish Record, Quarterly magazine, established in 1954

II. THE HISTORY OF THE CHINESE COMMUNITY IN NORTHERN IRELAND

Anna Lo

Chinese people came to Northern Ireland to better themselves economically. The majority of the Chinese community came from the rural area of Hong Kong called the 'New Territories,' between the border of China and the city area of Hong Kong. The New Territories were on lease to the Hong Kong Government for 99 years until 1997. After the Communist Regime took power in China in 1949, many refugees went to settle in the city area of Hong Kong which developed rapidly to become a prosperous world trade centre within a couple of decades. To cope with the population expansion, Hong Kong began to buy agricultural products from abroad, adversely affecting the livelihood of many of the small farmers in the New Territories. Many of them also found difficulties trying to find jobs in the city of Hong Kong.

The economic decline in the New Territories coincided with an economic boom in post-war Britain in the 1950s, causing a shortage in labour which attracted immigration from the Commonwealth countries including people from the New Territories of Hong Kong.

The first Chinese family arrived in Newry in 1962, with many others following and opening Chinese restaurants and carry-outs in Belfast and other parts of the province, so that by 2006 there were approximately 10,000 Chinese spread out into nearly every town in Northern Ireland. Most Chinese people came to Britain following a pattern termed a 'migration chain,' whereby someone who has settled here brings over a relative or friend to fill a job vacancy in their business, which are generally in the catering trade. Once they are here, they find houses near their workplace or sometimes live above the shop. For many, coming to Northern Ireland followed living in London or Birmingham, the move offering new opportunities, and a demand for fast-food outlets, and better housing. The Chinese form a close-knit community and local knowledge about where best to open a shop or live, is generally shared with the newcomers by other more settled Chinese people. Children are generally sent to the nearby school, often not being aware whether it is a state school or a Catholic school.

The majority of the first-generation Chinese community own their own businesses or are in jobs. They are content that many of them have achieved their ambition and are economically secure, and they are pleased to see their children receiving a good education and entering different professions in the wider society. Many parents do not want their children to work in the catering trade which involves long and unsociable hours The second generation of Chinese young people are well integrated. While many first-generation migrants intended to go home to China on retirement, (and many never became British citizens), most have stayed to be near their children as they married and made careers locally. This is now very much 'home,' and the second generation see themselves as Chinese/British/Irish, and this as their society.

Many Chinese people would like to see their community getting recognition for its contributions to the economic life and cultural diversity in Northern Ireland. They would like all sections of the community embraced, and for it to become an inclusive multi-ethnic society. Now with many other incomer communities, they have brought a wonderful increase in new ideas, and have contributed to the cultural diversity in Northern Ireland in the 21st century.

III. THE INDIAN COMMUNITY AND IRELAND

Nisha Tandon

Indu and Ireland are joined together by an imperial past but separated by language, religion and traditions. The imperial histories of these two countries are well known: the links between India, England and Ireland through the East India Company go back as far as 1600.

Many Irish men and women spent a large part of their life in India. Some of these famous people were Eyre Coote, George Thomas, Father Fennelly, Father Daniel Murphy and there were many more. The ties between the two countries became very strong in all avenues and the evidence exists in India until today, in the form of schools, missionaries, trade and religion.

India received its independence in 1947, and in the troubles which followed, many Indians fled to different parts of the UK, and some of them came to Northern Ireland. The first Indians to arrive in Northern Ireland were travelling to achieve better prospects in life. Some came in this country with as little as 11 shillings.

Those who came to Ireland can be divided into four categories. Firstly there were self-employed businessmen. These formed the majority of those that settled in the 1920s to 1950s. During that period they were particularly prominent in Northern Ireland and almost all were in the textile clothing business. They mostly prospered, and saved, and through their hard work and dedication they became tycoons of many industries in Northern Ireland. They gave priority to their businesses, and to family life. Though the first generation generally made their name in business, they did not mind when the next generation found professions outside the original businesses, and took an interest in education and more professional occupations.

Then there were students, most of whom had intended to come and study for a short while and then return to their country of origin, which was to India or to one of the British colonies with large populations. Thirdly there were professional workers, such as doctors, engineers, and chemists. Lastly a miscellaneous group included restaurant workers, sailors, embassy staff, Hindu priests and others.

As with the businessmen, many stayed and in the second and third generations 75 per cent of marriages were with locals (a higher percentage than anywhere else in the UK), and so were both intercultural and successful. The third generation is well integrated in Northern Ireland. Though they carry Indian genes, they are born Irish in many ways, and call themselves Indian-Irish.

In spite of all the troubles in Northern Ireland, the Indian community kept their heads down and never took part in any of the sectarian troubles. Within their own areas they integrated with both sides of the community, maintaining a good understanding of events, and carried on living a normal life. A few left, but now return to visit and are amazed to see how the Indian community here has progressed.

The early-settled Indians never suffered any racism in Northern Ireland, but in recent times, with a larger population of migrant nurses, hotel staff and call centre employees, coming from different regions of India, racial abuse is increasing and becoming more evident. To make this place welcome for our newcomers we have to learn about all different cultures and accept them the way they are.

The Indian Community Centre is based in the Carlisle Methodist Memorial Church Hall, which was built in 1876. The Centre (ICC) is a regional organisation, which provides a range of services and organises activities, mainly for the Indian Community in Northern Ireland, for whom it aims to provide services and facilities to maintain their philosophical, cultural and arts heritage.

To quote Mahatma Gandhi:

> Anger and intolerance are the twin enemies of correct understanding.

Chapter Eight

RECENT MIGRATION EXPERIENCES

Anthony Soares

O ver the past few months a substantial amount of construction work
has been taking place outside my office, improving access for
disabled people to all the university buildings along an entire street.
This has involved, among other things, the demolition of steps,
replacing them with permanent ramps, as well as connecting buildings with
wheelchair-friendly passages. We had been made aware beforehand that this
activity was going to occur by a foreman, who politely explained what this
might involve. However, when work actually began, the men handling the
machinery, the pickaxes, the shovels, those scurrying to and fro, did not,
unlike their foreman, engage us in any conversation. In fact, it quickly became
apparent, whenever one of them would shout out to a colleague above the din
of the machinery, or they were overheard talking to one another as they sat in
their van during their lunch breaks, that they were not local labourers – they
were, in fact, from Latvia. The construction company contracted by Queen's
to do this important work that will contribute to improving the university
experience of a certain proportion of students, has engaged labourers from one
of the newest nations to become a member of the European Union.

These men from eastern Europe are examples of a relatively recent trend
of foreigners coming (or being brought) to Northern Ireland in order to work.
They are men and women who will not find other natives of their countries
who have been living here for a considerable number of years, such as those

of the 'established communities', such as the Chinese or Indian communities. Neither are the recent migrant workers we will be discussing here examples of the recognized trend of the importation of professional or skilled workers, such as computer analysts, doctors, or university lecturers; instead, we will be concentrating on those who have arrived in Northern Ireland to take up generally low-paid and unskilled employment. Workers arriving in Northern Ireland from countries such as Latvia, Lithuania, Poland, Serbia or Brazil will have to negotiate many practical obstacles (such as linguistic barriers) during their stay, generally without recourse to an existing community of fellow countrymen and women who might have offered valuable advice and support. They will also have to overcome their initial lack of understanding of local cultures. However, be it voluntarily or through sheer necessity, the host communities among whom these migrant workers will live and work, will also have to face the nature of other cultures on their very own doorsteps: it is up to each individual from the host communities whether they engage in a positive manner with those from other cultural backgrounds, or whether they choose to react in less favourable ways. In either case, these encounters with migrant workers may very often lead to a deliberate or unconscious self-evaluation of the host communities' cultures and what it means to belong to a particular identity-grouping. This process is very often also being undertaken by migrant workers, who find themselves geographically distanced from their own countries through economic imperatives, and are 'carriers' of cultures that are alien and mark them as 'different', to a greater or lesser extent, to the local cultures that surround them. But what might be the major causes that have led these migrant workers coming to Northern Ireland in the first place? Why is Northern Ireland, despite its historical image abroad as an area suffering from substantial difficulties, apparently becoming attractive as an employment destination?

Firstly, it is important to note that it is not uncommon for migrant workers, responding to recruitment drives undertaken in their home countries by employment agencies, to be unaware, at the time they sign their contracts of employment that they will actually be working in Northern Ireland. Generally accustomed to primarily associate the destination 'United Kingdom' (which is where the recruitment agencies in these cases declare they are sending the migrant workers concerned) with England, a whole set of readjustments to their cultural (and financial) expectations must occur when many are unexpectedly sent to various locations throughout Northern Ireland. In these particular cases one could venture that there is a coincidence between some of the assumptions made about Northern Ireland by both prospective migrant workers and a percentage of local inhabitants, namely, that Northern Ireland has no 'tradition' of immigration, nor is it 'fertile ground' in which to initiate such a tradition. Many migrant workers unexpectedly arriving in such places as Dungannon, Portadown or Coleraine, having, until their arrival, pictured themselves in cities such as Manchester, Birmingham or, ideally, London, initially think of their temporary place of residence as an economic backwater, unsuitable for an individual seeking to earn enough to make a better life for their families back home. Consequently, even though many migrant workers may reformulate their initial negative cultural and economic assumptions about Northern Ireland, we cannot realistically attempt to identify any factors that may have 'pulled' these workers here, as the positive factors they had used to decide their migration were (mistakenly) based on their belonging to other (generally English) cities.

Nonetheless, there are other migrant workers who leave their own countries in the full knowledge that they will be employed in Northern Ireland, and have, therefore, made the decision to migrate here having considered the likely benefits. According to a recent report published by the Institute for Conflict Research, there are a range of 'push' and 'pull' factors that either encouraged people to leave the country they were living in or attracted them to move to Northern Ireland.[1] Limited opportunities for work was a prominent 'push' factor encouraging migration, while a range of positive attractions to Northern Ireland was cited. These included: a higher salary, opportunity for career development, a better standard of living, and the active recruitment process for specific occupations.

The range of factors identified in this report indicates, among other things, that we should, whenever possible, avoid seeing migrant workers as a homogenous group, even when it comes to their reasons for being here – a particular worker may have come to Northern Ireland due to a particular set of circumstances that are markedly different to those of another worker, even if s/he comes from the same country. In this regard, where the above report points to 'limited opportunities for work' as a single 'push' factor that causes individuals to leave their country, it would be useful to offer two further perspectives on what this might mean to separate individuals. These limits of opportunity may entail the relative difficulties of an employed individual obtaining another similar position with a higher salary within his/her own country; or someone without work being unable to obtain any employment whatsoever. Therefore, both these individuals may migrate to Northern Ireland, but they will have had very different circumstances in their home country, particularly in the case of a country which has little or no public resources to alleviate the greater economic difficulties experienced by the unemployed individual.

Despite the differing circumstances that lead individuals to migrate to Northern Ireland in order to work, there is a general reconciliation that often has to be made by many between their views of their own nations, and the fact that they have come to the conclusion that they must leave their own countries in order to attain a certain standard of life for themselves and their families. In other words, when a Portuguese or Filipino worker makes the decision to (very often) leave his or her family and a familiar culture in order to come to Northern Ireland, it can lead to a re-evaluation of the worth of Portugal or the Philippines, since neither of these countries have offered these workers the opportunity to achieve the desired standard of life they had envisaged. Furthermore, that standard of life, which is promoted as an ideal by general commercial advertising, and by many media products, such as films and soap-operas (whether imported or domestic), requires a level of consumption and acquisition of goods that cannot be generally sustained by large sectors of the population. Hence, many decide that, if they cannot find jobs that will pay them enough in order to purchase the goods that will make their families' lives more comfortable and offer them the standard of life they deserve, then they will temporarily migrate to where those jobs exist. And it this situation that presents the uncomfortable paradox: a certain ideal lifestyle is promoted by various means, and yet, for many, that very lifestyle can only possibly be obtained by leaving one's own country, and leading a type of life in a foreign land that is almost certainly far from that ideal.

Even though, as we shall see in greater detail later, many migrant workers have to endure a number of hardships and prejudices during their stay in Northern Ireland, it should not be assumed that the countries they are leaving are impoverished to such an extent that they are willing to endure living and working conditions that most of us would not tolerate. It is sometimes thought, when considering the presence of Portuguese, Timorese or Lithuanian workers in Dungannon and Portadown, for example, that they form part of a great wave of people leaving those countries in search of work in more prosperous parts of the world, as if their own countries were being emptied of their unskilled labour force or unemployed. Such a view fits neatly into many people's cultural perceptions of this part of Western Europe, perceived as more economically developed and, dare I suggest, somehow more culturally advanced, acting as a magnet upon people from less fortunate nations, who are coming here in droves. However, this world view can be reduced to the assumption that countries, such as the United Kingdom, due to their economic prosperity, have an immigration problem because they are attracting so many people from less prosperous countries. But how does the following quotation from a recent article in the Portuguese newspaper, *O Público*, entitled 'The Policy on Immigration', fit into this simplistic view of migration?

The development of an encompassing and coherent policy on immigration must be based on two interrelated concerns: on the one hand, the regulation of migratory waves and, on the other, the creation, by the State, of tools that will facilitate the reception and integration of immigrants.[2]

These considerations are not on how Northern Ireland, or the United Kingdom, should deal with immigrants moving to these countries in search of work; they are focusing, instead, on how the Portuguese government should deal with migration into Portugal. So, here we have a challenge to the perception of countries such as Portugal being merely exporters of unskilled labourers to other nations, as it is also a receiving nation, which should make us beware of assuming that, because migrant workers are arriving here from other countries, their own countries are so much poorer and less developed than our own that they are simply being emptied of large swathes of their populations.

Nevertheless, whether the migrant worker has come to Northern Ireland from a country receiving its own share of workers from abroad or not, and whatever the individual circumstances that caused them to be here, there are certain experiences that many of them share once they have arrived. These include, for example: poor accommodation; irregularities in the payment of wages by recruitment agencies; uncertainty as to their rights as employees; a lack of knowledge about the provision of public services; discrimination and racism both within and outside the workplace; linguistic barriers. And yet, in general terms, those whose presence here is due to the involvement of recruitment agencies tend to face a greater number of difficulties than those who have found direct employment. Problems arise from the fact that a migrant worker recruited by an agency may be working in a particular meat-processing factory, for example, but his/her employer is not the factory, but the agency, who pays the worker his/her wages, so that, in some cases, the factory does not have to take responsibility for the worker's situation, as it is not the employer. This may mean that a migrant worker who feels that they have not been properly paid for that particular week's work cannot seek any resolution to the problem in the factory that they are working, but have, instead, to seek assistance from representatives of the recruitment agency, which may not have offices in Northern Ireland, which will, at the very least, signify delays in rectifying the situation.

In fact, the role of the recruitment agencies and their treatment of migrant workers are not easily established, as Bell, Jarman and Lefebvre discovered when compiling their report (cited above, n 1):

It proved difficult to gather information from employment agencies themselves with regards to their involvement with migrant workers. Information was requested from thirty employment agencies across Northern Ireland on the numbers, origins and job sectors of migrant workers employed, methods of recruitment, and any liaison arrangements with employment agencies in other countries. Only one agency, based in Belfast, provided information. (p53)

Lack of clarity and obfuscation are among some of the determinant characteristics of the relationships between the recruitment agencies, the migrant workers, and the companies that employ those agencies, where the migrant workers are generally the ones to suffer when the lines of responsibility are left unclear. And the lack of information about the details of these recruitment agencies is not only due to their own reluctance to shed light on their businesses, but also because migrant workers themselves are very often unwilling and unable to provide insights into the agencies. Their inability arises from the fact that many of them are as unaware as everybody else as to the precise functioning of the agencies, whilst those who may have acquired some knowledge (perhaps individuals acting in a supervisory capacity) do not feel free to divulge it, through fear of intimidation, or simply because their very livelihoods, which they do not want to jeopardise, depend upon the recruitment agencies. The result is that inequalities may exist between the pay and conditions of migrant workers recruited by a particular agency and, not only local workers, but also other migrant workers attached to different agencies, where they are performing similar functions. Discrepancies arise, for instance, in the payment of fees by migrant workers to the recruitment agencies, where some may be charged a few hundred pounds, whereas others must pay thousands, as in the case of the Filipino nurse highlighted by Bell, Jarman and Lefebvre:

No information was gathered from nursing homes on how they recruit overseas nurses but we interviewed a Filipino nurse who had worked in a nursing home in Northern Ireland. He had been charged £2,000 by an agency in the Philippines who told him not to tell anyone in Northern Ireland about this fee. (p56)

Of course, the reluctance of individual migrant workers to reveal the details of the payments they make to the agencies makes it difficult for those workers to engage in a collective effort to establish equality of pay and conditions. That reluctance stems, in many cases, from a lack of knowledge of their rights as employees, as they apply in Northern Ireland, allowing recruitment agencies to give migrant workers the impression that they (the workers) will be the ones punished by the local authorities if they reveal certain details of their relationships to the agencies. Migrant workers' lack of knowledge of employment rights, as well as rights to public services and benefits have sometimes been compounded by the fact that some of those who attempted to gather information on these issues were dismissed by the recruitment agencies employing them. Such actions will send a clear message to others, who may be tempted to do the same, making them even more reluctant to risk their positions, especially when we consider some of the important functions that the agencies perform for the migrant workers, such as the provision of housing.

Accommodation is generally arranged by the recruitment agencies for the migrant workers, and is tied to their term of employment, so that, if the worker is dismissed or ceases his/her employment with the agency, then he/she will have to vacate the property provided by the agency. For many migrant workers, the prospect of jeopardising their accommodation would cause great anxiety, since renting another property would be relatively difficult, as very few would have the financial capacity to pay a deposit, as well as finding linguistic barriers hard to overcome. And yet, the accommodation the recruitment agencies provides is very often overcrowded, as migrant workers have to share houses that are not designed to hold the numbers put into them, as well as the fact that it frequently prevents those with families to arrange for them to join them. This can lead to feelings of isolation and a sense of instability, especially when we consider that the recruitment agencies may ask a migrant worker to move to different accommodation at any time. Compounding these difficulties is the fact that many recruitment agencies house their workers in interface areas, where there may be existing social and/or sectarian problems, and where the presence of foreign workers can attract unwanted attention from certain elements within the local population who may use racist abuse or even violence against them and their properties. Nevertheless, however unsatisfactory the housing may be, the migrant worker will have their rent deducted directly from his/her wages by the recruitment agency that has provided that accommodation, thereby denying them the opportunity to withhold rent when repeated complaints about the conditions of the accommodation have not been adequately dealt with and, at the same time, contributing to a feeling of powerlessness, whereby the migrant worker does not seem able to control something as essential as the place they live in.[3]

Such feelings of powerlessness can also be exacerbated within the workplace, where there may be a lack of clarity, for example, as to how overtime hours are allocated, so that an individual migrant worker may not know how to improve his/her salary, thereby being unable to control their economic situation. This aspect was highlighted by several Portuguese migrant workers, as my own 2002 work entitled *Relatório sobre trabalhadores portugueses na Irlanda do Norte/Report on Portuguese Workers in Northern Ireland*, shows, as in the following instance:

> Jorge refers to a perception shared by others that the allocation of overtime hours is unfair, since there are no clear guidelines as to who is given preference, and as to why certain individuals may be refused them. Giving priority to those who are deemed 'good workers' does not, in many individuals' view, make clear who is a 'good worker', as many of those that receive less overtime hours would place themselves in this category.[4]

Not only is the ability to take meaningful steps towards acquiring overtime hours taken away due to the absence of any clear and stable procedures as to how these are awarded, but the denial of this valuable means of improving one's economic plight may be used by those in a position of authority to unfairly punish those who are seen as 'difficult', which often translates as those who pursue what they are rightfully entitled to. As well as reinforcing the sense of powerlessness, this type of behaviour also contributes to the feeling amongst migrant workers that they are treated less favourably than workers from the indigenous communities, as they are not normally subjected to such irregular processes by their superiors. The ways in which absences from work or 'clocking on' have been administered by employers and recruitment agencies can clearly reflect disparities in how workers from local communities are treated differently to workers from elsewhere, as the following excerpt from my *Report on Portuguese Workers* demonstrates:

> The general type of behaviour that is seen by the majority of Portuguese workers as discriminatory is related to attitudes taken on absence from work, giving evidence of attending work, and the administration of payment of wages. In the first case, it was felt that, whereas their colleagues from Northern Ireland were entitled to take days off work due to illness or injury, Portuguese workers in the same situation were often pressurised by supervisors to return to work, and would not receive their wages if they refused. In the second example, some individuals were unhappy that their local colleagues had a system of clocking on and clocking off, whereas the Portuguese had to present themselves to their supervisors at the beginning of each shift to be signed in, and again when they reached the end of the

shift. […] As to the final case, many workers complained of delays and underpayments in their wages, which were blamed by supervisors on administrative errors. […] This was a major cause of resentment since they pointed out that such errors did not occur in the case of workers from Northern Ireland. (p68)

Feelings of powerlessness, subjected to arbitrary rules, and a sense that they do not receive the same kind of treatment as local workers, all contribute to making migrant workers feel insecure and at the mercy of those in positions of authority, both in the home (which may be provided by a recruitment agency), and in the place of work.

These feelings can also arise in the public sphere, such as when accessing public services or simply when interacting at a social level, as linguistic and cultural obstacles often arise at these points. Information on many public services has in the past only been available in English (although this situation appears to be improving, in the health and social services sector, for example), which automatically excludes many migrant workers whose English may be poor or non-existent, so that they are not even aware of the services that may exist for them. And yet, very often, when they do attempt to access some public services, such as a doctor, the linguistic barriers arise once more, as there has, until now, been a severe lack of interpreter provision, both because of a shortage of actual trained interpreters, and also due to the fact that some service providers have not thought to make such provision available.[5] In some circumstances, there is an assumption made that, if a migrant worker cannot speak English to a sufficient level, then that migrant worker should bring someone with them that will interpret for them on an unofficial basis when accessing a service. As well as such behaviour being unjust and unethical, it increases the sense amongst migrant workers that their well-being does not have the same priority as that of members of the local communities, causing them to increasingly believe that they are simply viewed as labourers whose usefulness ends as soon as they make any attempt to 'consume' local services, or in any way become a 'burden' if they are not working.

Even the hours of leisure can become a source of feelings of isolation and alienation, since migrant workers' local colleagues who may welcome them into their communities quite often socialise in public bars, which will not be affordable to individuals who have travelled to Northern Ireland in order to improve the economic situation of their families. This is the case particularly for the great majority of migrant workers who have come here on short-term contracts, where the imperative is to earn as much, and spend as little money as possible in the time they have here before returning to their own countries.

However, the effect is to reduce the opportunities for social exchanges with members of the local communities, which makes it difficult for any meaningful intercultural understanding to be reached. Many migrant workers, therefore, feel excluded from the lives of the communities they live and work in, despite the fact that they are usually eager to learn about the realities faced by local people, whilst they also consider that the same interest about their own cultures is not shared by local individuals. This was borne out during interviews undertaken with Portuguese migrant workers, which informed the following comments in my aforementioned *Report*:

> Interviewees often displayed an eagerness to know more about local history, politics and culture, while at the same time giving evidence of misconceptions and somewhat negative generalisations. But it must be emphasised that the will exists among the Portuguese to learn more about the communities in which they live, and that that will should be acknowledged practically. Allied to this is the fact that many interviewees also commented on the adverse comments made by individuals from their local communities about the Portuguese, as well as a reciprocal lack of knowledge about Portugal itself. (pp80-81)

These views are generally applicable to most migrant workers, whatever their nationalities and the lack of local knowledge of migrant workers' cultures initially experienced by the Portuguese has now even become evident in the language of mid-Ulster. According to various local sources, the term 'Portuguese' is now applied to any migrant worker, whatever their country of origin, displaying a total disinterest in finding out where an individual migrant worker has actually come from, and subsuming all of them into a general, indistinguishable category of 'Portuguese'.

Such a use of the term 'Portuguese' to describe any migrant worker may have, in its negative aspects, a possible historical equivalent, although this particular reference is in relation specifically to Portuguese migrant workers at the end of the nineteenth and beginning of the twentieth centuries, and it is made by a Portuguese academic, Boaventura de Sousa Santos, who tells us:

> In the Caribbean, the United States and Hawaii the Portuguese were always considered to be an ethnic group that differed from whites and Europeans, possessing an intermediary status between these and the blacks or natives. In the Caribbean and Hawaii workers on fixed-term contracts who had come to

substitute the slaves after the end of slavery were designated
'Portygees' or 'Potogees'.[6] [author's translation].

Although Sousa Santos points to the past use of negative terminology
specifically against Portuguese workers in other parts of the world, there are
two possible points of comparison with the use of the term 'Portuguese' in
mid-Ulster: firstly, it is the fact that, just like those called 'Portygees' in the
Caribbean and Hawaii, most migrant workers in Northern Ireland are
employed on fixed-term contracts; and secondly, Sousa Santos remarks that
racist attitudes underlying the terms used to describe the Portuguese were
especially to be found in the Anglo-Saxon world. Just as the expressions used
in the Caribbean and Hawaii, as well as the United States, through their
corruption of the word 'Portuguese', denoted a dismissive attitude on the part
of those who used them in relation to Portuguese migrant workers, refusing to
see them as individuals and, instead, lumping them together into a lowly
category of 'Portygees', so too the current application by some of the term
'Portuguese' to all migrant workers betrays the view that they are an
indistinguishable mass, without individuality; or perhaps it would be more
accurate to state that those who use the term 'Portuguese' in this way do not
think it worthwhile to distinguish the individual from the mass, as he/she is not
as important as someone who is not a migrant worker.

Despite these negative views, however, migrant workers make a positive
contribution to the communities they work and live in, enabling some
companies to fill a labour shortage and revitalising others, particularly in rural
areas, as well as spending some of their wages in local businesses, whilst
generally being law-abiding citizens. Although the great majority return after
the term of their contracts has expired, a few decide to make Northern Ireland
a medium-term home for them and their families, intending to go back to their
own countries after having saved enough to live more comfortable lives upon
their return. In these cases then, we could say that such individuals are no
longer migrant workers, but immigrants and, as such, their contributions to the
economy of the region should be welcomed, which is the attitude taken by
Roberto Carneiro, head of the 'Observatório da Imigração' (Immigration
Observatory), in Portugal, in relation to immigration to his own country,
according to an article in *O Público* of the 28th October 2004, entitled
'Immigrants are a "profitable business" for the National Insurance system'[7]:

> When an immigrant of around 30 years of age arrives here and
> starts to make National Insurance contributions, such an
> individual is someone in whom the State has not invested or
> spent anything and has already been educated and, presumably,

will be in good health [...]. Five per cent of the country's wealth is created by immigrants, which represents a total of over 40 million euros going straight into the state's exchequer. [author's translation].

Perhaps this is a somewhat narrow way of looking at immigration, but it serves to undermine the belief that some people have that immigrants, or migrant workers, are a burden on the State, instead of seeing them as positive contributors to the financial well-being of the country they are working in. Some of the blame for such misconceptions regarding migrant workers and immigrants must lie at the feet of those in positions of political authority, who rarely acknowledge the positive contributions they make to the Northern Ireland economy.

Perhaps the presence of migrant workers and immigrants may reflect the relative health of the economy here, as Northern Ireland may now offer such people the opportunity to earn sufficient money to attain the standard of life they want for their families back home. However, I would also like to offer the following possibilities to those who might point to those local people who are unemployed and ask: if the Northern Ireland economy is doing so well, why are they without jobs? Or, why are migrant workers taking jobs that the local unemployed may have filled? Perhaps the answer to both questions lies in the fact that what a migrant worker earns in Northern Ireland doing generally unskilled, monotonous and exhausting work, enables her/him to purchase much more in his/her own country than a local person may purchase here. That means that migrant workers may view the prospect of undertaking such employment on a short to medium term basis as worthwhile given the ultimate rewards that may be obtained in their own countries, whereas a local person will not be as likely to reach such a conclusion since they will not be able to obtain the same rewards, as the consumer goods that the migrant worker purchases in his/her own country will generally be cheaper than here.

I would also, in this concluding part, like to return to the Portuguese academic, Boaventura de Sousa Santos, and to his characterisation of Portugal in relation to its status within the wider world, to see whether it has any application to Northern Ireland and the recent trend of incoming migration. He states:

Portugal has since the seventeenth century been a semiperipheral country within the modern global capitalist system. This condition, which best describes Portuguese society's long-term modernity, evolved over centuries but maintained its fundamental characteristics: an intermediate economic development and an intermediary position between the centre and the periphery of the global economy'. (p23) [author's translation][8]

Although Sousa Santos constructs a theory of Portugal's current status in the light of its particular history as a colonial power and former head of an empire, the idea of being at the periphery or the semiperiphery of a modern global capitalist system may have some resonances for what we have been analysing here. If we think of the centre of this system not necessarily in geographical terms, but in terms of a certain type of discourse (although this discourse may originate from certain precise points), then we can begin to look at the migrant workers as individuals who are trying to reach that centre. That does not mean that Northern Ireland is the centre, rather that this place will become the means for migrant workers to achieve it, since the language of this discourse is made up of consumer goods that denote that their owner has reached the centre. The discourse that promotes the consumption of goods that will allow the purchaser to attain a lifestyle that shows that he/she has arrived at the centre reaches far and wide through all modes of the media, arriving at those countries whose citizens have migrated to Northern Ireland to work.

In this light, it is interesting to note that we now have Portuguese migrant workers, coming from a western European nation, a member of the European Union since 1986 and one of the euro club members, working alongside those from the new accession countries, such as Latvia and Lithuania, as well as others from further afield, such as East Timor. What may connect all these countries is that they all (including East Timor, which only became an independent nation in 2002) have free-market economies, although some of them are rather younger than others, and their citizens, therefore, have easier access to the type of discourse I have just outlined. However, ease of access to this discourse does not necessarily equate with the acquisition of what that discourse promotes, which is why many individuals opt to obtain the means to do so far from their homes and families. Often the incentive to do so arrives in the form of a recruitment agency, which has been asked to obtain workers for Northern Ireland, so that some of its companies may produce the goods that the modern global economy needs, and which its discourse will promote. The vacancies generally exist because the financial rewards that these jobs offer are not attractive to those who permanently reside in Northern Ireland, whereas these migrant workers can see benefits in coming to Northern Ireland to do these jobs in the short-term. However, one could question whether they will ever attain the centre of the global system, as the return from Northern Ireland to the country of origin may turn out to be a temporary one, since the lifestyle many of the migrant workers want to achieve may be costly to maintain, and the result may be that another temporary migration will occur, being employed in yet another country to produce goods that will be promoted as part of the lifestyle they are trying to achieve, in a cycle that will feed on itself. Northern Ireland has become a stopping point in that cycle, which could be viewed positively, since the alternative may be that it too will become (or return to) the periphery and, instead of receiving migrant workers, will have a population that could face the choice of migrating to do the same type of work that the Portuguese, Latvians and Lithuanians do here, hoping that their presence in others' countries will not be resented. Let us hope that this will not be the case.

Notes

1   Kathryn Bell, Neil Jarman and Thomas Lefebvre, *Migrant Workers in Northern Ireland* (Belfast: Institute for Conflict Research, 2004), pp 5-6
2   ['A construção de uma política de imigração global e coerente tem que ter por base duas preocupações indissociáveis: por um lado, a regulação dos fluxos migratórios e, por outro, a criação, por parte do Estado, de instrumentos que facilitem o acolhimento e a integração dos imigrantes'], Feliciano Barreiras Duarte, 'A Política de Imigração,' in *O Público*, 2004/10/04.
3   Recruitment agencies often also make deductions from the migrant workers' wages to cover the costs of return airplane tickets provided by the agencies to the workers. However, many workers complain that such deductions continue to be made even after the tickets have been repaid.
4   Anthony Soares, *Relatório sobre trabalhadores portugueses na Irlanda do Norte/ Report on Portuguese Workers in Northern Ireland* (Belfast: Multi-Cultural Resource Centre (NI), 2002), p 63.
5   The Northern Ireland Health and Social Services Interpreting Service entered service earlier this year, and should, given sustained adequate funding, improve the provision of interpreters in the health and social services sector.
6   [Nas Caraíbas, nos E.U.A. e no Havai os portugueses foram sempre considerados um grupo étnico diferente dos brancos e dos europeus, com um estatuto intermédio entre estes e os negros ou nativos. Nas Caraíbas e no Havai eram designados por 'Portygees' ou 'Potogees', trabalhadores com contratos a prazo que vieram substituir os escravos depois do fim da escravatura]. Boaventura de Sousa Santos, 'Entre Prospero e Caliban: Colonialismo, pós-colonialismo e inter-identidade,' in *Entre ser e estar: Raízes, percursos e discursos da identidade*, ed. by Maria Irene Ramalho and António Sousa Ribeiro (Porto: Edições Afrontamento, 2001), p 62.
7   ['Quando chega aqui um imigrante com cerca de 30 anos e começa a descontar é alguém em quem o Estado não investiu nem gastou nada e que já vem educado e, em princípio, será uma pessoa saudável […]. Cinco por cento da riqueza do país assenta na imigração, o que representa um valor superior a 40 milhões de euros só nas contas do estado'], http://ultimahora.publico.pt, accessed on 28/10/04.
8   [Portugal é desde o século XVII um país semiperiférico no sistema mundial capitalista moderno. Esta condição, sendo a que melhor caracteriza a longa duração moderna da sociedade portuguesa, evoluiu ao longo dos séculos mas manteve os seus traços fundamentais: um desenvolvimento económico intermédio e uma posição de intermediação entre o centro e a periferia da economia-mundo].

Chapter Nine

IDENTITIES IN NORTHERN IRELAND: NOTHING BUT THE SAME OLD STORIES?

Tony Gallagher

Introduction

I am a great fan of Ted Geisel, better known as Dr Seuss, the writer of children's books, who was recently restored to a wider audience by the adaptation of his book *The Cat in the Hat* in the Hollywood film.

The Dr Seuss stories began as a way of trying to help youngsters read – the challenge he originally set himself was to write luminous and engaging stories using only a limited number of simple words – but they also have, at their core, a strong moral argument. As he became increasingly successful and the range of books he produced widened, this moral core became more and more evident in his stories.

A particularly good example of this is provided by one of his last books, *The Butter Battle Book*, which tells the story of two communities, whom he calls the Yooks and the Zooks who live separated by a great wall. The story opens with an old Yook explaining to his grandson that the wall exists between the two groups as they have fundamentally conflicting opinions as to how bread should be eaten; on the Yook's side, butter-side-up is the rule regarded as sacrosanct, whereas the apparently degenerate Zooks are butter-side-downers, not to be trusted, to be watched carefully at all times. As the tale progresses this conflict of outlooks, fuelled by mutual mistrust and fear, leads to an arms race in which each side invents more and more destructive weapons such as the Yook 'triple-sling jigger', against which the Zooks deploy their 'jigger-rock snatchem'.

The Butter Battle Book is a satire on the Cold War and the spiral of conflict that develops in a context of fear and antagonism. The difference between the two groups – whether they eat their bread with the butter-side up or butter-side down – is obviously absurd. Indeed, it should make us grateful that our own sectarian antagonism is marked by clearly more logical differences, such as the fact that some of us play with different-shaped footballs or different-shaped sticks; or worship the same god, on the same day, in special buildings, but in slightly different ways; or the fact that some of us say 'haitch' while others say 'aitch'.

Another factor in our sectarian antagonism appears to lie in its longevity, for we are a community obsessed with history.

History

I was reminded of this a few years ago when the Minority Rights Group asked me to read a draft of John Darby's book on the Northern Ireland conflict entitled *Scorpions in a Bottle*. In the opening, historical chapter, Darby identified a series of key dates in the conflict, beginning with 1170. When commenting on a book like this I normally jot notes and thoughts on the page while reading, and I recall on this occasion I scored out '1170' and wrote in the margin '1169,' while semi-consciously wondering how the author had managed to get the date of the planned invasion of Ireland so obviously wrong. When I returned to this page later I was struck by how ridiculous it seemed to 'correct' a date, by one year, for an event that happened almost a millennium ago. (Nor, I should point out, was John Darby incorrect – while I was thinking of the year the invasion had been planned, he was referring to the year it actually took place.)

I was reminded of the ubiquity of history also when I interviewed a Loyalist paramilitary leader many years ago as part of the fieldwork for my PhD. 'Why,' I asked him, 'do Protestants feel so under threat from Catholics?' His reply began: 'You've got to remember, that since 1641...' almost as if he was referring to events that had occurred with living memory. And in one sense, I suppose, they had.

But we are not the only ones to live in the shadow of history. If one of the defining characteristics of modernity is that people developed a concept of the future and of progress, then another is that people also developed a sense of the past, a sense of history.

History and the past have long provided the stuff of cliché and aphorism. We are all familiar with Santayana's observation that 'those who cannot remember the past are condemned to repeat it,' or Karl Marx's comment that the 'traditions of the dead generations weigh like a nightmare upon the living.' Many will also recognise the comment attributed to Chou En-Lai who, when asked about the significance of the French Revolution, declared that it was 'too early to tell'. This comment takes on added significance if you read Isaac Deutscher's three-volume biography of Trotsky in which it becomes clear that the Bolsheviks had an almost obsessive concern with the course of the French Revolution as a potential template to guide their own actions. And Benedict Anderson, in *Imagined Communities*, illustrates how history is made real through the iconography and symbols of the modern state, and made socially effective through the promotion of nationalisms.

History is not, however, seamless and unchanging, as occasionally things change more fundamentally and old certainties melt away. There was a time in Ireland, for example, when resistance was based on an aspiration to restore the Stuart Pretender, but by the end of the 18th century the examples provided by the French and American revolutions offered a different route and launched a new discourse of Republicanism. Abraham Lincoln highlighted the same possibility as the United States lurched towards the Civil War when he said:

> The dogmas of the quiet past are inadequate to the stormy present. The occasion is piled high with difficulty, and we must rise with the occasion. As our case is new, so we must think anew, and act anew.

At the turn of the 19th/20th centuries Britain was racked by a emergent sense of crisis comprised of a number of elements: the inability to suppress the Boer rebellion in South Africa provoked questions on the physical character of the British soldier, a concern that was only heightened by the 'discovery' of poverty in the new urban centres of the industrial revolution. Added to this was a widespread belief that Germany and the USA were overtaking Britain in industrial production. These social, economic and military crises all combined to produce a political crisis in which liberal verities on the efficacy of the free market were questioned, then watered down, and later abandoned by the introduction of national insurance. All of this had the longer-term effect of leading to the establishment of the welfare state and, eventually, post-World War Two Keynesian interventionism.

Thus was a new set of economic and political assumptions established to form a taken-for-granted common sense, until they too were challenged by the economic crisis following the oil shock in the 1970s. This challenge was to open the way for the restoration of free market ideas in Margaret Thatcher's neo-liberalism.

Change, in these terms, normally follows some cataclysmic event, or series of events, which challenge fundamental assumptions. Once the old assumptions collapse in inadequacy, there normally follows an intense period of discussion and debate as different ideas compete to provide the best explanation on why things went so wrong and what now needs to be done. Eventually a new 'common-sense', or set of assumptions, emerge.

Northern Ireland: identity

Interestingly, however, this appears not to have happened in Northern Ireland, despite the cataclysmic events of the last 35 years. Well, perhaps that is not entirely true. With the outbreak of violence in the late 1960s there was a fundamental sea-change in Northern Ireland politics, perhaps best marked by the complete disintegration of the old Nationalist party and the partial collapse of the Unionist party. The only two existing political parties which predate this period are Sinn Féin and the Ulster Unionist Party, and the former hardly acted as anything akin to a normal political party until relatively recently. The other three main parties, the SDLP, DUP and Alliance, all emerged after the outbreak of violence. But while there was a realignment of parties, there was hardly a realignment of politics. Indeed, over the years since, the voting pattern suggests that there has been a consolidation of political support around Unionist and Nationalist groupings.

What is also striking, I think, is that the unionist parties proclaim a version of Britishness which seems idiosyncratic or unfamiliar to many people in Britain, while nationalists seem to assume a version of Irishness that probably disappeared many years ago in the Republic as a consequence of secularisation and Europeanisation. There seems, in other words, to have been a striking consistency in key aspects of proclaimed identity in Northern Irish politics. And are these identities better thought of as stable, or rigid, or stubborn, or set in concrete – fast-setting and long-lasting concrete?

Northern Ireland: equality

Another example seems to be provided by debates on the issue of equality. This issue was obviously central to the Civil Rights campaign in the 1960s, as was the Unionist defence at the time that a problem of inequality did not really exist. Curiously, contemporary debates seem to have a very similar character. On the one hand Sinn Féin spokespersons sometimes seem to suggest that inequality, and more particularly discrimination against Catholics, is as rife now as ever it was. By contrast, some Unionists argue that even if a problem once existed (and even that basic contention is not always conceded), it certainly has not existed for many years, and some go on to suggest that in fact the current problem lies in discrimination against Protestants.

The real contrast, however, lies in the changing nature of public attitudes on this issue. In the late 1980s, early 1990s, about twice as many Protestants as Catholics felt that both communities had equal chances to get jobs. As late as 1998, in the *Northern Ireland Life and Times Survey*, whereas 61 per cent of Protestants felt that both communities were treated equally, this was so for only 43 per cent of Catholics. However, in the 2003 survey 50 per cent of Protestants and 54 per cent of Catholics felt that both communities were treated equally. Opinion, in other words, seems to have shifted, but the nature of public political debates appears to have changed little.

Role of education

My main contribution and experience lies in the role of education in addressing these issues and it is to this that I now turn. When I have been talking to audiences of educationalists recently I have been suggesting that we ought to worry at the high expectations that the wider public has on the capacity of schools and teachers to solve some of our most basic and fundamental problems. This issue is something I have become particularly aware of recently, but it is possible to see this as something that has always had a ring of truth. Thus, for example, back in the early 1970s many commentators on the then-emerging violence in Northern Ireland took the view that the problem could be solved by the immediate introduction of integrated education or through the implementation of more immediate measures to address prejudice and antagonism. Over the next thirty years there has been significant investment in measures designed to promote reconciliation through schools, most of which implicitly or explicitly involve some attempt to mitigate the negative consequences of separate schools. I want to deal a little more later with the actual limitations in the effects of this work, but at this point I simply want to highlight the fact that schools often appear first in the spotlight when people look to someone, or some institution, to solve the problem.

This came up again more recently when a special meeting of the Northern Ireland Race Forum met to discuss the four-fold increase in racist attacks over the past five years. During the discussion on this issue, speaker after speaker suggested that schools and teachers could solve the problem of racist attacks if only an appropriate curriculum was introduced. I had to tell the meeting that the track record of education in dealing with sectarianism over a much longer time period is not actually all that strong and so they should be cautious in their ambitions both for what schools can do to deal with racism and the extent to which this problem will be dealt with easily or quickly.

When we look back over the record of education I think we will see that the track record is not that impressive. Over the past thirty years there have been three broad strands to work in education to promote reconciliation. One strand focused on the curriculum and tried to produce common textbooks and common programmes, mainly due to the realisation that some parts of the curriculum were delivered in an obscenely partisan manner. The second strand involved the promotion of contact between young Protestant and Catholics, initially through joint holiday projects, later through joint school projects and later still with financial support from the Department of Education through a formal contact scheme.

In each of these areas it is possible to identify some measure of success, albeit that this must be tempered by a realistic assessment of how much more might have been achieved. In the curriculum, for example, there were successes in creating new common history textbooks and a common religious education programme, and there was also success not only in developing entirely new programmes with a community relations dimension, such as Education for Mutual Understanding, but this work was given a place on the statutory curriculum in 1989. However, the evidence we have on the impact of these initiatives suggests that it has been limited. One of the basic problems appears to be a reluctance, perhaps even a fear, of dealing with difficult and controversial issues; or perhaps to put it another way, a sense of being too ready to take a safer, more comfortable option.

That teachers can be creative in their avoidance of risk is illustrated by two examples from the curriculum. There was a time when two options were available for studying the history of Northern Ireland: one option dealt with the period from 1945 to 1957, a period characterised by economic boom and growth, the establishment of the welfare state and the growth of free secondary education; the second option dealt with the period from 1960 to 1972 which saw the growth of the Civil Rights movement, the collapse into violence and the prorogation of the Northern Ireland Parliament. It seems that Protestant schools were much more likely to take the first option, while Catholic schools were more likely to take the second option.

The second example is provided by Religious Education. A significant success was achieved in this area when the four main Christian Churches agreed on a common Religious Education curriculum, albeit with various options to allow for denominational interests. One innovation that was agreed was that all pupils should study two denominations and while it was not written explicitly that this should involve one of the Protestant denominations and Catholicism, there was a clear sense that this was implicit. In the event, it seems that many Protestant schools opted to study Presbyterianism and the Church of Ireland, while many Catholic schools opted to study Catholicism and one of the Orthodox traditions.

Even when we consider the much larger body of evidence on the impact of the Education for Mutual Understanding programme, the emergent picture here is not too positive either. Although this was a statutory requirement and was supposed to inform the delivery of education right across the curriculum, there is little evidence that it was taken seriously in many schools or that it developed a whole-school character, as intended, in many places. This is one of those areas where it is important not to be overly pessimistic: there were, and are, some schools that demonstrate a significant commitment to this work and there are many teachers who provide inspirational example by their work on this theme. But the reality is that these inspirational examples are few and far between, and in most places the evidence suggests that Education for Mutual Understanding was only ever a low priority.

One of the main problems seems to be that many schools and teachers assumed that Education for Mutual Understanding and contact were synonymous and, therefore, if someone had specific responsibility for a school's contact programme, then the rest of the teachers had no responsibility in this area at all. Such a view misunderstood the essential position that Education for Mutual Understanding was first and foremost about the ethos and character of human relationships within a school and that contact work was a means through which the theme could be pursued, rather than the theme itself. In any event, the evidence we have on the experience of contact work is also not very positive. Despite the fact that a significant amount of money has been spent on contact programmes between schools and that a fairly high proportion of schools have been involved, the reality is that relatively small numbers of pupils were directly involved in these programmes and, in any case, the lofty aims of contact were rarely achieved in practice. The overt aims of contact were to bring young Protestants and Catholics together to build mutual awareness and understanding, and to challenge stereotypes and prejudice. In fact it seems that few contact programmes came anywhere close to meeting those aims and that much of the work was limited to safe issues, with little development or extension.

The third area lies in the development of integrated education, an initiative initially undertaken by parents who grew fed up at the rhetorical support of some official bodies towards the idea of integrated schools, allied with little or no action by those bodies to actually make the idea work. Since those beginnings in the early 1980s the integrated sector has grown to become an identifiable third sector in our education system, albeit that it involves only 57 schools and about 5-6 per cent of the school age population. While this sector remains small, the significance of the development was only brought home to me by a school principal from England who remarked that he knew of no-where else in the world where an entirely new educational sector had been developed primarily through the energy and commitment of parents, in conditions of political violence which hardly seemed to provide a particularly supportive context for such a development.

We also know that the pattern within the schools has its positive and not so positive aspects. There is undoubted evidence that some of the integrated schools have developed innovative curricular programmes and have worked to create an ethos which values and celebrates diversity. On the other hand, the pressure for standards and benchmarking appears to have reduced the priority attached to innovation in integration in some schools. Ironically, a problem of success has been the influx of new teachers, some of whom see themselves primarily as teachers of their subject, rather than teachers in an integrated school. Our education system divides young people in just about every way imaginable and so creates a myth that every classroom is homogeneous. Perhaps one consequence is that we do not give due appreciation, in teacher training and in schools more generally, to the actual diversity of every school and every classroom.

So what has gone wrong?

So, despite all the hope and promise invested in education to address issues of conflict and division, and to seek to encourage a more positive attitude towards reconciliation and diversity, why have the gains not been more significant? I think I got something of a clue to this a year or so ago. I had read a wonderful book by Neil Postman, *The End of Education* in which he examines the social purpose of US public schools. One of his contentions is that the United States is a vast experiment in which its citizens are permanently engaged in a process of trying to answer some fundamental questions on the feasibility of the state. These questions include whether it is possible to have a state which permits absolute freedom of religion, while itself endowing no religion; or whether it is possible to provide a basis for common loyalty in a state comprised of people from a multitude of, linguistic and ethnic origins. At different times, Postman suggests, the 'common sense' of the day has provided different answers to these questions, and so too the answers in the future will be different. But Postman then wonders what type of people teachers need to be in order to help young people participate in that great social conversation. One response he suggested was to identify a list of core texts he felt every teacher in a US public school should be familiar with if they wanted seriously to help young people be socially and civically engaged. What I find interesting about his list is just how familiar so many of the texts would be to us:

Thomas Paine's *The Rights of Man*
the Declaration of Independence
the US Constitution
Alexis de Tocqueville's *Democracy in America*
the Gettysburg Address
the Emancipation Proclamation
Mark Twain's *The Adventures of Huckleberry Finn*
Nathaniel Hawthorne's *The Scarlet Letter*
John Dewey's *Democracy and Education*
John F Kennedy's inaugural address
Martin Luther King's 'I Have a Dream' speech

Based on this notion I ran my own little experiment where I emailed colleagues and invited them to suggest a list of core texts that every teacher in Northern Ireland should know, if they were going to help all our young people play an active part in constructing the architecture of a new society here. However, after many suggestions, amendments, alterations, additions and iterations, I was only able to 'narrow down' the Northern Ireland list to some

250 items. And what was most interesting about the list was that it was not really one list at all, but many lists: for some, the items they suggested were blindingly obviously foundational documents, while at the same time others were completely oblivious to the existence of these documents.

This little experiment was a reminder that Northern Ireland is a place of many narratives, with few common narratives shared across society as a whole: we have many narratives, in parallel, and often none intersecting, almost as if we find ourselves in the ruins of the Tower of Babel, where many different voices co-exist, but do not communicate. But this is not a mere discursive curiosity: the recent consultation on the Shared Future document seemed to throw up two divergent visions of the future, one in which active attempts needed to be made to promote shared practice, and another which seemed to suggest that difference could only ever be managed or controlled, almost as if it would be possible to fashion a form of apartheid here which would be benign.

How have we found ourselves in this place?

I mentioned earlier that we try to make the differences between us appear real in all sorts of absurd ways, when we play with differently-shaped footballs or differently-shaped sticks; or worship the same god, on the same day, in special buildings, but in slightly different ways; or the fact that some of us say 'haitch' while others say 'aitch'. Despite its absurd features, however, this process of 'telling' is significant in that it is part of a process through which we are socialised into silence and avoidance. All of us recognise the cues that allow us to identify someone from 'the other community,' but for most of us the consequence of this recognition is that we avoid difficult or potentially embarrassing areas of conversation. Unfortunately this allows us to maintain a benign liberal sense of self, as we have friends and contact with 'the other side,' while at the same time means we have few opportunities to hear other accounts, experiences or emotions about the last thirty years. We have developed a culture of avoidance that places some issues beyond the pale of polite conversation.

Why have we found ourselves in this place?

The default condition in too many aspects of our society is to do things separately, as this is safer, more comfortable, more predictable and certain. But for all the safety and predictability this produces, it also renders us virtually incapable of breaking free of the sectarian binds that trap us.

If we recall the example of the Yooks and the Zooks, should we not be concerned that there are now more 'peace walls' in Belfast than there were in 1994 at the time of the ceasefires? But should we not be even more concerned at the continuing strength of the psychological walls that render us mute in the face of sectarianism and encourage the default option of separatism?

The political structures of the Good Friday or Belfast Agreement were intended to encourage cooperative interdependence between the political parties and thereby to build trust between them. This is not what happened in practice and it should be a matter of concern that some parties seek changes in the structures which will make separatist practice even more pronounced. While agreement is obviously desirable, hopefully those involved in negotiations will keep the point of an agreement uppermost in their minds, and not go along with pragmatic compromises on the fundamental principle and practice of partnership simply in order to make any sort of a deal possible.

The Shared Future debate cast a worrying contrast between those who argued that we had a shared future based on partnership, or no future at all, as compared with those who seemed to suggest that management of difference was all that was required, and that it was possible to establish in parts of Northern Ireland a form of apartheid that was benign. We have already gone too far in placing ourselves in silos, some physical, some psychological, when what we need is to try to find ways of breaking through all the walls that divide us. We are strengthening the institutional barriers that promote division and divisiveness, when we should be making these barriers more porous.

Conclusion

We have lived through an age in which 3,700 people have died as a consequence of political violence, in which one in four people know someone who has been killed, but we have not yet found a way to commemorate all the dead. In politics, and the wider identity discourses in society, it seems that we rely on the same old stories to render our past, present and future explicable. But do these old stories offer us anything more than further division and misunderstanding, perhaps 'myth-understanding'? The strength of these discourses highlights our continuing inability to establish a set of relationships between the communities which would promote reconciliation and allow for the possibility of some critique or challenge to essentialist identities.

Duncan Morrow, Chief Executive of CRC, put it this way in a speech at the conference on the 'Shared Future' document at Queen's University, Belfast in early 2004:

> To live in Northern Ireland is to live in a place haunted by its own memories of violence and discrimination or fears of destruction or massacre to come.

Later in his speech he connected this to our inability to deal more generally with diversity and difference:

> Even people arriving in Northern Ireland with none of this history got caught in its wake. New minorities found and find their concerns marginalised by the obsessive dominance of one question in politics, obliged to identify with one side or the other or, even worse, forced to hide and conform by the presence of paramilitary activity and a culture which has grown too tired to be shocked by violence and tolerant of ideas that protection means excluding those who are different rather than looking for renewal to those who bring fresh perspectives.

At this time of uncertainty in the political process, and our political future, it is probably more important than ever that we seek to arrest the separatist pressures that are so prevalent in our society and seek pathways which will bring us towards a shared future.

What are the new stories that might provide the basis for this shared future, or emerge once we embark on this path? I do not know, I do not think anyone knows, and I do not think anyone should attempt to prescribe the new stories. What we need is a willingness to encourage the conditions under which new stories might emerge; to see change as an opportunity, rather than a threat; to see diversity as a rich resource from which we can shape the future, rather than a signal to retreat to the laager of old certainties.

One of my favourite novels is Umberto Eco's *The Name of the Rose*. The main plot of the novel revolves around a series of deaths which occur independently of one another, but which only make sense when they are seen in relation to one another. Given our location here in the Linen Hall Library it is particularly appropriate to draw from the story at the end of my presentation as one of the central 'characters' in the novel is the library. One of the central themes of the novel lies in the control of knowledge which is derived from control of access to the books in the library. At one point in the story the hero,

William, explains the importance of this control to his apprentice Adso, for whom a library is a place where 'books speak of books, as if they speak among themselves'; a library is for him a place of a 'centuries-old murmuring, an imperceptible dialogue between one parchment and another', 'a treasure of secrets emanated by many minds, surviving the death of those who had produced them or had been their conveyor.' He asks if a library is 'an instrument not for disturbing the truth but for delaying its appearance', to which his friend Williams replies: 'Not always and not necessarily. In this case it is.'

If we think of the same old stories which inform our political discourses and identities as akin to the library, as part of a

> centuries-old murmuring, an imperceptible dialogue...a treasure of secrets emanated by many minds, surviving the death of those who had produced them or had been their conveyors.

Then we might also ask whether these same old stories are an instrument not for distributing the truth but for delaying its appearance? And we might echo William in our reply when we say:

> Not always and not necessarily. In this case they are.

Bibliography

Community Relations Unit (2003): *A Shared Future – A Consultation Paper on Improving Relations in Northern Ireland.*

Connolly, P, Smith, A and Kelly, B (2002) *Too young to notice? The cultural and political awareness of 3-6 year olds in Northern Ireland.* Belfast: Community Relations Council.

Darby, J (1997) *Scorpions in a bottle: conflicting cultures in Northern Ireland.* London: Minority Rights Group.

Deutscher, I (1954) *The Prophet Armed: Trotsky: 1879-1921*, Oxford: Oxford University Press.

Deutscher, I (1959) *The Prophet Unarmed: Trotsky: 1921-1929*, Oxford: Oxford University Press.

Deutscher, I (1963) *The Prophet Outcast: Trotsky: 1929-1940,* Oxford: Oxford University Press.

Eco, U (1985) *The Name of the Rose*, New York: Random House.

Gallagher, T (2004) *Education in Divided Socieites*, London: Palgrave/MacMillan.

Leitch, R and Kilpatrick, R (1999) *Beyond the school gates: Strategies for supporting children's learning in primary and secondary schools: responding to cultures of political conflict,* Belfast: Save the Children Fund.

O'Connor, U, Hartop, B and McCully, A (2002) *A review of the Schools Community Relations Programme,* Northern Ireland; Department of Education.

Seuss, Dr (1984) *The Butter Battle Book,* New York: Random House.

Smith, A and Robinson, A (1996) *EMU: the initial statutory years*, Coleraine: University of Ulster.

Chapter Ten

SYMBOLS IN PEACE AND CONFLICT

Dominic Bryan

We seem to spend a disproportionate amount of time in Northern Ireland displaying and arguing over symbols: we argue whether people should be allowed to wear a poppy or a black ribbon at work, or the content of a new mural, we have legislation that controls when parades can take place, what flags can be flown outside Government buildings and what symbols can be displayed in places of work. Barely a week goes by without a news story about a dispute involving symbols: flags on lampposts, the display of a royal crest or the wearing of football shirts. For many people such debates seem to be a waste of energy. On the other hand, debates over symbols are also ways of talking about fundamental issues. The Irish Tricolour and the Union Jack are not simply pieces of cloth but represent a whole range of beliefs and identities. If we are to start exploring how to deal with disputes over symbols it is worth exploring how symbols work. Why are they important?

Symbols are in themselves, meaningless; they do not have innate meaning. Human beings give them meaning. As such symbols become multi-vocal, that is, they gain layers of meaning. They do not communicate a single proposition, but rather a collection of propositions, ideas and emotions. Different people will invoke different meanings in the same symbol. A person may see a number of meanings in the same symbol and different people can see very different meanings in the same symbol. For example, the Red Hand of Ulster can be viewed as a Loyalist emblem, or on a GAA badge, or as the crest of the O'Neill family.

The context in which a symbol is used is all-important. The same symbol used in different places or, in the context of other symbols, can have its meaning altered. Think of the Union Flag wrapped around Linford Christie's shoulders at the Olympics, or held by a member of the British National Party in Oldham, or flying from a lamppost in Sandy Row or on a flag-pole in Dublin during the visit of a UK Prime Minister, or in the corner of the Australian national flag, or on the cover of a Sex Pistols album. Equally, the Irish Tricolour displayed over Government Buildings in Dublin, or on an advert for Guinness, or at a north Belfast interface, has different meanings. In each case, the context in which symbols are displayed suggests different meanings. The concept of the United Kingdom that includes parts of Ireland is an anathema to many Irish nationalists. Yet how many people in Ireland wear shirts that say FCUK (French Connection United Kingdom)? When the context changes the letters UK become fashionable, even in Ireland!

Interpretations of symbols are not static. They can change, sometimes dramatically, over time, depending upon how they are used and who uses them. The Red Hand of Ulster is a good example of this. It has moved from representing a 16th century Gaelic aristocratic family in Ulster to representing an Ulster that is no longer nine counties but the six counties of Northern Ireland. Though it still appears on many Gaelic sports tops. Yet, although the meaning of symbols might change over time they can also give the impression of continuity, of tradition. King William might have been displayed on banners in 1796 as he is in 2006 but does it mean the same thing? If the role of an organisation or event is changing, symbols may well be used to provide a link with the past or show a presence when the existence of an organisation is effectively under threat. Elaborate displays may be signs of confidence but they can also be a sign of insecurity.

The above properties of symbols mean that they are important in modern politics. Symbols can be used to represent, invoke or imagine a diverse community. Because symbols have layers of meaning and have different meanings for different people they can be used to represent a diverse group who may share almost nothing in common. This of course is what modern nations and communities are all about. Many people can share allegiance to a flag without necessarily sharing a common understanding of that flag. Symbols therefore condense identities.

This said, the valuable political properties of symbols has limits. When representing large diverse communities, symbols work best when they are ill-defined. As soon as a politician or group within a community attempts to *over-*

define the symbol, they inevitably begin to exclude those who have a different understanding of its meaning. The result is either a struggle over meaning or one of the groups stops using the symbol. The Union Jack and the Irish Tricolour, when used in Northern Ireland are in part defined by political groups and communities. Both are, in some contexts, symbols of party not simply symbols of nation. Does the Union Flag stand for a heterogeneous pluralist country of many peoples or a white Protestant people that once had an empire? There have even been suggestions in Britain that the blue on the Union Jack should be turned to Black to represent a new multi-cultural society. The colours of the Irish Tricolour are green, white and orange so why do many people say green, white and gold? Why is the orange turned to gold? Who is it excluding?

So symbols work to unite diverse groups and communities but also, in doing so, can exclude. But there is more to it. Symbols can evoke great emotion and help motivate people's actions. People will die for their flag or see it as an almost sacred object. As such, many people believe that national flags should be treated with respect. For example, there has been significant controversy in the United States over whether free speech should include the right to burn the flag of the country. The more a flag or emblem becomes associated with the identities of particular groups of people, the greater potential for an emotive response from those people. Those who use a symbol to define themselves in an exclusive way are likely to see any attack on that symbol as an attack upon themselves.

People in every walk of life use symbols but they are particularly the currency of the powerful. Those with power, particularly those in official positions, are better placed to define the meanings of symbols than those with less power. They can therefore use symbols to legitimise their position. That power can be either derived from having an official position, from popularity or from the ability to propagate ideas through the control of the media and other institutions. Heads of state are in a particularly strong position to take the lead to define and redefine symbols. As such, they will be involved in numerous ritual events when they will hope to define themselves through the use of symbols. For example, the coronation of a monarch is usually done through the manipulation of religious symbols suggesting that their position in society is God-given.

However the manipulation of symbols through ritual is open to the masses as well. Large gatherings of ordinary people can act as powerful moments at which symbols can be used to oppose structures of power. Similarly large displays of symbols can give the impression of power. If a large number of new symbols appear it would suggest that the social context for the use of those symbols has changed. The widespread use of loyalist paramilitary flags after the signing of the Multi-party Agreement suggests that the contexts in which those loyalists are behaving has changed. Equally the development of St. Patrick's Day has changed the way the Tricolour is used in Belfast City centre.

It is possible to set out a very simple model of symbolic conflict (see Harrison 1995). There are four basic strategies politicians and groups can use to manipulate symbols. Symbols are (1) invented; (2) more or less valued; (3) can be appropriated and; (4) can be destroyed.

At some point someone has to *invent* (design/construct/use) a symbol and attempt to give it value. The Irish Tricolour, the Union Jack and the South African flag have all at some point been invented and the use of the poppy, the green ribbon and the white ribbon are all practices that started at a particular point in time. Recently the use of wrist bands has become very prominent.

Symbols can have their *value increased or decreased*. People will undertake strategies to increase the value of a symbol. That strategy may include giving one symbol a greater value than another. Certain flags are given a greater status than other flags. For example, it is significant that in Quebec the provincial flag is given as much if not more status than the national flag of Canada reflecting, in some ways, the attitudes of French-speaking Canadians to the nation.

A symbol with existing value can be *appropriated*. Symbols can be utilised by more than one group and be competed over. Sometimes popular symbols are appropriated and then controlled by the State. In contemporary politics in Northern Ireland we see ongoing battles of ownership over The Red Hand of Ulster, Cuchulainn, and St. Patrick. Often symbols are appropriated by people in marketing in an attempt to sell products. Or alternatively politicians wishing to give themselves a particular image might try to be associated with particularly successful brands.

Symbols can be *destroyed or banned* as other political groups expand. It is crucial to understand what space exists in the public sphere for the display of symbols. Religion often provides the best examples. The most obvious recent example is the Taliban restrictions on all other belief systems in Afghanistan. But Hindus and Muslims in India, Jews and Muslims in the Middle East,

Christians and Muslims in Southern Spain, Christians and other Christian groups across Europe have attempted to destroy or restrict the symbols of others. A Soviet régime in Russia removed religious symbols and then has itself been removed from the public sphere. Ironically, and iconic-ally, the destruction of an opponent's symbol is in part recognition of its power. If a former symbol of power can simply be left and admired under a new régime it suggests that the power of the new regime is secure. Similarly, attempts to legally restrict the use of symbols can act to increase their status.

The above strategies are ideal types. Groups may well be using a combination of strategies at the same time. For example, loyalists in Northern Ireland may be giving greater value to the Northern Ireland/Ulster flag than accorded to the Union Flag by putting them on lampposts whilst still defending the use of a Union Flag when officials threaten not to use it on a Council building.

These strategies are also structured by relationships of power, feelings of identity, and senses of (in)security. They are also multi-layered. For example, the Union flag might be highly valued by unionists when it is threatened by Nationalists who argue it should not fly over a Council building. At the same time, however, those unionists may be putting up the Northern Ireland/Ulster flag or even Ulster Independence flags in their own areas where once Union flags flew. This is because the political strategy used inter-group is different to the intra-group strategy.

To conclude, we must never lose sight of the idea that symbols are a form of communication. The use of symbols should not be seen as peripheral to political debates but as a fundamental part of people's emotional attachment, as individuals, to political groups and communities. And the message given may be a complex one, interpreted differently by different individuals and groups.

Peace and Conflict in Northern Ireland

Given the importance of symbols in contemporary politics it is not surprising that the conflict in Northern Ireland, has, in part, manifested itself through disputes over symbols. Let me offer a small and by no means exhaustive list:

- use of the Easter lily – sticky or not?
- Orange Parades
- Cuchulainn
- St Patrick
- Ulster Scots
- Gaelic
- A whole range of symbols that have come and gone – eg Ulster Vanguard, Ulster Independence
- murals
- arches
- festivals
- badges – RUC or PSNI
- pictures of the Queen
- flags flying over buildings
- anthems played at graduation
- street names
- kerbstones
- memorials
- the Stormont Parliament building
- Council buildings
- what gets burnt on the top of bonfires
- appearing at war commemorations and wearing the poppy
- football shirts and GAA flags
- the Derry/Londonderry difference

All of this does not mean that people living in Northern Ireland are any different from people any where else in the world. Conflict over symbols is very common. It does however indicate the lack of agreement within our society over legitimated forms of representations. This was recognised in the 1998 Multi-Party Agreement which intended to provide a new political dispensation.

> All participants acknowledge the sensitivity of the use of symbols and emblems for public purposes, and the need in particular in creating the new institutions to ensure that such symbols and emblems are used in a manner which promotes mutual respect rather than division.

Since the Agreement there have been examples of symbols used to represent new beginnings or of consensus. At an early stage there was a relatively uncontested emblem produced for the new Assembly at Stormont. More significantly, after much debate, a new badge for the Police Service of

Northern Ireland was agreed upon in December 2001. Significantly the new badge was accepted by both the SDLP and UUP – giving it cross-community support. The new badge has the cross of St Patrick at the centre of a six-pointed star. The point of contention concerned the inclusion of six additional symbols; a harp, crown, shamrock, laurel leaf, torch and scales of justice. Unionists were insistent that some symbolic reference to the RUC had to be included in the new badge and this led to the inclusion of the crown and the harp (both of which originated with the older Royal Irish Constabulary). The SDLP may have been able to support the inclusion of these symbols because they were somewhat obscured by the other items contained on the new badge. Many options for this badge had been discussed including ones that utilised completely new and therefore neutral symbols as well as badges that included the symbols of both communities. In the end the badge decided upon used a selection of existing symbols, nationalist and unionist, although ironically they are all so small on the badge that few people could tell what they were.

Examples of symbols building consensus have, however been few and far between. The debate over the flying of flags over government buildings came into particular prominence with the devolution of power to local politicians in late 1999. Sinn Féin ministers refused to fly the Union flag over buildings for which they had responsibility. They argued that both the Union flag and the Tricolour should be flown, or neither. As a result the then Secretary of State, Peter Mandelson, introduced legislation naming a number of days on which the flag would be flown. The Flags (NI) Order 2000 was challenged by Conor Murphy in the Belfast High Court in October 2001 on the grounds that it breached equality legislation. Republicans argue that the terms of the Agreement guarantee equality between unionists and nationalists, 'parity of esteem,' and that both the Union flag and the Tricolour should be flown. The court ruled that flying the Union flag alone on a limited number of days was a reasonable compromise and a reflection of Northern Ireland's status within the UK.

Disputes over flags have remained acrimonious particularly within district councils. For example, in March 2004 the Sinn Féin Mayor of Limavady Council ordered the removal of the Union flag from the front of the Council Offices on St Patrick's Day (one of the designated flag days) to the fury of Unionists. Councillor Brolly stated that 'on a day when people celebrate their Irish heritage, I did not think this flag should be flying as it may have made some people feel uncomfortable.' (*The Chronicle*, Limavady, 31 March 2004). Even where policy has been changed the issue of flags can continue to be a source of contention. On 12 May 2004, for example, a DUP councillor wrote to the *News Letter* calling for unionist councillors in Ards Borough Council to support the flying of the Union flag over council property every day of the year irrespective of whether the councillors could face financial penalties as a consequence of this.

Some District Councils have developed their own flag. In some senses this makes great sense since District Councils are, by their very nature, representative of an area not of one, or two, national communities. To 'brand' an area through the use of a symbol can help in marketing for tourism. In doing so it might be possible that a flag could be produced that all in the council area could show some allegiance to. Following the model above, the flag needs to be invented then valued through its use on ritual occasions. Most councils however have not undertaken this strategy

Symbols in a new Northern Ireland

The range of disputes over symbols in Northern Ireland is indicative of the conflict over the legitimacy of the state. Disputes take place at an official level and in terms of control of territory. Nevertheless, just as symbols provide a language of division they also offer the possibility of cohesion. Because meanings and contexts change, and because symbols can be manipulated they can also provide solutions to problems. As such, the above disputes, whilst difficult, are not intractable. Imaginative solutions can be found that can draw upon what we know about how symbols work. Northern Ireland does not have lots of examples of new symbols arising out of peace, but it does have some. Symbols can play their part in transforming relationships of conflict.

Bibliography

Bryan, Dominic and Gillespie, Gordon (2005) *Transforming Conflict: Flags and Emblems,* Belfast: Institute of Irish Studies, Queen's University.
Harrison, Simon (1995) Four Types of Symbolic Conflict, *Journal of the Royal Anthropological Institute* (NS) vol.1 pp 255-272.

Chapter Eleven

TOWARDS AN ORAL HISTORY OF THE TROUBLES: *CONFLICT* AT THE ULSTER MUSEUM

Jane Leonard

T he main character in a recent novel set in Belfast after the ceasefires is a former loyalist paramilitary. Tormented by his memories of the Troubles, Martin only relaxes at work. He is a gallery assistant in the Ulster Museum. 'Strange to feel safest from the past in a museum,' he reflects.[1]

Martin would have felt even safer if employed prior to the ceasefires when museums in Ireland and Britain, while collecting artefacts relating to the conflict in Northern Ireland, rarely exhibited such holdings. When the Ulster Museum in 1978 hosted *Art for Society* (a touring exhibition from the Whitechapel Gallery), Martin's real-life counterparts refused, on sexual as well as political grounds, to hang work by five of the 102 artists represented in the show. Their action was supported by the Ulster Museum's trustees. The exhibition was staged minus the censored works (depicting rape, genitalia, sectarian killing, police interrogation and Bloody Sunday) which were shown instead at the Arts Council's gallery.

The censoring of *Art for Society* caused and continues to cause much controversy.[2] Less attention has been paid to the museum's permanent history displays. Its main gallery, opened in 1975, surveyed the province's history from 1590 until 1920. In noting the timidity of a national museum's omission of any historical developments after the founding of the state itself, one cultural historian failed to acknowledge that similar caution was displayed in the National Museum in Dublin.[3] With *Art for Society*, the Ulster Museum maintained that it 'had to weigh the relative evil of censorship against the evil of possible extremist reaction'[4]. This explanation, along with the frequent bombscares experienced by Northern Ireland's museums, galleries and libraries throughout the Troubles (not to mention the destruction six years earlier of some Ulster Museum collections in Malone House by republican bombers) is a sobering reminder of the perils and challenges of curating contemporary history. To embellish Seamus Heaney, it is not surprising that so many institutions resolved that whatever you display, display nothing.

The Ulster Museum, after the ceasefires, was no haven from the recent past. Four temporary exhibitions staged between 1998 and 2006 explored the legacies of political violence in Ireland. These were accompanied by workshops held at the museum and at venues throughout Northern Ireland and the Republic for community groups from areas that had experienced high levels of violence, polarisation or displacement throughout the Troubles. The final exhibition, *Conflict: the Irish at War,* ran from December 2003 until the museum closed in late 2006.[5] Eschewing a narrative approach, it instead offered snapshots of different conflicts within Ireland and of wars elsewhere in which Irish people served. Curated by a team of seven historians and archaeologists, the exhibition had five main chronological sections (the stone and bronze ages; the Vikings and Normans; sixteenth to eighteenth-century Ireland; twentieth-century Ireland; and the Irish in wars overseas, from Waterloo to Iraq, 1815-2003) and one thematic section on the aftermath and legacy of conflict. A contemplation area was provided where visitors could read, use multi-media resources or write comments for display on a notice-board.

The exhibition broke new ground. No national museum in Ireland or Britain had previously staged a major historical display that included artefacts and oral testimony relating to the Troubles. Artefacts on display spanned ten thousand years and were accompanied by recorded commentaries from 61 individuals whose personal perspectives on warfare and on political violence attempted to contextualise the past.[6]

Unsurprisingly, the majority of these focused on the post-1969 display. This chapter reviews how the oral testimony was gathered, presented and received.[7] Though the exhibition has closed, these recordings and the thousands of comment cards that the display attracted themselves still constitute a significant resource for historians of contemporary conflict.[8] This material, wide-ranging and forthright as it is, might usefully be consulted by the interim panel established in June 2007 to explore options for how Northern Ireland might deal with its past.

Exhibitions on war and conflict tend to highlight weapons, militaria and medals or the commemorative artefacts produced by veterans. It is not so easy to find objects that evoke the cost of war or the experiences and perspectives of civilian victims, witnesses to war and peace campaigners. A key aspiration of the curators was to convey the realities of war for its victims as well as to illustrate the experiences of those who waged it. Recording the voices of some whose experiences could not accurately or appropriately be conveyed through artefacts offered one way of ensuring that the exhibition's narrative was inclusive. A crystal trophy awarded to Dominic Pinto, a surgeon who treated the Omagh wounded, proved much more compelling when accompanied by his recollections of 15 August 1998.

The primary challenge was to ensure that the voices could adequately represent the diversity of experiences of conflict. Curators compiled a list of categories, including bereaved, wounded, ex-service personnel, ex-paramilitaries, civilian victims, medical staff, clergy, peace activists, police officers, prison warders, trauma counsellors and war correspondents. It was decided to include children. Pupils from primary and secondary schools in East and North Belfast, Lisburn, Omagh and Randalstown agreed to participate. To ensure that the voices reflected the experience of conflict throughout society in Northern Ireland, young farmers' clubs, women's centres and training projects for the unemployed and for migrant workers were approached. Communities in the Republic of Ireland and in Great Britain that had been bereaved or scarred by the conflict were contacted through projects based in Glencree, County Wicklow, Monaghan Town and Warrington. Participants from Belfast included members of the Roddy McCorley Historical Society in West Belfast, the 'Power to the People' adult education project in Sandy Row, the Indian Community Centre in North Belfast and the Society of Friends.

In finding individuals that matched these categories, personal contacts proved invaluable. Many were members of the community groups that had participated since 1997 in the museum's outreach programme. Appeals for victims' groups to participate in the recording exercise were circulated at events held as part of CRC's Community Relations Week. A *Voices* Advisory Panel, chaired by Sir Kenneth Bloomfield, was instrumental in persuading bereaved individuals in England to take part and in suggesting candidates from Northern Ireland's business community.

During the summer and autumn of 2003, preliminary workshops were held with groups interested in participating. These yielded useful suggestions for objects or themes to be incorporated in the display. The victims' support group, WAVE, noted the absence of any art work conveying the perspective of bereaved families. A stained-glass window designed by WAVE members, with nineteen panes depicting relatives killed in the Troubles, was subsequently lent to the exhibition.

Some categories proved impossible to fill. No serving or former prison officer or former loyalist paramilitary prisoner took part despite many attempts to secure such participation. The project rules sometimes complicated our task. A curatorial decision that no serving politicians or election candidates could participate ruled out some participants once the Assembly elections were called for November 2003. Last-minute cancellations by a civil rights campaigner and a mediator involved with the Drumcree parade likewise eliminated other important perspectives.

Recording and editing took place in the fortnight before *Conflict* opened in December 2003. In all, seventy people were asked to select three objects or images. It was left to each participant whether to select items related to their own experiences or views of conflict or objects from earlier conflicts which they found particularly significant. Their commentaries were then recorded. Once edited (individual contributions were limited to a few minutes in order to make possible several comments per object), the curatorial team then selected commentaries from 61 individuals for inclusion. Inside the exhibition gallery, visitors could listen to these contributions on hand-held audio wands.

The contemporaneity of the exercise was sharply apparent. The funeral of one of the 'disappeared', (those abducted and killed by the IRA and whose places of burial had not been disclosed to their families), Jean McConville, took place as the recordings were being made. A former Presbyterian Moderator, Dr John Dunlop, noted that the exhibition included an appeal issued eight years earlier by her family and the families of other such victims. This appeal:

> It first of all welcomes the new climate of hope and reconciliation and then goes on, 'however the violence is not over. Not finished and done with.' They continue to yearn for the return of the bodies of their loved ones. And it seems to me that those two statements are the two statements that always have to be made together: the welcome for the new climate of hope and reconciliation ...but there is always an 'however'. The 'however' is the continuing pain which people are going through.

Of 61 voices featured in the exhibition, the oldest was 82 and the youngest was 10; 35 voices were female and 26 male. Of 52 residents of Northern Ireland, 26 were Catholic, 24 were Protestant and 2 were 'other.' Three travelled from the Republic and two from England. Some overseas students temporarily based in Ireland also took part, including two Senator George Mitchell Scholars. Some participants had served in or witnessed wars elsewhere. They included veterans of World War II and trauma and mediation experts who had worked in Bosnia, the Middle East and with New Yorkers bereaved by the events of 11 September 2001.

The effect of the voices was to amplify, contextualise and humanise the objects on display. Comments on artefacts from 1922 revealed how recent that earlier civil war is in many familial memories. A West Belfast history teacher, Jimmy McDermott, chose a plaque displaying the Great War medals awarded to William Patterson, a Protestant cooper who 'survived Armageddon' only to be 'murdered in Belfast, 1922'. Although this plaque is intrinsically dramatic, the tension conveyed by this memorial is heightened by the commentary. Acknowledging the cruel circumstances of Sapper Patterson's death, McDermott also observed that his own great-grandfather was killed in Belfast on the following day, probably as a resprisal. Such empathy across eighty years and transcending the city's communal divisions was electrifying.[9]

Among the most intimate commentaries were those by bereaved women who had designed the stained-glass window commissioned by WAVE. Mary Treanor, a senior citizen from North Belfast, described how her pane was based on an old photograph of her son, Edmund (killed by the LVF), successfully changing a car tyre as a teenager:

> That is why he has the smile on his face. He was shot dead on New Year's Eve 1997 when he visited a bar on the Cliftonville Road that he didn't normally go to. And it was a few days after the killing of Billy Wright, in the Maze. I was very anxious about him going out that night and he said 'try not to worry, Mother, for I don't normally sit near a door.' He kissed me on the cheek and said 'when I get my new car tomorrow, New Year's Day, I'll do your shopping.'

The determination of people to continue going out at night was highlighted in a commentary provided by the late Jim Aiken which accompanied two covers of Miami Showband records.[10] Aiken had promoted the Miami Showband, three of whose members were killed by the UVF as they returned from a gig in 1975:

I thought that entertainment would never return to Belfast after the awfulness of this event. But it did, and the thing that brought it back, was the desire of people for normality and the resilience of people to look to the future.

Some commentaries questioned the inclusion of the artefact or expressed a revulsion for what was displayed. This helped to establish a dialogue with the exhibition visitor, confirming that there was no collusion between curator and commentator as to the validity or importance of an object. Such tensions also encouraged the visitor to indicate their views about what was on display. The most striking example of this was in the section relating to crafts made in 1974 in the Maze Prison by paramilitary inmates. These drew comments from ex-prisoners, clergy and prison visitors but the most gripping reaction came from Colin Parry, whose son, Tim, died of injuries received in an IRA bomb in Warrington in 1993. Parry discussed the iconography of a loyalist Twelfth of July banner fashioned from prison bed linen and of a republican roll of honour carved from a bed board. He then observed:

> It was hard for me to stand and read the roll call of names and appreciate that, as far as the IRA was concerned, these are freedom fighters, these are gallant men. I take the simple view that in a democracy, which this is here, even an imperfect democracy, the use of terrifying force by a self-appointed group, which the IRA is, as indeed the loyalist paramilitaries are as well of course, is entirely illegitimate.

Perhaps the most disturbing object in the exhibition was also the simplest: a handwritten story about a teddy bear written by a six-year-old child, David Hanna. It was displayed next to his photograph. The ordinariness of the item was shattered by the circumstances of his death, killed with his parents months later in an IRA car bomb as the family returned from holiday in 1988. One commentary, by Libby Keys, a community relations worker, acutely conveyed the universal reaction of the parent:

> The photograph is just a very typical school photograph, with the hair very neatly brushed and the school tie. And he does have that sort of long-suffering look that little boys have when they're getting their school photograph taken. I have so many of them, of my own son who is also called David and he would be just a little older. And it just, for me as a mother, is heartbreaking to look at this picture and to look into his eyes.

These commentaries connected objects and combatants from different wars and eras in a way that conventional captions and panels could not. A retired postman from Pomeroy, County Tyrone, was struck by how useless a bronze shield and an RUC riot shield from about 1970 both proved when deployed. Lawrence McKeown, a former IRA hunger-striker, selected two documents with powerful resonances for republicans: the 1916 Easter Rising Proclamation and a 'comm' (a written communication smuggled out of the Maze prison) in Irish ending the hunger-strikes. His third object, which he considered to be the most evocative item in the exhibition, was the Waterloo Quilt, formed from uniforms of soldiers killed on both sides in that distant battle. McKeown was particularly drawn by its connotations of 'warmth, comfort, safety and the luxury of sleep.'

As might be expected, many commented on the juxtaposition of objects proclaiming opposing loyalties, but the perspectives these provided were not always so easy to anticipate. Here is Katerina Gerstig, a Swedish student looking at two banners, Orange and Hibernian, with memorial portraits of brethren killed respectively by republicans and loyalists:

> My mother was born in Northern Ireland. She married my father and moved to Sweden where she converted to Catholicism. We were all raised Catholics. My grandparents were never told, and when I was younger, they used to take me to Orange marches when I was over here on holidays. These two banners remind me of this inner family conflict and that, in Northern Ireland, you can't always be open even with those closest to you.

The voices also provided an instant review of the exhibition. In some cases, the museum was able to act on this feedback even before the exhibition opened. Repeated criticism of the absence of the Ulster Defence Regiment resulted in a final addition to the display, a steering wheel scarred by bullets when the IRA fired on a UDR vehicle. Other omissions noted by the commentators went unrectified. Trina Vargo, President of the US-Ireland Alliance and an advisor on Irish issues to Barack Obama during the US presidential election in 2008, queried the absence of objects illuminating the cease-fires and the peace process of the 1990s. Colin Parry felt that the exhibition vividly conveyed the 'bloody handprints' left by Britain on Ireland but asked why no objects evoked IRA attacks carried out in Britain. Rita Restorick, the mother of the last British soldier killed in Northern Ireland, was moved by a photomontage of all RUC officers killed since 1969:

...especially those killed after Stephen, in 1997. It is so much more powerful seeing their faces rather than just their names. I find it sad, though, that there is nothing in the exhibition about the British soldiers, many of them aged only 18 to 25, who were killed in the conflict.

Conflict attracted large crowds during its three-year run. In 2004, for example, museum visitors increased by some 23,000 on the previous year. *Conflict* won a major award (the Heritage Council of Ireland/Northern Ireland Museums Council Best Exhibition of the Year 2005) and it brought new audiences to the museum, especially community groups from rural areas and from the victims' sector. Workshops were also provided for victims and survivors of conflicts elsewhere. Sometimes their perspectives were unnerving, as when a Sri Lankan group queried why so few photographs of atrocities were used in the display. Most academic and general reviews welcomed this experiment at displaying multiple perspectives and experiences but considered that more voices were needed.

Many of the community groups using the exhibition have since begun to record their own conflict-related experiences and several have found the strategy of focusing on objects and images useful starting points for their reminiscences. Though overseas tourists were sometimes confused by the multi-voiced approach, the use of oral testimony proved popular with the general public. One visitor felt:

> The artefacts and memorials are at once gut-wrenching, and at best talismans of hope...the audio portion reinforces those emotions.

Several museums have since included the Troubles in their displays or have expanded the space devoted to this topic in existing galleries. The new permanent military history gallery in the National Museum in Dublin, opened in 2006, includes a few items relating to the role of the Irish Army and of the Garda Síochána in policing the border during the Troubles.[11] The National Army Museum in London recently staged an art exhibition depicting the British Army in Northern Ireland, 1971-74.[12] In 2008, an inventory of Troubles-related artefacts held by museums or in private hands was produced by 'Healing Through Remembering', a group investigating the feasibility of establishing a new museum of the Northern Ireland conflict and what engendered it.

If there is one paramount lesson to be learned from the *Conflict* exhibition's use of oral testimony, it is the importance of inclusivity in recounting or displaying the stories of the innumerable communities scarred by the Troubles. Among the comment cards were many contributions from emigrants who left Northern Ireland in the 1970s and 1980s and who visited the exhibition as part of an attempt to understand why they had left and to decide whether they should return. Their story deserves to be recorded too.

As the exhibition progressed, some of those recorded occasionally returned to view the display again and to continue the dialogue. The Revd Harold Good, a former President of the Methodist Church and one of the two clergymen who witnessed the IRA's decommissioning of weapons in 2005, reiterated this core value of inclusivity. His concerns are pertinent to any exercise in gathering and displaying testimony from a divided society. This is what he wrote:

> Very eloquent, graphic, troubling and moving experience. Did I miss it…or have you overlooked the pain and grief of families and colleagues of prison officers who lost their lives? They had a most difficult responsibility and, knowing some of them personally, it must add to their pain not to be acknowledged. A similar point to that being made by Rita Restorick. Focusing on some and ignoring others is not conducive to healing.

Notes

1   David Park, *Swallowing the Sun* (London, Bloomsbury, 2004), p 210.

2   Brian Ferran, 'Emerging from the grey mists', Conrad Atkinson's exhibition, *Some Wounds Healing: Some Birds Singing* (Belfast, Belfast Media Group, 2007), pp 4-7.

3   Richard Kirkland, *Literature and Culture in Northern Ireland Since 1965: Moments of Danger* (London, Longman, 1996), pp 1-2.

4   Letter from the museum's chairman, *The Times*, 30 November 1978.

5   The others were *Up in Arms: the 1798 Rebellion in Ireland*; *Icons of Identity;* and *War and Conflict in Twentieth Century Ireland* (a CRC-commissioned exhibition which toured 15 towns and cities in Northern Ireland and the border counties).

6   Funding from the Victims Strategy Implementation Fund via the Office of the First Minister and deputy First Minister covered the costs of the recording project.

7   I wish to thank the CRC for administering the outreach initiative which employed me as the museum's Community History Outreach Officer from 1997-2006, a post funded by the European Union Peace and Reconciliation Programme. This role included curating *War and Conflict in Twentieth Century Ireland* in addition to the *Aftermath* and *Voices* segments of *Conflict:The Irish at War*. I am grateful to those who participated in the recording project

and in the outreach workshops. I wish to thank former colleagues who worked with me in recording the voices, especially Peter Carson, sound engineer, for his invaluable contribution, Linda Ballard, Clifford Harkness and those who served on the *Voices* Advisory Panel. My thanks also to Mike Houlihan, former Chief Executive of the National Museums and Galleries of Northern Ireland, for his comments on this paper (when it was first presented at the Museums Association Conference in Edinburgh in 2004) and for his original suggestion that the exhibition incorporate the perspectives of those directly affected by conflict.

8   These recordings are deposited in the sound archive at the Ulster Folk and Transport Museum, Cultra, County Down. The comment cards are retained by the Ulster Museum's Department of History, also based at Cultra pending the re-opening of the Stranmillis site after renovation.

9   The Patterson plaque was lent to the exhibition by the Linen Hall Library.

10   I wish to thank Angela Reid and Emerald Records for tracking down these items.

11   Northern Ireland since 1969 merits half a page in the exhibition catalogue, *Soldiers and Chiefs. The Irish at War at Home and Abroad from 1550* (Dublin, National Museum of Ireland, 2007) p 31.

12   Jenny Spencer-Smith, *Painting the Troubles. An Artist in Northern Ireland. Paintings and Drawings by Ralph Lillford* (London, National Army Museum, 2006).

Chapter Twelve

OUR TANGLED SPEECH: LANGUAGES IN NORTHERN IRELAND

Aodán Mac Póilin

B efore I got inside the skin of a second language, I thought that people who talked about the ultimate impossibility of translating from one language to another were a bit affected, perhaps a bit precious. I have since tried my hand at transferring both the meaning and feeling of Irish language poetry into English, and have come to the conclusion that my pretentious friends were right.

Some of you may be already know another language well. In that case I don't need to explain anything. For those who do not, I'll try an experiment that concentrates on the tangled speech of Ulster English, and involves a bunch of words that will be familiar to anybody who can remember black and white television. The experiment is to translate the following into standard English: 'I couped into the sheugh, and sprauchled out again, clabber an glaur to the oxters.' I'm not asking for a functional translation, which is easy, 'I fell into the ditch, and scrambled out again, covered with mud.' What I'm looking for is a translation that also captures the essentially liquid and muddy quality of a *sheugh,* the ungainliness of a *sprauchle*, the stickiness of *clabber* and the adhesiveness of *glaur*. Above all, one that captures what can only be called the totality of the word *coup* – more than a fall, more than a tumble, something like the kind of prat-fall that a child's comic would mark with 'splat!'

The flavour of that sentence has for most of us a particular expressiveness that is more than the sum of its etymological parts, although the etymology is not to be sneezed at. The particular linguistic tangle here involves *coup* from French, *clabber* from Irish, *sprauchle* from Old Norse, *sheugh* from Middle English, *oxter* from Anglo-Saxon, and *glaur* from God knows where. All these words are alive in Ulster Scots. Possibly surprisingly, you'll find *seoch* and *glár* in the Ulster dialect of the Irish language, and a *spriúchálaí* is 'one who makes awkward gestures, throws his arms about' in Dineen's Dictionary.

Languages are more than their words, and there are enormous areas of structure, syntax and grammar, never mind culture, that remain to be explored, but it may be simpler to stick to words for the moment. In fact, I want to look at a single word, one that has been the subject of a minor but intense controversy.

The word is 'crack'. All over the south of Ireland you will come upon notices painted on the side of pubs indicating that 'Ól, Ceol agus Craic' were available, if not inevitable, and almost certainly unavoidable. As the first two words, *ól* and *ceol,* meaning drink and music, are in the Irish language, it is widely assumed that *craic,* is also Irish, although Kevin Myers in the *Irish Times* has complained of the 'pretentiousness, witless posturing' of the Irish version.[1] The use of the word by Irish-speakers, and English-speakers who salt their discourse with phrases of Irish, has caused even greater offence in Northern Ireland, where everything is contested. In October 1997, the *Irish News* and *Belfast Telegraph* published a number of letters which variously attributed the origin of the word to Old English, Middle Dutch, High German, Scottish Gaelic and Ulster Scots. The controversy provided more heat than light, but gave a number of correspondents an opportunity to insult the Ulster Scots movement, 'this glorified Ballymena accent masquerading as a language.'[2]   Ulster Scots enthusiasts can, of course point to the likes of Hugh Porter of Moneyslan, who had published as far back as 1813:

> Among the rest that me attracts
> There's one of which I hear great cracks
> An' that's the *Elegant Extracts...*[3]

This word has been in my vocabulary since before I can remember. 'One more crack out of you ...' meant an utterance, usually a cheeky one, and seems to be embedded into standard English. But all the other forms seemed to be more local – I restrict myself to the Belfast dialect here. My auntie used to talk about 'crackin' with friends and neighbours – that meant a conversation full of enjoyable gossip. 'What's the crack?' or "what's this crack about ...?' means what's new or what's going on – you'll hear both senses in Donegal Irish: 'Cén craic? Caidé an craic seo faoi ...?' 'A good night's crack' meant you had enjoyed yourself. Someone who was good crack was somebody who was entertaining company. You'll hear the last two senses of the word throughout Ireland in both languages.

Sometimes 'crack' seems to mean not so much enjoyment as a form of exuberant drink-fuelled excess. Dominic Behan's version of 'McAlpine's Fusiliers' is the best-known expression of this sense of the word, which is, oddly enough, remarkably close to the Middle English 'Crak,' meaning loud conversation, bragging talk.[4]

> The craic was good in Cricklewood
> And they wouldn't leave the Crown
> The glasses were flying and Biddy was crying
> The Paddies have hit the town
> Oh mother dear, I'm over here
> And I'm never coming back
> What keeps me here is the reek o' beer
> The weemen and the craic

More than thirty years ago a Celtic scholar, who, because he was from the south of England and had never been exposed to it, mentioned to me that he found this extraordinarily eloquent word *craic* to be in use in every dialect of Irish – but not only was it not be found in any dictionary, it didn't have the feel of an Irish word. It happened that the previous week I had met the word in a review of a book on William Wordsworth. Somebody had wandered around the Lake District in the late 19th century asking the local peasantry what they thought of the poet. One horny-handed son of toil had described him marching gloomily around the hills with his sister, his enormous brood of children straggling behind, and 'no crack from him'.

What conclusions can you draw from this word 'crack' about our tangled speech. One is that the word, whatever its origin, was definitely established in English about 1300, and survives, in the senses outlined above, in modern Scots, dialects of northern England, Hiberno-English and Irish. It also illustrates how porous languages can be – as Irish borrowed 'crack' from either English or Scots, Ulster Scots has borrowed 'gub' and 'clabber' from Irish, and Scots has borrowed 'coup' from French. The language that most spectacularly borrows words is English – 99 per cent of the words in the *Oxford English Dictionary* came from other languages.[5] Finally, the row over who owns 'crack' says more about our society than it does about the word, in particular an unhealthy obsession with exclusive ownership of anything that is of value. 'Crack' is a good word, an expressive word, however you spell it. It's a good word that belongs to anybody who is interested in the concept.

Linguistic diversity is a very big subject, even for a place as small as Northern Ireland, and I am not in a position to speak for all the language communities in our society. In particular, I have no insight to offer on a whole range of experiences relating to, say, ethnic minority language communities who are far away from the epicentre of their culture. Nor have I lived in a society where I did not have to have a firm grasp of the majority language, or one where the colour of my skin marked me as an outsider. But I can make some points about the phenomenon of language, and about the phenomenon of fragile languages.

First point. Except for sign languages, languages are essentially a series of grunts, pops, whistles, groans, moans, hisses, whines, hums, snuffles and occasionally clicks. What turns these noises into a language is that sometime in the past they were codified according to an agreed pattern, and by this pattern you could pass on information to somebody who snuffled and moaned in a similar way. These patterns of grunts and groans evolved over thousands of years, changing constantly, gathering new meanings, new nuances and new structures which extended the range of what could be communicated in each language, as well as a series of accidental and arbitrary accretions, excrescences, baubles and whirligigs.

Second point. A language can be a way of asking someone to pass the salt, but it also communicates at a level far beyond the utilitarian. A living language is the expression of an evolving civilization which is itself diverse. Or to put it another way, each language is a complex of ways of interpreting the world.

Third point. The Donegal writer Seosamh Mac Grianna once wrote that 'The whole world is beyond the little shadow of words we put on it.' In other words, language simplifies and distorts the real world. It is of course obvious that a language in some way reflects the reality that surrounds it, but it is equally obvious that no language captures all of reality. However, and this is close to one of the really important points which I am trying to make, every language has a different pattern for simplifying and distorting reality, every language provides a unique lens, a unique window – a unique partial view – of the world. The sum total of these distortions is the sum total of that part of human wisdom that can be put into words. And we need all those distortions.

Fourth point. You may have guessed by now that I am making an argument for cultural and linguistic ecology. It seems to me that the cultural ecology argument is irrefutable. I am always fascinated by those who are happy to see the death of a language, the death of a culture, the death of a civilization. They all belong to that class which knows the price of everything and the value of nothing, but they can be broken down into sub-categories; philistines, vulgarians, cultural cringers, lumpen-utilitarians and begrudgers.

Fifth point. Just when we are beginning to understand the importance of linguistic ecology, most of the languages of the world are in danger of extinction. We are on the brink of a linguistic holocaust. There are between 6,000 and 7,000 languages in the world at present, more than half of which are spoken by fewer than 10,000 people. To take the statistics another way, 96 per cent of the world's languages are spoken by just 4 per cent of the world's population. On average, one of these languages dies every fortnight.[6] In a hundred years, it is calculated that there will be only about 500 languages left – a handful of major world languages and the rest hanging on in there. The linguist John McWhorter speaks about a future in which most of the world's peoples will be 'subsumed into a slurry of multiethnic urban misery and exploitation voiced in just a couple of dozen big fat languages.'[7]

Let us be clear about this: languages do not die because they are incapable of surviving *as languages*; languages die because their speakers have been economically, socially and (usually) politically marginalised, and often because their speakers have been oppressed for speaking them. James McCloskey has written eloquently of the cultural loss involved in the death of a language:

> Every language that succumbs to the economic, political and cultural pressures being applied all over the globe today, takes to the grave with it an encyclopaedia of histories, mythologies, jokes, songs, philosophies, riddles, superstitions, games, sciences, hagiographies – the whole cumulative effort of a people over centuries to understand the circumstances of its own existence. It is an enormously frightening thought that nine tenths of that accumulation of wisdom, speculation and observation is to be lost within the next century or so.[8]

Sixth point. Language preservation. Let me make one thing clear, there is not a single linguistic eco-warrior in the world who wants to preserve a language. A language is not jam, conserve or marmalade. It cannot be put into a deep-freeze, salted, pickled, tinned, smoked or dehydrated. Languages and their cultures are not static, they do not live in libraries and archives and theme-parks. They live in communities, in a constant dynamic between a complex past and a complex present. The survival of a language is the survival of a language community.

Seventh point. The complete, total and irreversible disappearance of a unique language and culture can happen with astonishing speed. McCloskey again:

> It is a very, very easy thing to lose a language. All that is required is one short period of inattention or complacency or deliberation, and the community can find itself with a generation of children none of whom speak the older community language. With that single break in the chain of generational transmission, language, and all that goes with it, becomes a walking ghost.[9]

Eighth point. Whatever your personal experience has been, language activists are actually quite a diverse bunch, not all looking or acting the same. However, endangered minority languages tend to attract nutcases. The Irish language movement, to take but one example, is infested with a disproportionate number of tunnel-visionaries, impossiblists, messiahs, linguo-masochists (people who are attracted solely to lost causes), grammarians and grant-pimps. And I haven't even started on the politicians.

Ninth point. If you belong to a linguistic minority in an overwhelmingly monoglot society, you live your life through two languages and two cultures. You see the world simultaneously through two different lenses and from two different perspectives. Among the advantages and irritations of being inside two cultures is that you can both understand the majority perspective and be infuriated by its assumptions.

Tenth point. Linguistic diversity also benefits the majority culture. Is there any society that would not profit from the creative tensions of being interrogated from every possible angle by people living in it and who look at it with a different set of assumptions? Having said that, I would also like to say that we speakers of minority languages are not here just for the benefit of the majority – our purpose is not solely to leaven the lump of a monocular monolingual society.

Eleventh point. There's no point in getting excited about the linguistic ecology of far-away places when there is an issue of linguistic ecology on your own doorstep. I would argue that, however strongly we feel about the survival of Mohawk and Arapahoe and Bobangi and Liboko, we have a particular responsibility for those languages within our own society whose very existence is threatened. McCloskey, in his small but enormously valuable book, *Voices Silenced*, which focuses on the Irish language within a global context, has made this case far better than I can:

> In a broader, global perspective, there are excellent reasons for trying to maintain Irish, but those reasons have nothing to do with nationalist sentiment, nor with any search for an authentic, distinctive, or exclusive *Irish*-ness (whatever that might mean). Far from being driven by an insular or inward-turning impulse, the effort is worth making because it is our contribution to a much larger effort, a global struggle to preserve a kind of diversity which human society has enjoyed for millennia, but which is being lost in our time. Like the Maori and the Inuit, we have the good or the bad fortune to be sole custodians of one threatened strand of that diversity.[10]

This brings me to my final point. Those of us living in these islands who are involved with threatened languages see the world, not only through the multiple lens of our languages, but also through the lens of a powerful, expanding juggernaut of a world language and one that is, like Maori and well over five thousand others, hanging on by its finger-nails.

Languages in Northern Ireland

What forms of linguistic diversity do we have? I will take the languages of Northern Ireland more or less in the chronological order of their arrival in Ireland, with one significant exception. English, the dominant language of our society, is so pervasive that it is enough to know that it first made an appearance in Ireland in the 12th century, and that since the 17th century it has been eroding the position of both Irish and Scots.

Irish

Irish has been around for anything from 3,800 to 2,300 years. It is a Celtic language closely related to Scottish Gaelic and Manx, and more distantly related to Welsh. Only one speaker from an organic Gaelic-speaking community within Northern Ireland - Rathlin Island - is still alive in 2008; the last native speakers of Irish in Armagh and Tyrone died in 1969. However, the language has survived among learners of Irish and children of learners who were brought up with Irish as their first language. The 2001 census records 167,000 positive answers to the Irish language question, around 10 per cent of the population. This figure over-estimates the number of fluent speakers of Irish and under-estimates the number of people with some knowledge of it. Until we get a better census question, we will not have accurate figures to work with.

Ulster Scots

Like English, Scots first established a permanent presence in Ulster at the end of the 16th century. The variant we now call Ulster Scots developed through an interaction with English and Irish. There are some difficulties in estimating the number of speakers of Ulster Scots. Although Scots and English both derive from Anglo-Saxon, they had diverged significantly by the 16th century. However, as both Scots and Ulster Scots have been converging towards an English norm for centuries, they range along a spectrum from a Scots-flavoured English to a dense form of maximally differentiated Scots. It is essentially at this latter end of the spectrum that the claims for Scots being a distinctive language rest. It is unlikely that the Ulster Scots Language Society's claim that there are 100,000 speakers of Ulster Scots refers to this end of the linguistic spectrum, but the Household Survey's figure of about 2 per cent of the population as identifying themselves as speakers of Ulster Scots appears to me to be a bit low, and possibly a reflection of the uncertainty that people have in defining Ulster Scots.

Sign Language

The two forms of Sign Language spoken in Northern Ireland have grown organically, and can claim distinct linguistic status, as their structure is quite different to that of English. British Sign Language, for example is a topic-comment language 'What is your name?' becomes 'Name (you), what?' 'Turn right at the traffic lights' becomes 'traffic lights' (one sign) 'turn right' (one sign). Not only is the word order changed, but because sign language uses, simultaneously, three-dimensional space, movement, shape, speed, direction, facial expression, some of its grammatical features are simultaneous rather than sequential as in English or Irish. There are also dialects – British Sign Language has 10 or 12 ways of signing the word 'holiday'. Irish sign language has nothing to do with the Irish language, and has developed with a different grammar from that of British Sign Language – it was based on American Sign language which itself derived from the French system.

Cant, Gammon or Shelta

Cant or Gammon, the speech of Irish Travellers, is less a distinct language than a specialised vocabulary designed to ensure that outsiders do not understand what is going on. It is a vocabulary-based speech-form, which appears to have been used with both Irish and English in the past, and is now used exclusively with English structures.

Migrant languages

The oldest surviving migrant language is Italian, which first established a presence in the late 19th century and is still spoken, but only a minority of people of Italian descent still speak the language. As far as I know, there are no firm figures yet on other languages spoken in Northern Ireland. Daniel Holder of the Multi-Cultural Resource Centre has produced a guestimate of at least 18,000 speakers of other languages. Of these, the Chinese, speaking mainly Cantonese, but with some speakers of Mandarin and Hakka, are the largest group (8,000). About 3,000 are from Europe, including speakers of German (800), French, Italian and Spanish (500 each), but to the latter must be added Spanish-speakers from Latin America. There is also a small number of speakers of east European languages such as Polish and Romanian. Other languages (few of which appear to have more than 1,000 speakers, and some as few as 30) include Hindi, Punjabi, Swahili, Fulani, Xhosa, Urdu, Punjabi, Mirpuri, Vietnamese, Malay, Thai, Arabic.

Linguistic diversity and government policy

Cultural diversity is currently one of the flavours of the month at Westminster. This welcome move is informed by both moral and pragmatic imperatives. The moral imperative is fuelled by a sense of justice. The pragmatic imperative comes from a desire to begin to deal with ethnic tensions in British society before that particular powder-keg explodes, and points towards various subtle and unsubtle forms of social engineering.

I do not believe that the Westminster government has worked out the implications of this policy, which resounds with the sound of well-meant incoherence. Well-meaning confusion is, of course, an honourable state in a human being; it is rather less useful in a government.

There is a further complication. Scotland and Wales both have indigenous minority languages to deal with, as well as significant numbers of speakers of migrant languages, but England does not. On this issue, England, devolution or no, still calls the shots, and an English perspective, which concentrates exclusively on migrant languages, dominates the debate on linguistic diversity. This essentially English issue is then exported to Northern Ireland, where honourable confusion is honourably confounded by the fact that we have a home-grown set of ethnic tensions that involve everybody except the ethnic minority communities, who wisely keep well away from them.

The UK Government has also ratified the European Charter for Regional and Minority Languages since March 2001. In Northern Ireland, this commits the UK Government to undertake 'resolute action' to promote Irish and Ulster Scots as 'an expression of cultural wealth'.[11] This commitment comes under Part II of the Charter. Only Irish has commitments to specific measures under Part III of the Charter. Article 12, which deals with cultural activities and facilities, commits the Government to a number of specific measures relating to Irish.[12] Implementation of the Charter is monitored by a Committee of Experts, but there are no legal sanctions to back it up.

The terms 'linguistic diversity' and 'cultural wealth' also appear in the Good Friday Agreement. This time the frame of reference is broadened to include the languages of the various ethnic communities of Northern Ireland in the context of 'respect, tolerance and understanding'.

> All participants recognise the importance of respect, understanding and tolerance in relation to linguistic diversity, including in Northern Ireland, the Irish language, Ulster-Scots and the languages of the various ethnic communities, all of which are part of the cultural wealth of the island of Ireland.[13]

The Irish language again receives particular attention in the Agreement. While the commitment to 'resolute action' for Irish and Ulster Scots in the Charter involves moral sanctions only, the commitments in the Agreement, which has the legal force of a treaty, are arguably enforceable by law, although we do not yet know what legal mechanisms can be invoked.[14]

Under another piece of international legislation, a statutory Cross-Border Language Body was set up for Irish and Ulster Scots. The body has two separate agencies, each of which has a statutory right to advise government and public bodies on language policy. In Northern Ireland, this advisory function refers directly to the commitments of the Good Friday Agreement and the Charter.

This legislation also defines the status of Ulster Scots, which is recognised as 'the variety of the Scots language traditionally found in parts of Northern Ireland and Donegal.'[15] (This is the first time that Scots has been given legal recognition as a language in the UK.) The cultural remit of the Ulster Scots agency is not restricted to language-related culture, and also involves 'the cultural traditions of the part of the population of Northern Ireland and the border counties which is of Scottish ancestry and the influence of their cultural traditions on others, both within the island of Ireland and the rest of the world.'[16]

On the administrative side, the Department of Culture, Arts and Leisure has set up a Linguistic Diversity Unit to develop and monitor linguistic diversity policy in Northern Ireland. Its remit involves, as well as Irish and Ulster Scots, Travellers' speech and the two sign languages in use there as well as the languages of migrants and their descendants.

One other recent development on the legal front should be noted. The Northern Ireland Human Rights Commission published a consultation document containing preliminary proposals on the new Bill of Rights, which includes a section on language rights. It proposes to provide legal protection to all languages, and has widened its remit to include dialects and other forms of communication. The introduction to the section argues that all languages and dialects 'contribute to the cultural richness of the whole community and they enable individuals to express their needs and identity ... and to participate in cultural life through literary and artistic expression.'[17] We have no idea what is going to happen to the Bill of Rights.

This, briefly, is the context in which language policy is to be developed. Irish currently has the strongest legal protection, followed by Ulster Scots. Irish and Ulster Scots also have the strongest institutional support. Other linguistic traditions do not yet have this level of legal or institutional support. However, they are now firmly within the debate, have been mentioned in legislation, are being considered for further legislation, have emerging administrative support structures within a Northern Ireland government department, and, in the UK context, are reasonably high on the list of the Westminster Government's priorities.

I will finish with a brief comment. Although the principle of linguistic diversity is recognised in law, and there are stronger support structures for linguistic diversity than there have ever been in Northern Ireland, none of our threatened languages is necessarily safe.

Notes

1 Kevin Myers, "An Irishman's Diary", *Irish Times*, 1 Sept 2004. *Craic* is not to be found in Dineen's 1927 Dictionary, but is in Ó Dónaill's (1977).

2 *Irish News*, 15 Oct 1997. I am indebted to my colleague Gordon McCoy for references to the various newspaper controversies. This one ran from 8-19 October.

3 *Rhyming Weavers*, p 30. The *Elegant Extracts* was the *Golden Treasury* of its day.

4 According to the *Oxford English Dictionary*, this sense emerged as early as the 14th century, and survives as a dialect word in the south of England. Spenser uses this sub-meaning of the word in the *Faerie Queen*, TP Dolan, *A Dictionary of Hiberno-English*, Dublin, 1998, p 77.

5 John McWhorter, *The Power of Babel*, (2001) 2003, p 95.

6 David Crystal, *Language Death*, Cambridge, 2000, pp 14-15.

7 McWhorter 2001, p 277

8 James McCloskey, *Voices Silenced*, Dublin, 2001, p 36.

9 McCloskey 2001, p 39.

10 McCloskey 2001, p 41.

11 *European Charter for Regional or Minority Languages*, Strasbourg, Council of Europe, 1992, Part II, Article 7a, p 44.

12 *ibid*, Part III, Article 12, pp 55-6.

13 *The Belfast Agreement*, 'Rights, Safeguards and Equality of Opportunity: economic, social and cultural issues,' Para 3.

14 *ibid*, Para 4.

15 *The British-Irish Agreement Bill, 1999*, Dublin, Stationary Office, Part 5, 'Language: exercise of functions,' Para 1.7, p 46.

16 *ibid*.

17 *Making a Bill of Rights for Northern Ireland*, Belfast, Northern Ireland Human Rights Commission, September 2001.

Chapter Thirteen

THE NORTHERN IRELAND PEACE PROCESS IN COMPARATIVE PERSPECTIVE

Adrian Guelke

L et me start with a very simple proposition. Peace processes are generally the product of a mix of internal and external influences. The mix varies, but few societies are so cut off from political developments in the rest of the world that the prevailing climate of international opinion makes no difference to whether a peace process can be launched. Similarly, few peace processes make any headway simply on the basis of external opinion alone.

Northern Ireland is no exception to this general rule. Its peace process occurred in an era of peace processes. Formally speaking, the Northern Ireland peace process was launched on 15 December 1993, with a joint declaration by the British and Irish governments. Of course the launch would have meant little if it had not been followed up in August and October 1994 by ceasefires by the main Republican and Loyalist paramilitaries. Further, the ceasefires required to be underwritten by a political settlement if the truce was to become the basis of an enduring peace. This was achieved with the Good Friday Agreement of 10 April 1998. It has not been plain sailing since then, however. I will come back to this issue later.

For the moment, I want to focus on why the 1990s proved to be an era of peace processes across the world, though it should also be noted that the 1990s also witnessed the outbreak of conflict in areas of the world that had been tranquil in previous decades. The obvious example of this point was the violence that engulfed the Balkans in the 1990s. It is not difficult to identify the major external influence on both these sets of events. It was the end of the Cold War and even more fundamentally of bipolarity, that is, the ending of the division of the world on the basis of two blocs, one centred on Washington, the other on Moscow. The event that signalled the end of the Cold War was the coming down of the Berlin Wall in November 1989. The implication of that event was the end of Communist rule in Eastern Europe. When the old guard in Moscow sought to reverse this process in the summer of 1991, they merely accelerated it. At the end of 1991, the Soviet Union itself was dissolved, underscoring the revolutionary change to the world that had resulted from the dismantling of the Berlin Wall.

The change quite naturally had an immense impact on conflicts where the local protagonists appeared to be fighting proxy wars on behalf of the global rivals. But it also affected conflicts that very clearly had a basis which was unrelated to the rivalry between Washington and Moscow. And two obvious cases of relevance to Northern Ireland were the conflicts in South Africa and in Israel/Palestine. In the case of South Africa, the coming down of the Berlin Wall loomed large in President FW de Klerk's decision to remove the ban on the African National Congress and to release Nelson Mandela from prison in February 1990. De Klerk's assumption was that the ANC would be damaged in the new era of world affairs by its links to the South African Communist Party. The alliance between the ANC and the SACP was epitomised by the fact that MK or Umkhonto We Sizwe ('Spear of the Nation' - the vehicle for the movement's armed struggle), had been formed jointly by the ANC and the SACP in 1961. In fact, de Klerk's calculations proved entirely mistaken. Indeed, the end of the Cold War meant that countries such as the United States and Britain were less, not more, concerned about the ANC's links with the SACP.

There was a somewhat more complex connection between the end of the Cold War and the Israeli-Palestinian Peace Process than in South Africa's case. However, one element certainly was a similar calculation by the Israeli government that the demise of the Soviet Union had weakened the PLO and made it more amenable to a settlement on Israel's terms. Another factor in the Middle East peace process was the Israeli government's realisation following the Gulf War of 1991 of the extent of state's dependence on the United States. What was more, in the absence of the Cold War, there could be no assumption that America would automatically come to Israel's aid for strategic reasons.

Professor Michael Cox of the London School of Economics has advanced the thesis that the Northern Ireland peace process too was strongly influenced by the end of the Cold War.[1] He demonstrates the extent to which the Republican movement was influenced by the spirit of the times in its development of a peace strategy. The end of the Cold War also made it possible for the British Government to facilitate the process by adopting a stance that helped to persuade nationalists to accept the principle of consent, if in the case of the Republicans somewhat ambiguously and grudgingly. This was the statement in November 1990 by the Northern Ireland Secretary of State, Peter Brooke, that the British government had 'no selfish, strategic or economic interest' in Northern Ireland. Brooke had wanted to make the statement a year earlier but it had been vetoed by Prime Minister Margaret Thatcher as the wrong signal to send to the Soviet Union. So in this case, the influence of the end of the Cold War is very clear. But also very important in the Northern Ireland case was the comparison of Northern Ireland with both South Africa and Israel/Palestine. With the South African transition initiated in 1990 and optimism as a result of the Oslo peace process in the case of the Middle East in 1993, politicians in Northern Ireland came under pressure to emulate their progress, particularly Sinn Féin politicians who had promoted the comparison so assiduously.

Before saying more about comparisons of the three cases in the context of the peace process of the 1990s, let me say a little about the history of the comparison. I will look first at academic comparisons before examining the more obviously prescriptive and political comparisons. The point of departure for academic comparisons of the three situations was a concept that became increasingly influential in Comparative Politics during the 1970s. This was the concept of a 'deeply divided' society, with the recognition that resolving conflict in such societies presented special difficulties. A landmark in this concept was a book by Eric Nordlinger that was published in 1972. Its title was *Conflict Regulation in Divided Societies.*[2] (I should point out that notwithstanding the book's title, in the text Nordlinger used the term 'deeply divided' not just 'divided', since obviously all societies could be said to be divided to some extent.) What made deeply divided societies special was the existence of fundamental conflict over the nature or even existence of the prevailing political system.

Thus, in Israel/Palestine, there was a fundamental conflict between Zionism as a political project and Palestinian nationalism. In South Africa, the conflict was between the Afrikaner nationalist scheme of apartheid entailing the partitioning of South Africa and the African nationalist demand for one man one vote in a unitary state. In Northern Ireland the conflict was over the province's membership of the United Kingdom versus the nationalist aspiration for a united Ireland.

At the time the comparison became popular in the 1970s and 1980s these different political aspirations looked utterly irreconcilable, so the basis of much academic analysis of the three situations was the intractability of conflict in the three cases. Bernard Crick, in a contribution to a conference on the three cases held in Bonn in the autumn of 1989, described the three as 'insoluble' on the basis of the declared positions of the parties. At the same time, none of the three was politically stable. All three were caught up in political violence and in each there was a crisis of governability that put in question the continuance of the status quo. That added to academic interest in the comparison as scholars could debate the applicability of this or that mechanism from their toolbox of political initiatives for addressing conflict.

But academics were not alone in making the comparison. Politicians also made the comparison, though in their case it was not necessarily to promote structural comparison of the conflicts. Apartheid provided the basis for comparison for the purpose of condemnation. Thus, the comparison of Northern Ireland with South Africa at this juncture was a shorthand way of condemning the status quo here as illegitimate and intolerable. That implication was one reason why the comparison attracted so much hostility from Unionists. Unionist recognition of the propaganda possibilities of the comparison with South Africa has an interesting history. In 1960 the British government was seeking to promote popular support for the British Commonwealth within the UK. It hit upon the idea of holding exhibitions across the UK. One of these exhibitions was to be held in Belfast. The Conservative government wanted the Belfast exhibition to be opened by the South African High Commissioner. The Unionist government objected. For the most part, the objections related to the Afrikaner nationalist and republican nature of the South African government.

South Africa was about to hold a referendum to turn the country into a republic. This did not go down well with Unionists, some of whom harked back to the Anglo-Boer War at the turn of the century and to the alliance between Irish nationalism and Afrikaner nationalism. However, one of the Unionist ministers struck a more modern note. Brian Faulkner suggested that South African involvement would encourage mischievous people to compare sectarianism in Northern Ireland and apartheid. Faulkner was not misconceived in his concerns.

Comparison is a very common aspect of political discourse. Sometimes the comparison is quite superficial as in comparisons before the Iraq war of Saddam Hussein with Adolf Hitler, as if a broken-backed Third World regime could be compared to an industrial world power. Sometimes a comparison may be fortuitous. An example is the debate that took place in the United States in 2002 over the lessons of the Cuban missile crisis 40 years earlier for the conduct of policy towards Iraq. One can quite see why the field of Comparative Politics in general provokes scepticism. It is easily characterised as the exaggeration of the similarities between unique situations. However, it is a mistake to dismiss comparison, not least because of the role which imitation plays in political behaviour.

At the same time, it is important to stress that imitation can as easily have malign consequences as benign ones. A remarkable transformation took place in Belfast's urban landscape in 2002 following Israel Prime Minister Sharon's offensive against the Palestinian Authority at the end of March. Henry McDonald described the scene in a piece in *The Observer* in May 2002:

> Israel has found a new ally in its war against Yasser Arafat and the Palestinian Authority - Johnny Adair's dog. Rebel, Adair's pet Alsatian, has become the latest member of the Ulster loyalist community to display support for Ariel Sharon's assault on the West Bank and Gaza. Last Monday afternoon the UDA commander's four-legged friend was seen being taken for a walk along Belfast's Shankill Road with the Star of David flag wrapped round its body.
>
> In UDA redoubts such as the Lower Shankill and Tiger's Bay it seems every lamppost is now festooned with the Jewish state's flag. In response, Palestinian flags have been put up in large numbers across Republican strongholds. The INLA in particular has been keen to express support for the PLO and even more extreme forces in the Palestinian controlled areas. 'Victory to Jenin' and 'We support the suicide bombers' are commonplace on the walls of Duncairn Gardens, Newington and Ardoyne.

The message on the Loyalist side was unmistakenly that Loyalists preferred Sharon's war process to Tony Blair's peace process. That is, instead of the Israelis and Palestinians resuming their negotiations inspired by the model of conflict resolution embodied in the Good Friday Agreement, as Blair was urging, Loyalists wanted Blair to copy Sharon's methods. The message on the Republican side was that there would be a very aggressive response to any such imitation, whether by Loyalists or ultimately perhaps by the British government. At a more sophisticated level than Israeli flags or slogans in favour of suicide bombers, Unionist politicians underscored their dissatisfaction with government policy by denouncing its failure to treat Republican terrorism the same way as it treated international terrorism.

Now, sceptics may object that there was a large element of opportunism in this comparison-making. If they want evidence to support their interpretation, they can cite the fact that the Loyalists in two of their strongholds took down Israeli flags and covered up some of the graffiti celebrating Israeli victories, temporarily at least, to accommodate visitors from the British National Party. Be that as it may, I think it would be wrong to underestimate the power of comparison in peace processes.

For far more constructive reasons than I have hitherto discussed I think that comparisons tend to be important in peace processes, for five practical reasons.

First, in so far as the objective of a peace process is the achievement of a fresh political dispensation, there is a need to legitimise new arrangements, new institutions and new processes of decision-making. An obvious way of doing that is to demonstrate their similarity to good practice elsewhere.

Secondly, there is also a need to provide an overarching framework for viewing the changes. International comparisons and the field of Comparative Politics come into their own in providing such models.

Thirdly, during the process of negotiations it is important that the parties are provided with the reassurance that a successful outcome to the process is achievable, is possible. Successful outcomes in societies with similar problems are significant in this context. South Africa's successful transition to democracy provided an inspiration for the Northern Irish process. The Good Friday Agreement in turn has been an inspiration to others. An example is provided by the establishment of an Irish forum by Basque nationalists which led on to the Basque Country's short-lived peace process in the late 1990s. Of course, that example shows that the attempt to transplant a model of conflict resolution from one situation to another does not always succeed.

Fourth, almost all peace processes require external goodwill to have any chance of success. Consequently, meeting current international standards looms large in most peace processes. To put it another way, models of what the international community considers legitimate inevitably matter.

And fifthly, the wider international context also matters. In a television interview he gave on the eve of the ceremony at which he received the Nobel Peace Prize, the Israeli Foriegn Minister, Shimon Peres, spoke of the importance of the end of the Cold War to the Middle East peace process. 'We moved' he said 'from a world of enemies to a world of problems.'

With the events of September 11 2001, it is hard to avoid the conclusion that we have returned to a world of enemies. The logic of that and the politics that go with it seem bound to affect peace processes in the years ahead.

At the conference in Bonn in 1989 that I previously mentioned, an Israeli sociologist, Sammy Smooha, spoke on the prospects for political settlements in the three cases. He was most optimistic about the case of Israel/Palestine. He argued that the two-state solution required only a divorce between the two sides and that a divorce is easier to arrange and is more durable than a marriage. In the case of Northern Ireland, he wondered whether things were bad enough to persuade the parties to reach a compromise. Finally, he thought the gulf in conditions between whites and blacks to be too large to make possible a political settlement in South Africa. Prediction in politics is difficult at the best of times and this illustrates the point.

The three societies have diverged in ways that few would have imagined conceivable in 1989. In 2004 South Africa celebrated ten years of democracy as well as holding its third democratic election. To all intents and purposes, South Africa is a done political deal far beyond the point when anything is likely to disturb its new dispensation. That is also reflected in the negligible impact that 9/11 had on its politics.

Interest in the South African case these days is principally from the perspective of whether lessons can be learnt from its success. In a paper I gave in 2004 to a conference on international dimensions of the crisis in the Northern Ireland peace process, I referred to this as 'the lure of the miracle.' The focus of my paper was the interest in Northern Ireland in South Africa's Truth and Reconciliation Commission as a mechanism that could work here. I would certainly agree that one of the main problems here is that our peace has been a cold peace without reconciliation. However, despite the name, South Africa did not achieve reconciliation through the Truth and Reconciliation Commission. Indeed, it might almost be said that reconciliation was achieved in spite of it. The main agent of reconciliation in South Africa was not the TRC but the figure of Nelson Mandela and Northern Ireland has no conceivable equivalent of Madiba, as Mandela is popularly known.

In the case of Israel/Palestine, the peace process was in a severe crisis well before 9/11. The failure of the Camp David negotiations in mid-2000 and the al-Aqsa intifada that followed Ariel Sharon's coat-trailing exercise on the Temple Mount in the autumn of that year had already plunged Israel/Palestine into a downward spiral. However, matters were unquestionably made worse by the outcome of the Presidential elections in the United States that year. George W Bush was determined to be different from Bill Clinton, so in the crucial first six months of 2001 he decided that America would not intervene and that parties should be left to discover that a new cycle of violence would not serve their interests. By the time wiser counsels began to prevail, it was too late. Thus 9/11 effectively put paid to US Secretary of State Colin Powell's efforts to revive the peace process. In particular, Bush backed off after Sharon made his opposition to an American initiative clear with a speech in which he declared that 'we will not be Czechoslovakia.' Bush was said to be furious over being compared to Neville Chamberlain, but left Sharon alone.

Blair has periodically made efforts to get Bush to intervene more energetically in the conflict. In particular, Bush was persuaded during his brief visit to Hillsborough in April 2003 to connect the peace process here with the Middle East. But as agreement in Northern Ireland failed to materialise, this was inevitably something of a damp squib. There has been speculation that Yassir Arafat's death and the election of a new Palestinian leader may create the conditions for reviving negotiations among the parties. We shall see. The backdrop of continuing violence in Iraq and the opposition in Israel to the very idea of a Palestinian state are not favourable conditions for making progress. Further, it would be dangerous to underestimate the influence in Washington of neo-conservatives opposed to the very concept of an Israeli-Palestinian peace process and who reject the need for any political accommodation with Palestinian nationalism.

Northern Ireland lies somewhere between the success in South Africa's case and breakdown in the Middle East; but certainly closer to the South African case than to that of Israel/Palestine, whatever deal may remain to be secured. The impact of 9/11 on Northern Ireland has been mixed. The war against terrorism has made it more important for Republicans not to be seen as connected, conceptually as it were, with the activities of al-Qaeda. And it does seem to be the case that the first act of decommissioning by the Provisional IRA in October 2001 occurred in part because of the political repercussions of 9/11. However, for Unionists, the launch of a global war against terrorism makes their sharing of power with Sinn Féin a harder pill to swallow. If Colombia, which had a peace process in the 1990s, can now be part of the war on terrorism and be covered by the precept of no negotiations with terrorists, then why not Northern Ireland? It is fortunate that what is at issue in Northern Ireland now is fixing a political process against a background of relative peace. In the present international climate it is difficult to imagine that the much harder task of reaching a political settlement – what was achieved in 1998 – would be possible.

I opened this lecture by arguing that peace processes were the product of a mix of internal and external influences. Similarly, their implementation depends not just on domestic conditions but also on the external backdrop, though I would expect domestic factors to loom larger in the case of implementation. That is borne out by what has happened in Northern Ireland since 1998. However, we should not discount the significance of external factors even while acknowledging their secondary role.

In a number of respects the external backdrop has become more difficult since 1998. Thus, at the time of the Good Friday Agreement it appeared that a facilitating factor was the existence of a pro-human rights, pro-European, post-imperial British government in power at Westminster. Few people would characterise the Blair government in such terms today. Blair's ambition to set the world to rights in tandem with George W Bush has put paid to the idea that imperialism is dead. By contrast, the commitment to European integration seems close to dead, while the politics of fear has taken over from the human rights agenda. It is not a very encouraging prospect.

The external backdrop might matter less if domestic conditions were not also quite difficult. This is not intended to strike a note of pessimism about the future. In fact, I don't propose to make any predictions. Northern Ireland's politics endlessly surprises, so I doubt my guesses would be any good. Whatever value there is in examining the peace process here in a comparative perspective, it does not extend to telling us either when or whether there will be a deal or if there is a deal, whether it will prove durable.

Notes

1   'Northern Ireland after the Cold War' in Cox, Guelke and Stephen (eds), *A Farewell to Arms? From 'long war' to peace in Northern Ireland,* Manchester University Press, 2000.
2   Harvard University Center for International Affairs.

Chapter Fourteen

CONTEMPORARY POLITICS IN NORTHERN IRELAND

Paul Arthur

Timing, they say, is all in politics. Indeed it might be asserted that the organisers were percipient in choosing as a seminar series 'What makes Now in Northern Ireland?' We may have a much clearer idea shortly but we can say this: we have been facing a new dispensation since November 2003. The task now is to delineate the institutional and constitutional architecture. But that is a role for politicians and policy makers.

In a reflective article on the tenth anniversary of the release from Robben Island of President Nelson Mandela the distinguished South African novelist, André Brink, recalls a sense of existential disorientation when he noted a blank wall in the airport building in Port Elizabeth announcing 'You are now here'. That was it – a blank wall, no map, no plan. It served as a useful metaphor for a peace process. A certain amount of disorientation is inevitable as is the roller-coaster between hope and despair. For us the question is which one we 'would choose to define ourselves by: the moment of light or the dark intervals in between. Perhaps neither should be thinkable without the other. If humanity makes sense, it is not because it is capable of the best, or the worst, but of both'.

Let that be our starting point. We start with a blank wall where the question 'where is here?' may be incredibly daunting: and 'we may not be yet' as Brink asserts, 'where we'd like to be, but at the least we are no longer "there" any more'. Most importantly, we seem to be on our way to 'somewhere'. Drawing on the small cell that Mandela occupied for 18 of his 27 years in prison Brink concludes: 'Our peculiar cell may yet expand to the dimensions of a larger and more human world.' This paper will be concerned with such a journey, with the larger issues of 'time' and 'space' rather than with more practical concerns of the modalities entailed in conflict transformation.

'There'

One of the characteristics of an intense conflict is the growth of a cottage industry in navel-gazing. The assumption is that 'our' conflict is unique; that we have nothing to learn from elsewhere; and that indeed the rest of the world is as consumed with our quarrel as we are ourselves. It is incestuous and dangerously static. The Irish poet, Louis MacNeice, employs a useful metaphor: '...bottled time turns sour upon the sill.' In the Middle East, in eastern Europe and in Central America I have encountered similar mind-sets – a selective obsession with the past, a narrow insularity about the present, and no proper concern for the future. The Czech novelist, Milan Kundera, captured its essence in *Slowness*: '...the source of fear is in the future, and a person freed of the future has nothing to fear'. Those who are engaged in peace processes know that they have to confront the future. Senator George Mitchell recognised as much in his original Report on Decommissioning. In paragraph 16 he wrote that 'if the focus remains in the past, the past will become the future, and that is something no one can desire'. So when we speak of 'there' we are thinking less about place and more about space in a temporal and emotional sense. We are acknowledging the baleful role of 'victimhood,' which Robert Elias has defined as 'the political economy of helplessness.'

It has to be said that we operated under an intimidatory political culture long before the recent 'Troubles' became a reality. Towards the end of the last century an Irish Nationalist MP stated that 'violence was the only way of securing a hearing for moderation.' In his comparative analysis, Frank Wright comments that in place of what 'metropolitans call peace,' Northern Ireland enjoyed at best 'a tranquillity of communal deterrence.' This view is complemented by John Darby's longitudinal study of political violence from the North of Ireland from the beginning of the nineteenth century. Darby depicts a polity in which 'the power of intimidation springs from its essentially defensive nature. Local minorities were driven by violence and fear to move to other communities in which they could become part of a majority. They were often willing to encourage the expulsion of ethnic opponents from their new community.' But despite the mayhem, the picture is not totally bleak in that his research indicates that Northern Ireland's conflict 'is remarkable for the limitations on its violence rather than for the violence itself.' That condition produced a paradox that was to be a constraint on mediation. Violence neither reached genocidal levels nor was it sustained enough to induce compromise: '...there has been no resolution because the violence has not been intolerable. By whatever calculus communities compute their interests, the price of compromise is still thought to be greater than the cost of violence.' Later we will need to examine the reasons for the changing calculus.

Given the sad turbulent history of Ireland, violent acts were revisited after 1969 that were (according to J Bowyer Bell) 'so natural as to be beyond comment... (A)ll that was needed was to exploit the existing reality.' Our auditors of violence have classified this 'importance' in 1993: 'This small but deeply divided population has generated the most intense political violence of any part of the contemporary UK, the highest levels of internal political violence of any member-state of the European Community, and the highest levels of internal political violence in the continuously liberal democratic states of the post-1948 world.' They went on to make comparisons elsewhere: 'If the equivalent ratio of victims to population had been produced in Great Britain in the same period some 100,000 people would have died, and if a similar level of political violence had taken place the number of fatalities in the USA would have been over 500,000, or about ten times the number of Americans killed in the Vietnam war'. They conclude with the devastating remark that our record is not quite so bad as the Lebanon but being 'second to the Lebanon' is an unenviable classification.

Those figures might be said to represent the darkness inbetween the light. They could be countered by another bald fact: this tiny piece of earth, this 'narrow ground,' has produced no fewer than five Nobel Laureates in the past 25 years – the Peace People (Mairead Corrigan and Betty Williams) in 1976, Séamus Heaney in 1995, and David Trimble and John Hume in 1998. I want to spend a little time examining this phenomenon because we may be faced with a conundrum: how do we explain so much violence and so many peacemakers? How do we explain the facts that Corrigan and Williams were recognised by the Nobel Peace Institute at the height of political violence? That the movement they led had a more spiritual, than secular, dimension? That it was briefly in the political firmament and that it could be more easily compared to a shooting star that blazes across the skyline only to burn itself out? We might ask, too, whether a Literature Laureate belongs in this particular pantheon. And we might query (gently, respectfully) whether John Hume and David Trimble – permanent fixtures in that violent maelstrom of the past three decades – were truly worthy of the award? My instant reply to the latter is that indubitably they deserve their recognition but that it has to be seen in the context of conflict transformation. In other words, we are concerned with the temporal and how we got from 'there' to 'here' in our search for that visionary 'somewhere'. Ultimately we are concerned with 'transcendence'.

'There' has the timeless quality of any intense conflict of which I am aware. I always fall back on an aphorism from another Nobel Laureate, Czeslaw Milosz: It is 'possible there is no other memory than the memory of wounds.' That is one of the more profound statements about the condition of victimhood. It calls into play the concept of the 'Long War' and a tradition of martyrology. It was part of Irish Republican theology encapsulated in the words of the hunger striker, Terence MacSwiney in 1920 that it 'is not those who inflict the most but those who suffer the most who will conquer.' There can be perfectly understandable reasons why people insist on remembering. It is a way of avoiding oblivion. A Guatemalan human rights activist provides one reason: 'the war created fear, a lack of communication, a lack of confidence, an inability to solve conflicts. You can't reconcile with the living if you can't reconcile with the dead.' The inmates of Majdanek concentration camp produce another: 'Should our murderers be victorious, should they write the history of this war... their every word will be taken for gospel. Or they might wipe out our memory altogether, as if we have never existed... But if we write the history of the period... we'll have the thankless job of providing to a reluctant world that we are Abel, the murdered brother.' It is also the case that those who ask the question, should we remember 'is usually asked by people who have a choice. For many... there is no choice about remembering... (it) is not an option – it is a daily torture, a voice inside the head that has no on/off switch and no volume control' (Smyth).

But if we are in the business of conflict transformation we need to make the distinction between individual and communal suffering on the one hand, and the appropriation of historical trauma for political purposes on the other. The latter is explored by Ian Buruma who asserts that it 'becomes questionable when a cultural, ethnic, religious, or national community bases its communal identity almost entirely on the sentimental solidarity of remembered victimhood. For that way lies historical myopia and, in extreme circumstances, even vendetta'. A similar view is expressed by the distinquished French jurist, Roger Errera: 'One of the sound foundations of a political society is a true knowledge of its past... But the affirmation of the rights of memory does not mean that the past must be the only, or the main, value'. I would contend that one of the reasons why we have moved from 'there' to 'here' is that we have been prepared to move beyond memory (as a negative motivation) to acknowledgment (as a form of catharsis.) I would go further: our peace process is not solely the property of those who have been rightfully honoured but it belongs to the wider community – to the grass roots including the former combatants, to the diaspora, to the poets, to the transcenders. While there is some merit in the theoretical literature, in the concepts of hurting stalemates and ripe moments, we ignore at our peril the quiet attitudinal changes being nurtured in the undergrowth. Unquestioningly political leadership has a primary role to play in transforming conflict, in building up trust and credibility but at the end of the day there has to be a sense of ownership.

'Here'

> A peace agreement is merely one element of a larger peace process, an element that may create some new opportunities but hardly alters all aspects of the conflict. One thing that is imperative is to establish realistic expectations about how much and how quickly a weak and tentative peace agreement can alter the basic nature of a long and profoundly bitter conflict. It is also very important for the leaders on both sides to recognise that the game has changed, that the behaviour necessary to get to a provisional-agreement period is not always the behaviour appropriate for the post-agreement period: needs and priorities change, interests must be redefined and revisioned, and a joint learning process must be institutionalised and accelerated. (Rothstein).

'Here' is 'The Agreement' signed on Good Friday 1998 and all the problems it has encountered in the meantime. The fact that it is described under different nomenclatures – The Good Friday Agreement, the Belfast Agreement, or 'The Agreement reached in the Multi-Party Negotiations' to give it its correct title – is indicative of the necessity for an accelerated joint learning process. If we examine the life-span of a conflict we can detect three phases – analysis, negotiation and implementation – not all of them totally autonomous   Analysis takes many shapes and forms. It can be part of the normal thrust of political discourse; of informed commentary in the media and academia; in exercises in Track Two diplomacy; in our capacity to tell stories to one another.

I want to linger on that last point for a few moments. Telling stories, creating narratives, is non-threatening. It can be done in a structured manner as it was in South Africa in what was called the Mont Fleur Project. Pierre Wack suggests that that project was about 'the gentle art of reperceiving'. It was about establishing networks and understandings and ultimately changing hardened opinions. It was about communication:

> Communication entails recognition of the other, and 'the awareness of being separate and different from and strange to one another' opens up potentials of creative search for dialogue and for understanding the other. This is also the essence of negotiations. Reaching common ground is not necessarily a product of similar opinions. (Sasson Sofer quoting ZD Gurevitch)

Lack of communication, lack of dialogue, can lead us to having a wrong cognitive framework 'which is what happens if you prematurely close in on an understanding. There are no correct understandings but there are very bad ones' (Arthur). I would suggest that one of the reasons we were so slow in reaching the negotiation stage was that we were operating under wrong cognitive frameworks – we were not even agreed on the nature of the problem, hence we could not begin to address the elements of the solution.

Can I illustrate this point about the power of dialogue and communication by quoting from one of our Nobel Laureates. Séamus Heaney entitled his 1995 Nobel Lecture 'Crediting Poetry'. In it he mused on the fact that only 'the stupid or the very deprived can any longer help knowing that the documents of civilisation have been written in blood and tears, blood and tears no less real for being very remote. And when this intellectual predisposition coexists with the actualities of Ulster and Israel and Bosnia and Rwanda and a host of wounded spots on the face of the earth, the inclination is not only not to credit human nature with much constructive potential but not to credit anything too positive in the work of art'. He was reflecting on Brink's 'dark intervals in between... the moment of light': or on the philosopher's (Edith Wyschogrod) portrayal of the twentieth century as 'the century of man-made mass death' in which a death-world manifests itself in the slaughter of the Great War which created a postmodern culture of mass death, of necropolis, of impersonality, of the slave labour and concentration camps, of 'the Red Guards in the Cultural Revolution (who) set out to destroy the four olds: old ideas, old culture, old customs and old habits'. Whither the role of the artist in this bleak environment? 'Which is why for years I was bowed to the desk like some monk bowed over his prie-dieu, some dutiful contemplative pivoting his understanding in an attempt to bear his portion of the weight of the world, knowing himself incapable of heroic virtue, but constrained by his obedience to his rule to repeat the effort and the posture. Blowing up sparks for a meagre heat. Forgetting faith, straining towards good works'. Nevertheless he believes that 'art can rise to the occasion'.

Heaney employed his art in this lecture to tell a story based on one of the most harrowing events in our conflict. He recounts what was known as the Kingsmills massacre in January 1976 when eleven workmen were held at gunpoint on a lonely stretch of road on their way home. One of the masked executioners asked if there were any Catholics among them they were to step out of line. As it was there was only one Catholic and the assumption was that this was a loyalist gang. Heaney continues:

> It was a terrible moment for him, caught between dread and witness, but he did make a motion to step forward. Then, the story goes, in that split second of decision, and in the relative cover of the winter evening darkness, he felt the hand of the Protestant worker next to him take his hand and squeeze it in a signal that said no, don't move, we'll not betray you, nobody needs to know what faith or party you belong to. All in vain, however, for the man stepped out of line; but instead of finding a gun at his temple, he was pushed away as the gunmen opened fire on those remaining in the line, for these were not Protestant terrorists, but members, presumably, of the Provisional IRA.

Having told this story the poet reflected that it 'is difficult at times to repress the thought that history is about as instructive as an abatoir: that Tacitus was right and that peace is merely the desolation left behind after decisive operations.' But this dread is surely followed with a moment of light: 'The birth of the future we desire is surely in the contraction which that terrified Catholic felt on the roadside when another hand gripped his hand, not in the gunfire that followed so absolute and so desolate, if also so much a part of the music of what happens.'

I have dwelt on this particular story for so long because it is significant. Heaney was describing an act of transcendence that can take many forms: an act, a narrative, a person. Its importance lies in the definition provided by Byron Bland – 'connecting what violence has severed.' This particular incident was important in its own right – the unnoticed acts of heroism by those who don't make history – and in its telling in the sumptuous surroundings of the Nobel Prize ceremony. Its sentiment was reinforced three years later when in the Oslo Radhus John Hume said: 'I think that David Trimble would agree that this Nobel prize for peace is in the deepest sense a powerful recognition of the compassion and humanity of all the people we represent between us... Endlessly our people gathered their strength to face another day and they never stopped encouraging their leaders to find the courage to resolve this situation so that our children could look to the future with a smile of hope.' One can take examples from other conflicts. Mozambique, at one time listed as one of the poorest countries in the world by the UN, underwent a civil war lasting fifteen years and claiming over one million lives. Yet the anthropologist Carolyn Nordstrom depicts an ethic behind a culture of peace constructed across the wastelands of war: 'Average Mozambicans configured peace as an act of resistance against violence, people reconstructed a new political culture, one that delegitimized the politics of force.'

It would be foolish to place too much weight on the role of the average person in conflict transformation. I have emphasised it because it seems to me that it has been underplayed. The high politics is much better-known because it is in the public domain. One can easily list the landmarks on the road to the 1998 Agreement: a statement by President Jimmy Carter in August 1977; the burgeoning Anglo-Irish diplomatic relationship from 1980 culminating in the signing of the Anglo-Irish Agreement in November 1985; talks between the SDLP and Sinn Féin in 1988, and between an emissary of the British Government and a Republican representative in 1990-93; the Brooke and Mayhew talks; the Downing Street Declaration; the Framework Document and finally the Agreement itself. Indeed one can examine virtually every Green and White Paper emanating from the British Government since 1972 and find elements of them in the final Agreement.

Equally, obeisance has been paid to the exogenous factors: the collapse of the Berlin Wall; the demise of communism as an aggressive ideology in geopolitics; the end of apartheid and South Africa's removal from pariah status; the Oslo Accord; the role of the Clinton Presidency. All of these freed republican and loyalist paramilitaries to reassess their old modes of thinking and to learn from peace processes elsewhere. One could mention, too, the place of Track-Two diplomacy. And that raises the place of conventional diplomacy that may have less to offer than heretofore imagined.

For example, the United States Advisory Commission on Public Diplomacy has commented on the effects of the information revolution at a time when the number of societies in transition is unprecedented and where globalization of issues 'is blurring the separation of foreign affairs and domestic politics.' This calls for the practice of a new kind of diplomacy where 'policies and negotiated agreements will succeed only if they have the support of publics at home and abroad.' The Commission borrowed Joe Nye's concept of 'soft power' – the 'ability to set the agenda in ways that shape the preferences of others,' which 'strengthens American diplomacy through attraction rather than coercion.' Soft power was invoked in Northern Ireland in ways that worked outside the parameters of formal conventional diplomacy. It appealed beyond the paramilitary and political élite levels to the wider public at a crucial phase of the process – somewhere between negotiation and implementation – when the public was invited to slough off its historic fatalism and to become proactive in the search for peace. It was yet another indication of the demotic nature of Northern Ireland's political culture whereby political leaders had been unduly influenced by their more extreme supporters to follow an intransigent agenda.

The Agreement had an inversionary effect in that demos ceased being fatalistic and began to urge their politicians to work for peace. Beyond American diplomacy we could mention the significance of the European Union (EU) and of eminent persons such as Senator George Mitchell and General John de Chastelain, as well as that of NGOs ('non-governmental organisations'). External actors can have a role to play in depoliticising extremely contentious issues and can be an enormous asset in assisting countries making the transition out of conflict. The Commission asserts that in 'many ways they can do things better than government. They foster a flexible style that encourages innovation... They offer the world a winning combination of... professional skills, a wealth of experience, fresh perspectives, and enormous good will.' Nevertheless, NGOs, EPGs ('eminent persons groups') and soft diplomacy have not been enough to move a peace process based on strategic ambiguity forward. Indeed, central to 'here' has been what Prime Minister Blair has called 'four and a half years of hassle, frustration and messy compromise.' He may have following Brink when he went on to say that '[a]fter the dawn of the Agreement itself, there have been no moments of dazzling light when the decisions are plain, the good and the bad illuminated with crystal certainty, the path clear, the clarion call easy to sound' (17 October 2002).

Instead we have had four suspensions of the Northern Ireland Assembly, allegations of collaboration with the FARC in Colombia, of raiding a police station and of spying inside the Northern Ireland Office (all by the IRA); evidence (or at least enough to satisfy the International Commission on Decommissioning) of the IRA putting some of their armoury beyond use; of growing mistrust between the parties to the Agreement and of a tendency to a wishlist culture.   It is in these circumstances that Tony Blair recognised that under these circumstances '[t]here is no parallel track left.   The fork on the road has finally come.   Whatever guarantees we need to give that we will implement the Agreement, we will.   Whatever commitment to the end we all want to see, of a normalised Northern Ireland, I will make.   But we cannot carry on with the IRA half in and half out of this process.   Not just because it isn't right anymore.   It won't work anymore'.   So 'here' sets its own time constraints.

Despite this hiatus we need to acknowledge certain givens.   In his speech Mr Blair admitted that the British had not been able to eliminate the IRA militarily and that the Adams/McGuinness leadership had 'taken great risks to bury the past' and that '[e]specially post-11 September, there is a complete hatred of terrorism.'   We need, too, to remember that at the height of the Troubles nearly 500 people died from sectarian violence in one year.   And yet the recent IMC Report covering the period March to October 2004 indicated that in that period there were four Troubles-related deaths.

'Somewhere'

'The Future, Not The Past': some may recognise this as the title of the Ulster Unionist Party manifesto for the Assembly elections.   Here was an acknowledgement that both George Mitchell and Milan Kundera were correct in asserting that a person freed of the future has nothing to fear.   The vehicle for this transition in values is the 1998 Agreement in which '[d]evolved self-government and transnational institutions have created a new political space' that allowed both communities to 'live together, not only sharing power, but sharing cultural space with one another' - a space that has been encapsulated by Fintan O'Toole in the *New Yorker* (27 April 1998) shortly after the Agreement was signed: 'The search for peace has turned a place that nobody quite wanted into a place that nobody claims.   Northern Ireland has become a new kind of political space.   Its people are in an extraordinary position – free to be anything they can agree to become.   They have escaped from nations.'

If that suggests a profound shift in outlook the political philosopher Richard Bourke suggests another when he states that the core value of democracy is that of political equality, 'a democracy is a regime founded on equality, and not a political organisation belonging to a majority.'   He reminds us of the essential difference in political analysis between democratic governments and democratic status whereby Northern Ireland always had some kind of democratic process, albeit in the absence of a democratic state. He sets out to review the 1998 accord 'as merely pointing to the possibility of a democratic settlement which could evolve in operating the provisions of the Agreement.' And he sees the conflict as a product of 'a set of recent circumstances where the burgeoning of modern expectations had collided with the absence of democracy.' In that respect the 'loyal' majority had had to recognise... that Northern Ireland 'remained an integrated part of the United Kingdom, yet not an integral part of its politics.'

In this reading it was the fate of David Trimble and of Ulster Unionism (and we could say that of the SDLP as well) to act as precursors for Ian Paisley and Gerry Adams. They did the heavy lifting by teasing out the modalities of decommissioning and policing. The electorate delivered the verdict at the Assembly elections. The strong centre was dismantled and has been replaced by a curious hybrid. They have been in the driving seat particularly since the Leeds Castle meeting in September. An *Irish Times* editorial (20 September 2004) concluded that negotiations may have disguised the 'seismic advance' that could be made: 'The promise is held out that the IRA is prepared to decommission its arms and effectively stand down in a relatively short period of three to four months. For democratic parties on this island the prospect is finally held out that our day has come.' But the usual health warning needs to be borne in mind: 'Hence Mr Blair's "original" deadline of April, which became May, then June, then September, then the first fortnight in October, and which is now, according to the Taoiseach, the last week in November' (Frank Millar, 17 November 2004).

Inherent in a healing process is a capacity to deal with the past - and with the actions of the 'spoilers' in the present. We need look no further back than August 1998 and the grotesque tragedy of the Omagh bomb and another 28 lost lives. It was President Clinton on his visit to Omagh on 3 September 1998 who remarked: 'By killing Catholics and Protestants, young and old, men, women and children, even those about to be born, people from Northern Ireland, the Irish Republic and abroad – by doing all that in the aftermath of what the people had voted for in Northern Ireland, it galvanised, strengthened and humanised the impulse to peace.' There have been too many Omaghs. The wounds are raw and deep, the memories scarred and traumatised. But we have come to terms with all of this. The 1998 Agreement was a start. Besides embracing institutional change it gave implicit recognition to attitudinal change through its comments on Rights, on Decommissioning, on Policing and Justice, on Prisoners, and on Validation. It is implicit when it addresses Reconciliation: '...it is essential to acknowledge and address the suffering of the victims of violence as a necessary element of reconciliation... It is recognised that victims have a right to remember as well as to contribute to a changed society... An essential aspect of the reconciliation process is the promotion of a culture of tolerance at every level of society...'

Our primary task is to establish a culture of tolerance. We have begun. BBC Radio Ulster ran a two-minute radio programme, 'Legacy', every morning for a year in which victims told their stories. It was a powerful indictment of our past and an endorsement of the centrality of narrative. Another had been a monumental tome from four local journalists. The title speaks for itself: *Lost Lives: The stories of the men, women and children who died as a result of the Northern Ireland Troubles.* In their Introduction the authors state that they hope that 'anyone tempted to think of resorting to violence will find in these pages more than 3,600 reasons to think again.' There are other examples. The more crucial point has been made by *The Economist* (1 November 1997):

> In their efforts to deal with the past, new democracies have given victims their chance to speak. Wrongs have been exposed. A few culprits have been punished. These are considerable achievements. And by investigating the sins of former regimes, the new governments have invited their own people to judge them by a higher standard of behaviour. This is the most important achievement of all. The trials and truth commissions of recent years have not really been about the past. Rather, and rather more sensibly, they have been about building a future in which the rule of law prevails, especially over the rulers themselves.

This paper has been more concerned in describing the human condition than in presenting a manual on the modalities of conflict transformation. Each conflict and its resolution create its own rules. In Ireland the emphasis has been on inclusion, on politics as process rather than zero-sum and on a proper sense of time-scales. As early as 1992 the Sinn Féin strategist, Jim Gibney, argued that 'a British departure must be preceded by a sustained period of peace and will arise out of negotiation.' In 1995 John Hume spoke of 'the real healing process [which] will take place and in a generation or two a new Ireland will evolve.' I want to close with some considerations on this healing process because in many respects the most difficult is that of implementation.

Indeed it may be one of the reasons why David Trimble's authority has been so undermined in recent years. According to Frank Millar '...while he saw the Belfast Agreement as a "settlement" and a line in the sand over the IRA's challenge to the Northern Ireland state – Sinn Féin characterised it as a "process" pushing remorselessly towards a united Ireland. And, of course, a great many Unionists were prepared to believe Adams rather than Trimble'. (p81) Trimble recognised as much in an interview with Millar:

> I actually take the view that what we did in the talks is the basis of the solution to what people call 'the Northern Ireland problem'... history is also going to record George Mitchell's closing comment about getting the Agreement being one thing while implementing it is going to be just as difficult. The judgement that people are going to make about Blair, about how Blair handled implementation, is going to be a bit more variable... that many of those weren't good decisions, that throughout the implementation there was a tendency by government to be too solicitous of republicans and to great willingness on the part of Blair's government to assume that unionism could carry greater weight. (pp137-8)

This can be our starting-point on the road to 'somewhere'. But we need to move cautiously. In his work on 'Impunity, Reparation and Reconciliation in Latin America' Michael Foley reminds us that is unseemly for anyone to demand of the victims of violence that they forgive. It is reasonable, he argues, 'and much more respectful, to insist that conditions be created in which it is possible to forgive, to heal, but above all to reclaim one's human dignity.' The South Africans may have shown the way with their Truth and Reconciliation Commission. Brink considers the exercise to be flawed, perhaps even a failure: 'Yet any comparison with situations elsewhere in the world, where a transition has been attempted without such a process, brings to light the profound need for it.' Perhaps failure or success is not even important; the test is the 'will' to move towards truth, and towards reconciliation.

Bibliography

Arthur, P. *Special Relationships: Britain, Ireland and the Northern Ireland problem* (Belfast: Blackstaff Press, 2001).

Brink, A. in the *Observer Magazine*, 13 February 2000.

Bland, B. *Marching and Rising: The Rituals of Small Differences and Great Violence in Northern Ireland* (Stanford Calif.: Center for International Security and Arms Control, Stanford University, 1996).

Bourke, R. *Peace in Ireland: The War of Ideas* (London: Pimlico, 2003).

Darby, J. *Intimidation and the Control of Conflict* (Dublin: Gill and Macmillan, 1986).

Errera, R. *Memory, History and Justice in Divided Societies: The Unfinished Dialogue between Mnemosyne and Clio* (Bellagio: unpublished paper, 1999).

Foley, M. 'Impunity, Reparation and Reconciliation in Latin America', (unpublished paper: University of Ulster, 1999).

Heaney, S. *Crediting Poetry* (Stockholm: Nobel Literature Lecture, 1995)

Millar, F. *David Trimble: The Price of Peace* (Dublin: The Liffey Press, 2004).

Milosz, C. (Stockholm: Nobel Literature Prize, 1980).

Nordstrom, C. *Memory, Forgiveness and Reconciliation: Confronting the Violence of History* (unpublished paper: University of Ulster, 1999).

O'Leary, B. and J. McGarry *The Politics of Antagonism: Understanding Northern Ireland* (London: The Athlone Press, 1993).

Rothstein, R. (ed.) *After the Peace: Resistance and Reconciliation* (Boulder: Lynne Rienner Publishers, 1999).

Smyth, M. 'Remembering in Northern Ireland: Victims, Perpetrators and Hierarchies of Pain and Responsibility' in Hamber, B. (ed.) *Past Imperfect: Dealing with the Past in Northern Ireland and Societies in Transition* (Derry: INCORE, 1998).

Sofer, S. 'The Diplomat as a Stranger', *Diplomacy and Statecraft*, 8, 3, (1997).

United States Advisory Commission on Public Diplomacy: *A New Diplomacy for the Information Age* (Washington DC. 1996).

Wyschogrod, E. *Spirit in Ashes: Hegel, Heidegger and Man-Made Mass Death* (New Haven: Yale University Press, 1983).

Wright, F. *Northern Ireland: A Comparative Analysis* (Dublin: Gill and Macmillan, 1987).

Chapter Fifteen

THE MEANING OF HISTORY AND EXPERIENCE FOR THE FUTURE

Duncan Morrow

There is a danger in the fashionability of the term 'cultural diversity' that it is treated as some kind of bland, self-evident policy without relation to the politics of power and domination. Little could be further from the truth. In practice, the demand for 'diversity' tends to arise in social and political life as a direct result of coping with competing pressures of political, social and economic change. At one level or another, cultural diversity expresses a demand for making public space for previously suppressed or hidden differences in a context of actual or potential uncertainty. The political space in which the challenges of diversity emerge is never neutral, but always already occupied by cultural and political systems which carry presumptions and assumptions about citizens and citizenship drawn from a previous era. Paradoxically, as we become more alike in terms of power and assertiveness, so the demand for the formal recognition of the reality of difference grows. No absolute separation can be made between cultural diversity and politics.

Secondly, the present discussion about the balance to be struck between assimilation, accommodation and integration may be haunted by more radical questions of exclusion and inclusion which, if not resolved through transcendent principle, may be resolved by violence. This may be true, even where it is not acknowledged. It is even more the case if and when cultural difference becomes politicised or territorialised, when the debate about cultural diversity is infected, if not overwhelmed, by the politics of ethnic antagonism.

The politics of exclusion on a national or ethnic basis have serious 'form' in Europe. The nineteenth-century response to the claims of divinely-sanctioned Empire was the nation state rooted in popular sovereignty. Self-determination of the eternal nation was posited as the liberating alternative to being subject the illegitimate rule of others. But within the simple elision of kinship, power and ethics is a potentially unacknowledged dependence on violence. Because unless the nation can be defined and identified and the territory claimed without opposition, national sovereignty is not just a declaration of war against a class enemy enjoying unjustified privilege, as the French Revolution and the republican tradition which emerged would have it, but becomes a declaration of enmity against others, who are now defined or define themselves as being of different nationality and live in 'our' territorial space.

Seeking a nation-state means, as Max Weber understood, making a claim for 'the nation' to the monopoly of the ultimate weapons of political force. But post-imperial Europe was not a place of neatly separated ethno-national territories. Instead it was a complex patchwork of historical interaction shaped by centuries of politics, war, economic and cultural change. But in fighting for 'national' democracy, nationalism emphasised and reproduced the ritual points of internal homogeneity and external distinction – language, religion or customs – and declared them sacred. In these circumstances, majority rule by the ballot box inevitably generated a series of mutually exclusive nationalist demands.

In contexts like Habsburg Austria or late Ottoman Turkey, where no single national power could dominate the whole territory in the absence of the overarching empire, claims to democratic national self-determination radically undermined the existing imperial order without providing a viable alternative. The result by the late nineteenth century was pragmatic governance by a series of unwieldy administrations under the tired gaze of the old imperial machinery. In a context like Germany, where one nation could claim a massive popular majority, the empire was understood by its supporters as the embodiment of the national purpose, and smaller challengers (such as the Poles) suppressed and treated as obstacles to German national destiny.

The defeat of all three empires in World War One reversed the political order across east-central Europe. Without German or Russian power, Polish claims to independence were supported by the victorious allies. Polish demands for land connected easily with French and British interests in weakening Germany. But Polish nationalism could only be successful by ignoring the claims of the previously insulated German-speakers. The situation in Bohemia and Moravia was even more complex as three and a half million Germans found their claims for *Anschluss* with Germany ignored at the expense of Czech claims for an independent state. Hungarians found themselves in similarly reversed circumstances in Serbia, Slovakia and Transylvania.

Wherever there was dispute over the political destiny of a given territory, the assertion of ethnic political supremacy was always also an assertion of threat to others. Liberation for some was always occupation for others. In the logic of victory and defeat, freedom for one side was automatically a catastrophe for others. Democratic self-determination, the utopia of liberalism, had an unacknowledged underside: it inevitably also went against the self-expressed wishes of considerable groups of others. More importantly, it could only be ensured by the threat of coercion, not free choice. In its radical form, the claim to national sovereignty was and is also a claim to the ethnic purity of a claimed territory and to the transcendent right of the nation to impose itself against all comers. As always, the deceptively attractive lure of 'purity' was actually a euphemism hiding the 'necessary' suppression of others.

All of this was visible in the failure of Woodrow Wilson's attempt to replace imperial rivalry with the friendly co-operation of free nations in 1919. In 1923, the Turks killed thousands of Greeks and expelled millions in their conquest of Anatolia, thereby destroying a Greek culture that had lasted for millennia. The Greeks responded in kind in Western Thrace. Successive eastern European regimes fell under the sway of radical and authoritarian nationalism. But it was when Germany fell under the spell of the ethnic poison of Nazism that the disease spread into a major economic power with potential to do untold damage even outside its own disputed borders. By first invoking self-determination to invade Austria and coerce Czechoslovakia, Hitler gained a military/political advantage from which he was able to pursue his dream of absolute racial supremacy justifying the acquisition of *Lebensraum*. Even more disastrously, Hitler expanded the logic of national superiority to justify the concentration camps and the 'final solution': elimination of – for the historic non-territorial minorities of Europe – first and foremost the Jews, but also the Roma.

In the traumatic aftermath of World War II, and in the face of continued repression in the east, western Europe grappled desperately for a distinctive ethical framework for democracy. The outcome – universal human rights and equal citizenship – put the emphasis on limiting the potential and proven violence of the state in its dealings with individual citizens each of whom is endowed with inalienable rights.

At the core of both rights and citizenship is an ethical determination to put the force of the state at the service of the defence of the person. Because the legitimacy of the use of violence is severely constrained, the bias in the system moves from a presumption of assimilation to the will of the state, to one favouring accommodation of the differences of citizens. But what is a relatively clear issue in the context of striking balances between citizens and the state in one context has become transformed in the context of the retreat from Empire and the advent of mass migration into western Europe from the Middle East and North Africa. Both of these movements generated new and less intimate relationships between nation-states and their new citizens and workers, and also generated group-based political and cultural tensions which were particularly tense around inherited presumptions about the shape and form of the public space. At stake is the relative authority of resident majorities, incoming minorities and the state to determine the outcome. Suddenly, political societies are confronted with critical questions about the limits of enforcement around the balance to be struck between freedom of speech and incitement to religious hatred, the shape and structure of the family, the status of language and religion in public life and the identification of common public rituals such as festivals, public holidays and traditions which were previously part of the unquestioned inheritance of a cultural tradition so deep and presumed that it could claim the title of 'normality'.

None of the resulting political and ethical dilemmas can be simply resolved. But as globalisation continues apace, so finding workable and acceptable answers to these and similar challenges lies at the heart of the project that goes by the name of 'cultural diversity'. It is already obvious that this task has moved from being the interest of a dedicated minority to becoming one of *the* defining issues of our times in western democracy, as states struggle to reconcile equality of citizenship, social cohesion and the reality of difference within a viable political and social framework.

Northern Ireland and antagonism

Although geographically on the edge of a continent, the north of Ireland was close to the middle of the great British maritime empire. The historic alignment of religious conviction and political identity were planted by the politics of expansion and imperial competition in Ireland in the sixteenth century and the resulting injuries were nourished and often refreshed through the subsequent generations. Unlike other parts of the empire, Ireland was also a 'home nation,' ultimately part of the United Kingdom itself, even if a majority of people living on the island felt antagonistic to 'English' rule. As numerical majorities began to matter – that is, as head-counting became the central mathematical mechanism for democratic government – so this contradiction grew in political significance. By the early twentieth century the division in the north of Ireland had polarised into an impermeable political antagonism on the basis of religious identity. Behind nationalist demands for liberation and Home Rule, Protestants saw effective Rome rule and suppression, and where Unionists clung to Britain as a protector of liberty, many Irish Catholics were more easily persuaded that it was a ruthless and humiliating imperial presence.

Britain was part of the winning coalition in World War I. But it was a victory which almost destroyed its economy and ended its global political hegemony. A radicalised Irish nationalism now demanded independence along the lines of the nation states being established on the ashes of Empire in continental Europe. Britain proved unwilling to sustain the military or political cost of prolonged nationalist guerrilla war in Ireland where there was widespread support for it (across most of south, central and western Ireland). But the conservative-liberal government had neither the appetite nor the intention of suppressing the pro-British Protestants in the north east. Thus, although initially proposed as part of an all-island political compromise, Northern Ireland was ultimately separated by an international border from the rest of the island. For unionists, the new arrangements were an expression of the democratic will of the people of the six counties. For nationalists, the same outcome was the result of a gerrymander which allowed Britain to justify ongoing occupation of part of Ireland. And from the outset, this antagonism was characterised by violence, inter-community polarisation and deeply ritualised antagonism.

Politically, the outcome was what Paul Arthur calls 'a decorative constitution'. In theory Northern Ireland was a harmonious democracy characterised by the blessings of equal citizenship, long-established British liberties and full participation of all. In everyday experience, however, all of that had to be set against ingrained hostility between the dominant political traditions manifested in a tradition of violence and permanent 'emergency' derogations from normal habeus corpus in law, a consistent pattern of economic distribution which suggested ingrained discrimination and the institutionalisation of the 'Orange' view of history within public life as well as through a Unionist monopoly on power, the declaration of two public holidays to celebrate the Protestant settlement in Ireland and the anathematisation of the Irish Republic in symbol, history or reality.

Some of this had counterparts in the rest of Ireland. But the overwhelming nationalist and Catholic majority south of the border made any thought of ongoing resistance by Unionists largely counter-productive and certainly futile. As a result, remaining Unionist-Protestants faced a clear if stark choice to accept the outcome and integrate into the new Ireland or, eventually, to depart. Over time, the twenty-six-county state evolved into an unusually homogeneous and internally stable political entity, However, the continued existence of a substantive and alienated nationalist Catholic minority in Northern Ireland, allowed for the development of 'internal opposition,' which embedded and nurtured in both majority and minority a sense of mutual threat which lasted through decades and exploded into active rage and violence in the late 1960s and early 1970s.

Unsurprisingly, antagonism was barren ground for any concept of cultural diversity. For republicans, an identity claimed by all of the active political parties in the new Irish Free State, Irishness was now defined in opposition to Britishness rather than integral to it. History teaching emphasised the continuity rather than complexity of Gaelic, Irish and Catholic suppression at the hands of the invader. When World War II broke out, Ireland chose neutrality rather than be forced back under British military protection. After 1949, the new republic gave a primary constitutional role to the Catholicism of its majority and eulogised the Rising of 1916.

It took very little to convince Catholics within Northern Ireland that the new political settlement was but the latest twist in this unhappy tale. The Unionist majority set out to secure 'the imperial province'. As Irishness was now aligned with republicanism so it became anathema to Unionists. While the concept of both Irish and British continued to linger, a possibility nourished by the fact of devolution itself, Unionism remained vigilant against any possibility of Catholics in power. For the new majority, however, Northern Ireland had to be a Protestant parliament for a Protestant people if it were to remain British and free. Emergency powers and nearly entirely

Protestant special police forces supported the existence of the state against its internal enemies. Irish symbolism and culture, especially anything associated with Irish political independence, were suppressed or neglected. Orange celebrations of Protestant victory over Catholic power became the de facto national holiday. Unionist support for British troops during World War II was contrasted with the attitude of de Valera in the Irish Free State. Under the Flags and Emblems Act, the display of Irish flags was made illegal.

Although precluded in practice from participation in government, Catholics and Irishness could not be finally eliminated from the political scene. In some places, Catholics formed the local majority including much of Tyrone and Fermanagh, South Armagh and Down and the city of Derry/Londonderry. Furthermore, the tradition of separate schooling continued to nurture a strong sense of separate Irish identity, through religion, sports and, at times, the teaching of history and language as well as generating a significant professional and academic class.

All of this underpinned a relationship characterised by two simultaneous but apparently paradoxical features: internal cultural developments which approximated to the Québécois idea of *deux solitudes* and an attention to every perceived or actual change in the political balance of power to the point of obsession. Cultural separation was matched with political intimacy. Political life reduced to a question of Protestant or Catholic, Unionist or Nationalist. Cross-cutting alliances on other issues emerged only weakly and temporarily. Polarised experiences of cultural identity were often the product of opposing experiences of the same historical or political events. The argument for separation was paradoxically driven by the relationship with the other.

As modernity eliminated many of the actual differences in everyday life, so the tensions of the past obstructed Northern Ireland's engagement with the post war western world of civic equality and human rights. The unanticipated spark for inter-communal explosion was thus the liberal/social democratic demand for civil rights. When Stormont was abolished in 1972, it is now clear that the old balance of power in Northern Ireland went with it. Putting Northern Ireland together again could now only take place on a 'new deal' about the balance between Unionism and Nationalism. In the context of antagonism, it was clear to almost all external observers that this could not be done on the basis of an assertion of uniform belonging to Britishness or Irishness, but would require a complexity and accommodation that had never characterised affairs in the Northern Ireland. On the other hand, the dominant political drive on both sides was to eliminate the threat which the other apparently posed to their cultural and political existence, making the rationality of diversity and compromise appear to be dangerous, treacherous and (critically) unrealistic.

Northern Ireland was held back from the brink only by massive military, political and economic intervention from the UK, often acting without local mandate in either or both political communities, and by an unusually co-operative relationship which developed gradually between the UK and the Irish Republic after 1970. Problematically, the imperative to restore order and reduce the level of direct political violence also led the state to invest in greater segregation and numerous compromises with the realities of power politics in many neighbourhoods. Peace when it arrived was a peace based on military-political exhaustion rather than a peace shaped by transformed political relationships. As the tide of violence, so the evidence of the scars of conflict on the prospects for a shared future came into renewed focus.

At the same time, and no matter what the underlying dynamic towards ceasefire, the new trajectory of politics could only be away from victory through violence or suppression. Nonetheless, a decision to abandon violence does not necessarily mean a decision to embrace the other. While the new direction of co-operation and engagement was strongly supported by the UK, Ireland, the USA and the European Union, engagement remained tentative at best at local level. Finding a viable social and political way for people to live in peace together in Northern Ireland remains a goal to be reached.

With no military, political or cultural victory in sight, the alternative to conflict leads inevitably towards dialogue and the implication of accommodation, compromise and transformation. What emerged after 1998 was a prolonged struggle to define the new balance of power between the traditional enemies including debate about the degree to which each tradition would be formally protected from change or would be obliged to embrace it. What was evident by 2006 was that the political leadership of both traditions was strongly attracted to a policy of minimal concessions, while at the same time decrying the consequences of antagonism when it appeared to create costly consequences for their political interests. Thus Unionists demanded shared space for Orange celebrations but sought to protect 'Protestant areas' from the encroachment of 'Catholic housing,' while Nationalists demanded shared governance but were anxious to reduce Britishness wherever possible, especially in areas with nationalist political majorities. Unsurprisingly, the result was political stasis.

From Cultural Traditions to Cultural Diversity?

Even in Fermanagh and Tyrone, nothing stays the same. The years since the ceasefires of 1994 have also served to make the question of cultural diversity both more complex and more prominent. The transformation of Ireland from an island of poverty and emigration to the place with the highest rate of immigration in the western world took most people by surprise. Most of the change was driven by the explosive growth of the Republic's economy, but the ebb of conflict in Northern Ireland also contributed to significant changes. While measurement is notoriously inaccurate, the arrival of large numbers of eastern Europeans forced social and political thinkers to recognise that Northern Ireland was indeed part of the wider western world, even as the narrative of number-driven politics remained determinedly local and parochial.

Modern economies prize flexibility and movement, and the ability to match supply and demand across the globe. Between 2001 and 2006, the number of people not born in the UK and Ireland but resident in Northern Ireland increased by up to five times. On the island of Ireland, the number of people of eastern European origin now exceeds the population of the city of Belfast.

On arriving in Northern Ireland, new arrivals found themselves in a place where the notion of territorial ownership by a 'single' cultural identity, political tradition or even political grouping had become deeply ingrained. Spatial segregation, which has become even more widespread in urban areas of Northern Ireland since 1972, is also usually accompanied by paramilitary organisation which gains local legitimacy through their claim to act as 'defenders' of communities.

New arrivals inevitably disrupted this pattern. This was especially true in areas where the availability of vacant cheap accommodation allowed for the influx of larger numbers. As this was largely in previously Protestant areas, the interface was particularly violent in loyalist areas. Rapid change was thus marked by an increase in the number of violent attacks on people motivated by racial or ethnic hatred often associated with local paramilitary groups.

Both the underlying economics of migration and the potential for economic development to become entangled in the violence of the past created renewed impetus towards cultural diversity. In a world of multimedia communication and cheap airfares, new arrivals would not be assimilated into Northern Ireland by simply abandoning their countries of origin.

Some of the consequences of this new context are already visible. First, global dynamics have raised not reduced the social and economic necessity of finding ways to accommodate and integrate difference into a socially cohesive whole. The challenge is visible across Europe and is likely to become more rather than less urgent in coming years. Secondly, the challenges of the future in Northern Ireland cannot simply be shaped as an answer to the bipolar past. Answers which bring short-term stability in one context, especially if they freeze current relationships in a permanent political pattern, may store up difficulties for the future. The challenge of finding principles for living together into the future is bigger than the challenge of finding answers to the injuries and injustices of the past. Given that parties designed to represent the competing interests of Northern Ireland's traditional polarity predominate, this is a considerable challenge. Thirdly, the concept of diversity points both to the existence of a 'whole' to which all belong and to a huge variety of particular circumstances. The policy challenge is therefore to find and define the unifying principles of belonging and to devise and apply policies in various particular circumstances.

What all of this suggests is that 'once and for all' structural answers to fluid questions of inter-relationship are unlikely to be forthcoming. 'Cultural diversity' is therefore not an easily circumscribed set of policies but a statement of principle and an indication of method. It cannot be a simple question with a clear-cut answer, but instead is a pointer to a profoundly challenging set of human challenges; how to welcome, engage and integrate people with different expectations and cultural knowledge into a coherent and cohesive society, how to find working balances between cultural specificity and the rapidly advancing inter-penetration and relationship of modern life and how to find politically viable balances between the theoretically neutral and equal public space of secular constitutionalism and the reality of group interests and fears. Resolution to these issues is likely to depend as much on learning from practical experience as on straightforward planning and theoretical rigour. But we should be under no illusion that a failure to engage publicly with this complexity will result in the emergence of antagonisms and enmities which may only acknowledged when they explode into violence and rage. Cultural diversity has become a necessity because its alternatives lead to ethnic cleansing and from there to other 'final' solutions.

A Shared Future?

The search for a basis for inclusion takes place against the backdrop that no single all-embracing national identity based on origins has emerged in Northern Ireland. In its absence, and given the continued need to accommodate difference within a territorial space, the integrating transcendence must therefore necessarily be political and ethical. Cultural diversity is in effect one of the names given to this search.

After 1945, cultural diversity is part of the search in western Europe for a less violent and inclusive relationship between citizens and between citizens and the state, including the right to change the allegiance of the state through agreed electoral mechanisms. For this reason, it can never be a value-free endeavour. But in recognising difference and seeking to make space for it, states are also confronted with the dilemma of how also to ensure social cohesion: how to ensure that diversity does not become a synonym for new forms of segregation and antagonism.

Cultural diversity is therefore inadequate if it is simply a statement of political difference and a demand to institutionalise difference on the basis of today's balance of power. Social relationships formed in relation to political power do not necessarily fade into deep-rooted tolerance, even when there are periods of relative calm and widespread examples of personal relationships which run in contrast to the dominant axis of conflict. The first lesson of Northern Ireland is that, untreated, such relationships can modernise into endemic and violent antagonism.

On the other hand people who come to believe that the public space is aimed at actively undermining their political and personal identity are likely to resist, and seek protection from, the movement to integration. What Northern Ireland shows is that democracies rooted in antagonism do not convince the minority to become willing partners, if resistance can be successfully organised. Democratic mechanisms to determine the 'will of the people' (counting votes) in these contexts fail to resolve the dispute.

In moving beyond this conundrum, several things seem to be important. First of all, there needs to be recognition that violence is no longer legitimate within political affairs. Without this, all sides feel that the possibilities of accommodation are largely fictional. Secondly, the public space cannot be characterised by any single version of national allegiance but must include a genuine commitment to a new agreed political dispensation with its mechanisms for law-making and dispute resolution alongside and beyond any differences of aspiration. Thirdly, beyond the current reality, there needs to be commitment to principles for engaging new issues and recognition that agreements in the present will have to be able to accommodate future changes to meet new circumstances. Principles remain, institutions evolve.

In Northern Ireland, the international principles of human rights and equality have provided a useful framework within which to limit and define inter-community relationships. What is potentially absent in both, is any recognition that both must co-exist within a whole community in which the pattern of relationship is complex and fragile and that the numerically dominant partners can no longer claim to represent all vital of the population. The demands of social justice and distinctiveness must be set alongside a consistent recognition of the interdependence of all to ensure the success of the whole. Likewise, interdependence must be created on a basis of a real commitment to equal citizenship and fairness, a notoriously elusive concept which requires constant readjustment and redefinition, as well as a commitment to protect core cultural freedoms.

All of this leaves open huge areas for political dispute and agreement. The precise balance to be struck between multiculturalism and inter-culturalism will depend in part on the relationships that can be established between people and groups and the institutional trust that can be evolved. But if antagonism and exclusion are to be tackled, the critical task is to establish real mechanisms of open communication and dialogue between people of different backgrounds, to promote the existence of open spaces where people meet each other in unexpected and unpredicted ways and to design and operate institutions in which people engage at a practical level in common tasks.

Central to that task is telling and retelling the story of who 'we' are. *What made Now in Northern Ireland* is our contribution to that discussion in a complex but important moment in our history. That is why CRC was keen to establish the original series of seminars on which this book is based: not to close debate or to draw a final line under the public dispute but to set all such discussion within a tone of mutual interdependence. We are convinced that the establishment of that tone and context, including an honest assessment of where exclusions on our part have contributed to the predicaments of the present, is not a matter of mere aesthetic interest, but potentially one of survival, and certainly the key quality of life issue facing many people in Northern Ireland for the foreseeable future.